D1565618

PUBLICATIONS ON ASIA
OF THE SCHOOL OF
INTERNATIONAL STUDIES
Number 34

Origins
of the
Japanese
Language

LECTURES IN JAPAN DURING THE
ACADEMIC YEAR 1977-78

Roy Andrew Miller

UNIVERSITY OF WASHINGTON PRESS
SEATTLE AND LONDON

This book was published with the assistance
of a grant from the Japan Foundation.

Library of Congress Cataloging in Publication Data
Miller, Roy Andrew.
    Origins of the Japanese language.
    (Publications on Asia of the School of
International Studies ; no. 34)
    Bibliography: p.
    Includes index.
    1. Japanese language—History. 2. Japanese
language—Grammar, Comparative—Altaic.
3. Altaic languages—Grammar, Comparative—
Japanese. I. Title. II. Series: Washington
(State). University. School of International
Studies. Publications on Asia ; no. 34.
PL525.M49   495.6'09   80-50871
ISBN O-295-95766-2

Contents

[v]

Maps

Introduction

During the academic year 1977-78, most of which I was fortunate enough to be able to spend in Japan, thanks to support provided by a senior faculty fellowship from the Japan Foundation, I was asked to deliver four public lectures on the general topic of the origins of the Japanese language. The invitations were advanced at different times by different groups, and originally I hoped to fulfill the obligations they represented by using the same lecture, or at least parts of it, for each occasion. But as the year went on, it became clear that these opportunities to address audiences of varied interests and backgrounds on this topic also provided me with a welcome opportunity to sketch out a series of connected, if not comprehensive, remarks on the subject, which also happened to be one that had occupied my own research interest for some time. Accordingly, I prepared a text for four different lectures, in the form of a rough, working manuscript, and it is that text, revised for publication and edited to remove at least some of the repetitions and unclarities that pass unnoticed (or so one always hopes) in oral presentation, that is now published here.

My experience over the past decade or more in teaching courses dealing with the history of the Japanese language in American universities has convinced me that there is a need for a nontechnical, simply written introduction to the subject aimed especially at American and other English-reading students. This is especially true of that important segment of the study of the history of the language that is involved with the genetic relationship of Japanese to other languages. Little if any of the important literature on the history of the Japanese language, particularly of the literature that deals with the genetic relationship of Japanese to other languages, is available to our students in English. The few titles available in English versions that can realistically be assigned as "additional readings" for our classes are mostly clumsy translations of Japanese originals that ought not to be recommended to students in the first place, even if they could read them in their original versions. Most of the recent and more important literature on this general subject is in German and Russian, and as a result unavailable to most of our students, who rarely are able to read these languages with any facility.

The lectures on which this book is based were originally written for Japanese university audiences, mostly students; but the needs and interests of such audiences are not that much different from the needs of the students in our American classrooms; they, too, rarely handle German or Russian with any practical facility, and they suffer the additional handicap of seldom being able to read English well enough either—a formidable linguistic handicap, which pretty well restricts them to the largely unimportant literature that exists, on this subject, in Japanese. For all these reasons, it seemed worthwhile to make the effort necessary to turn these lectures into a form in which they would be available to our own students in America, as earlier they had been made available to students in Japan.

But it must be stressed at the outset that this book is only a short introduction to the general subject of the genetic relationship of the Japanese language, something that may be given in its present form to our American university students interested in Japanese studies, and something that is at one and the same time accurate, up to date, and written in a language they can read—nothing more than that. It does not aim at being a specialized academic monograph, nor does it present any particularly new or original ideas or research findings, even though it does incorporate many ideas and results from fairly recent research that are still far from well known or understood in many circles.

This same desire—to make the result as useful to the American student as possible—has motivated the addition of bibliographical information and three maps to the present volume. The additional bibliographical information will be found at the end of the volume, in a section headed "Further Reading and Documentation." These notes, again with the needs of the American student particularly in mind, stress works available and written in English when such exist; however, works in other languages have also been mentioned when necessary, or when they happen to cover aspects of the subject for which no treatment is available in English, or no treatment that can be recommended. This section also provides the necessary bibliographical documentation, which will be of interest largely to the specialist, for a number of statements or claims advanced in the text for the first time, or which are controversial, or which for some other reason require documentation. References to works in languages other than English have been kept to a minimum; but perhaps they will serve a useful purpose if they encourage at least a few of our students to study the languages in which some of these essential titles are to be found. The section on further readings and documentation begins with a general account of the field at large; following this, topics are treated in turn for each of the four lectures, in the order in which they appear in the text.

Thus the book that has resulted is essentially general in nature and designed as general reading, aimed primarily at the university student, not the professional scholar or specialist in these matters. But so also were the lectures as originally delivered in Japan, and in this sense the book does not diverge very far from the original aim of the lectures out of which it has grown—another reason for not abandoning the lecture format of the original presentation, notwithstanding the many changes introduced in the course of preparing the work for publication.

Three of the lectures were originally written and delivered in Japanese, the other one in English, according to the following schedule:

1. "Nihon ni okeru gengogaku no shōrai no kadai ni tsuite no shiken." Lecture at the 74th General Meeting of the Linguistic Society of Japan, at Tokyo Women's Christian College, June 19, 1977.

2. "The Origin of the Japanese Language: Who, When, and What?" Convocation Lecture at International Christian University, Mitaka, October 20, 1977.

3. "Nihongo wa doko kara kita ka?" Lecture at the Nihongo Kyōiku Kokusai Kaigi, at Aoyama Gakuin University, Tokyo, March 18, 1978.

4. "Dōshite Nihongo no keitō wa wakaranai?" Lecture at the Nihongo Kyōiku Kokusai Kaigi, at the Yomiuri Bunka Center, Senri, March 20, 1978.

None of these materials have appeared in print before, but after the first of the lectures, I was asked by the Taishūkan Publishing Company to contribute an article to their monthly magazine *Gengo* that would summarize some of the points I had made at the meeting of the Linguistic Society of Japan. The article that resulted, "Nani ga Nihongo no keitō wo fumei ni shita no ka?" *Gengo,* vol. 6 no. 9 (1977), pp. 76-81, 109, considers some of the same issues touched on in that lecture, but does not directly duplicate anything in this book. (My lecture at the meeting of the Linguistic Society was also reported on in the same issue of *Gengo,* p. 82.)

To prepare the manuscript for this book, it was necessary for me, in the case of three of the lectures, to translate my remarks out of the original Japanese in which they had been written and delivered. Whatever the advantages of this rather involved procedure, at least it means that no translator other than the author is to be blamed either by him or by the reader if passages still survive that make less than good sense.

Apart from this actual business of translation, preparing

[x]

the manuscript for this book has largely involved two different processes. The first was to rearrange some of the material originally presented in these lectures in a more useful order than a literal transcript would have provided. This has also meant that each of the four chapters does not simply report on each of the four lectures, even though by and large their order and content remain the same. Chapter 3 in particular has been considerably rearranged, and now incorporates a number of remarks from the second lecture. A few explanatory notes, particularly for Japanese technical terms and expressions that may not be familiar to the reader, have been added to the translations of lectures originally delivered in Japanese; but I would at the same time wish to emphasize that most of the explanations of technical terms and issues in historical linguistics found in this book were part of the original lectures, since they represent an area of scholarship with which Japanese audiences are generally unfamiliar, and one where I felt I could make the greatest contribution by explaining my views, and my approach, as fully as possible.

The second process grew out of the readers' review conducted on behalf of my original draft manuscript by the publications committee of the School of International Studies, University of Washington, after I had submitted my original version to them with a view to possible publication, in September 1978. The detailed comments of the five different readers from both inside and outside the University of Washington faculty who studied my original draft provided me with many extremely useful suggestions for modifying, correcting, and generally improving my manuscript, almost all of which I have most gratefully incorporated into the final version. This has meant the addition of certain ideas and items not in the original lectures, as well as the correction of more than a few errors that were. On both scores, I count myself fortunate.

I wish that I could thank individually the five readers who in the course of the review process so greatly enhanced the quality and effectiveness of this book; but since their reports were anonymous in the form they reached me, this is unfortunately impossible. But I can and do thank the chairman of the publications committee of the School of International Studies, Professor Jack Dull, and the other members of his committee, together with the school's publications editor Ms. Margery Lang, for their much appreciated assistance, not only in seeing this book through the press but also in helping to improve its quality and form of presentation through their reader-review procedures. I am appreciative, as well, of the physical form and the maps of this book, both of which were the work of Ms. Cynthia Louie.

In addition to the chance to prepare and present these four lectures, the academic year 1977-78 also provided me with the opportunity to lecture once a week in Japanese on the history of the Japanese language to a class of Japanese undergraduates at Kyoto Sangyō University, a rare and rewarding experience for which I am most grateful. Many of the ideas that are elaborated in this book were first tentatively broached in one of these long Wednesday afternoon lectures at Sangyō University, where the easy and friendly attitude of the students made it possible for me to prepare myself for the more formal reception generally afforded by the lecture audiences.

Neither the opportunity to write and deliver the lectures upon which this book is based nor the leisure to study and prepare for them would have been possible without the assistance of the Japan Foundation. I also owe a particularly great debt of gratitude to Professor Murayama Shichirō of Kyoto Sangyō University, for his encouragement, assistance, and instruction during the year, and for extending to me the academic hospitality of his department and university. Since I am also in debt to many other Japanese scholars and friends, it is impossible to name any individuals without doing an injustice to all the rest; but at least the names of Professors Izui Hisanosuke, Okutsu Kei'ichirō, and Yoshida Kanehiko must find a place here, even at the risk of appearing to slight others. To Professor Karl H. Menges, professor emeritus at Columbia University and now at the Orientalisches Institut der Universität Wien, I owe the original suggestion to make these lectures available in a language more widely read by scholars in Europe and the West than Japanese. Finally, I must surely also mention in this connection the nearly fifty students at Kyoto Sangyō University who persisted in attending my weekly lectures on these and related subjects throughout two entire terms of the academic year. They should know that they were the most rewarding, and certainly the most courteous, of all the captive audiences I have yet enjoyed, even after some three decades of university teaching both in Japan and in America.

R.A.M.

Seattle, Washington
July 31, 1979

ORIGINS

OF THE

JAPANESE

LANGUAGE

LECTURES IN JAPAN
DURING THE
ACADEMIC YEAR 1977-78

1. The Search for Origins

The opening lines of the Chinese Confucian classic known in the West as the *Mencius*—the contents of which are today probably better known in Japan than they would be in modern China, with its repudiation of both Confucianism and its texts— describe a famous and often-quoted encounter between the king of the ancient Chinese state of Liang and the philosopher Mencius. The king addresses Mencius, "Since you have not considered a journey of a thousand miles too much to undertake (in order to come to Liang), it must necessarily follow that you know something that will profit our kingdom." Mencius replies, "Why must your majesty invariably ask about profit? I know nothing, apart from those things that I believe to be right and true."

In accepting the invitation to give these lectures in Japan, I felt somewhat like Mencius. Certainly I resemble him at least in the sense that I did not consider the trip to Japan as one too great to undertake. And perhaps I can be forgiven for feeling that I resemble him in not claiming to have any special secrets or news of striking discoveries with which to startle—or profit—my listeners. Like Mencius at the Liang court, all that I can do is share what I and others engaged in the study of the origins of the Japanese language in the West now hold to be a consistent and viable hypothesis concerning where this language came from, how it reached Japan, and what other languages in the world it is related to historically.

Titles, like outlines, are not only important indications of the directions that the study of a subject may take: titles for their part can also help to determine those directions, and so they properly deserve careful attention at the outset of any scientific or intellectual investigation. If here we are to concern ourselves with what I have called *Origins of the Japanese Language,* it is a matter of some importance to consider together, and in some detail if necessary, just what this title implies, and if possible agree on what we mean by the words that make up the title, before we embark on a treatment of the the subject itself.

The meaning of the last two words of the title is relatively easy to agree on. By "Japanese" we of course mean the language of the nearly 115 million people who live today on the four "home islands" of Honshu, Kyushu, Shikoku, and Hokkaido, as well as on Okinawa and many other smaller islands that lie to the south of the principal island chain. The language is also used daily, especially in the home, by many residents of Hawaii, and in other parts of the world, such as Brazil, that have significant numbers of Japanese immigrants. Given the current remarkable influx of Japanese tourists and businessmen throughout the world, one finds Japanese in use, for one purpose or another, in every major city of the world. In this sense, at least, it is now an international language. But even apart from this, as the language of one of the world's major industrial nations, and particularly as the language that has transmitted one of the world's important literatures and cultural traditions, Japanese certainly has an importance that far exceeds the narrow geographical confines of its original, and continuing, island home.

The earliest written records for the Japanese language

[4]

consist of a few names that appear in late fifth-century inscriptions; but from the eighth century on we begin to have substantial literary texts from Japan. From then until the present day, Japanese literary culture has been as notable for the variety and excellence of its production as for its bulk.

The Japanese language, of course, has not been uniform throughout all its long history; no language ever is. Moreover, all languages undergo various kinds of change as time goes on. The linguist takes notice of this phenomenon of linguistic change by assigning names, sometimes rather arbitrarily, to various periods in the history of a language, simply because without such concise designations or terminology it is difficult to deal comprehensibly with the history of a phenomenon that, like the Japanese language (or like any human language, for that matter), embraces millennia rather than simply centuries.

Thus, we usually call the variety of language that is found in the earliest texts from Japan, largely dating from the eighth century, Old Japanese. From some time following the transfer of the capital to Heian-kyō—the modern city of Kyoto—in 794, we may speak of the language as "late Old Japanese," a somewhat changed variety of Old Japanese from which it particularly differed in the number and nature of its vowels. One of the greatest monuments of Japanese literary culture, the *Genji monogatari (The Tale of Genji)*, dates in the main from the period ca. 1001-1010, and its language may be described as late Old Japanese. But from the early part of the thirteenth century until nearly the end of the sixteenth century, we must speak instead of Middle Japanese, another stage in the history of the language that is quite clearly demarcated from both Old Japanese proper and late Old Japanese. From about 1600 on we begin to have texts in what linguists call New Japanese (or Modern Japanese), and even though much of this variety of the language is rather far removed from the contemporary language of Tokyo, Osaka, and the other major cities of Japan, it is still closer to that language than it is to the two major earlier stages that have been mentioned. But of course, assigning terms for periods in linguistic history such as Old Japanese or Middle Japanese should not make us think that there ever was an abrupt transition or shift from one to another. Linguistic change is not only continual but constant,

[5]

and—at any given time, at least—it is imperceptible. It would not be at all misleading to compare linguistic change to the flow of a glacier: the movement of both is extremely slow, but steady; and after much time has elapsed, it is not difficult to see evidence that the language has changed, or that the glacier has indeed moved.

The criteria on which the linguist bases terms such as Old Japanese or Middle or New Japanese are mostly concerned with differences on two separate levels that may be identified in all languages: he observes differences between one period and another in the pronunciation of the language, and differences in the forms of words and what they mean. (The first level is called "phonology," the second "morphology" and "semantics," in the usual technical terminology.)

We know, for example, that Old Japanese differed greatly in its pronunciation from Middle Japanese as well as from the modern language. Old Japanese, for example, had eight different vowels, while most varieties of Middle Japanese had six, and the modern standard language of Tokyo has only five. (Each of these five modern vowels may be long or short, with a significant difference in the meaning of a word as a result, but Old Japanese had no such difference in the length of its eight different vowels.)

We also know that Old Japanese was not a uniform or monolithic language. Like all human languages of all times and places, it had a number of dialects, distinguished from each other by different pronunciations, and sometimes different words for the same thing, or words that were pronounced the same but had different meanings in different dialects. These dialects have survived down through all the historical periods of the language; today scholars generally divide the modern Japanese dialects into three major groups, those of Eastern Japan (Tokyo and its environs), Western Japan (Osaka, Kyoto, and the other older cultural centers), and the isolated island of Kyushu. A few of these surviving modern dialects may still be so different in pronunciation, and in their words and the meanings in which they employ them, that a speaker of another dialect nearby, or especially a speaker of the Tokyo language, may not be able to understand what is being said. But such major differences between dialects

[6]

are fast falling by the way in contemporary Japan, partly because the language of Tokyo is taught in the schools throughout the country as a national standard, and also because of the tremendous impact of national television and radio broadcasting throughout the islands. Radio and TV now bring this standard language of Tokyo into even the most remote rural areas.

As a result, persons who have never been to Tokyo—or perhaps will never visit it in their lifetimes—early acquire fluency in speaking as well as understanding the Tokyo language. Local dialects continue to be employed in the home and within the family group. But since most younger Japanese now have considerable fluency in the language of Tokyo as well as their own local dialect, one finds increasingly little use of the local dialects for public or formal occasions, such as speeches and lectures. Nor is a person using the Tokyo language likely to encounter any serious difficulties in understanding or being understood by Japanese speakers from any other part of the country, no matter how remote it may be—a linguistic situation that was quite different a century ago, and throughout all of earlier Japanese history.

Thus, there is not much question about what we mean by the words "Japanese language" in our title. But what do we imply by "origins," and what facts or concepts do we suggest studying when we take on this topic as our subject of inquiry? Unfortunately, "origins" is potentially a dangerous as well as a difficult term. This is because the word "origins" does not immediately announce that it is a technical term—by which is meant a word with a special, delimited sense—in the way that, for example, a coined term such as "phonology" or "morphology" does. "Origins" is an ordinary English word; it gives no warning that it will be used only in a technical, carefully defined meaning. "Common sense" might argue that origins are origins, and that any attempt at scientific precision is as impossible here as it is out of place; if so, then a "common sense" approach to the question would be—as is so often the case—wrong.

Japanese scholars, or others of us who sometimes speak and write in that language, have here a somewhat different problem concerning terms and their definitions. The usual Japanese equivalent for "origins," in the sense it is used here, is *kigen*. This Japanese word has many of the same problems that the English "origins" does. Like the English term, Japanese *kigen* is not specifically marked, or easily identified, as a technical term for the treatment of problems in historical linguistics. As a result, this Japanese word also finds its way into the titles or outlines of writing and speculation on these same topics, but often with little attention having being paid along the way to precisely what the term means, or to the question of just how, in its narrower, scientific usage, its sense may differ from its larger, "common sense" implications.

The Japanese term *kigen* has one additional problem that is worth mentioning. Like all Japanese nouns, this word is not overtly marked for either singular or plural, since number is not a compulsory grammatical category in the Japanese language. There are many ways of expressing plurality in Japanese when such expression is necessary or desirable, or of stressing that a noun is singular and not plural if that is what one wishes to do. But normally, any Japanese noun serves equally well in sentences where it may be correctly translated as an English singular as in sentences where it may be translated as an English plural. It all depends—as language teachers so often like to say—on the context.

This means that from the outset of our discussion, if we set ourselves to study the "origins of the Japanese language," we have set our course in a somewhat more closely defined direction than if we were to take instead as our topic the closest Japanese equivalent of this phrase, *Nihongo no kigen. Nihongo* means "the Japanese language"; but *kigen* might be either "origin" or "origins." The fact is, of course, that *kigen* is neither singular nor plural, and our need to decide on a singular or plural form when it comes to English "origin" or "origins" is a necessity forced on us only because of the structure of the English language. It is a necessity from which the Japanese scholar, or anyone else who chooses to write and lecture in Japanese, is mercifully free.

But most freedoms carry their corresponding responsibilities; and the genial linguistic freedom of the Japanese language in this matter of singular and plural, at least as illustrated by this specific example, is not a responsibility that we can say that Japanese scholars have, in general, lived up to very well. *Nihongo*

[8]

no kigen is not only the title of one important book on the subject; this phrase or some variation on it figures in the titles, or outlines, of hundreds of recent works in this field. But one almost
always looks through this enormous literature in vain for any
indication that, in setting *Nihongo no kigen* as their topic, the
authors have given serious thought to the definition of *kigen*
as a technical linguistic term—or to its possible distinction from
kigen as simply another word in the Japanese language—any
more than they have paid sufficient attention to whether what
they are writing and studying about is the "origin" of the language
or its "origins."

Whether from the outset we go looking for a single, unique
"origin" for this language of more than 115 million people or
search instead for multiple, pluralistic "origins," matters a great
deal. The decision we make will inevitably do much to determine
the nature of our findings, as well as the conclusions we eventually
base on them. In English, we cannot escape the formal tyranny
of grammatical number: we must decide whether we will look
for an "origin" or for "origins."

As it turns out, this particular case of grammatical tyranny
is probably a fortunate one; by forcing our studies from the outset into a more carefully defined frame of reference than that
with which our Japanese colleagues may operate, we in the West
are compelled to make a number of theoretical and methodological decisions that greatly facilitate our subsequent study of
this question. No one believes that the grammatical facts of any
language are anything but arbitrary and fortuitous; but this does
not imply that sometimes these arbitrary grammatical facts may
not enhance the progress of scholarship in one case or inhibit
it in another. In the striking contrast between the liberty, if not
the license, to employ undifferentiated Japanese *kigen* and the
strict necessity to pick and choose between English "origin" and
"origins," we have certainly identified one of the former cases.

This should not be taken to imply that the vocabulary
of modern Japanese scholarship is meager or lacking in terms.
If there is any essential problem about the lexical resources available to our Japanese colleagues, it lies in quite the opposite
direction. Japanese *kigen,* like English "origin(s)," is not really
a technical term of linguistics at all; it is an ordinary term that

we may, if we wish, agree to use in a technical—that is to say, a carefully defined and delimited—way. But besides *kigen,* Japanese scholarship has two words, both clearly marked by their form in the language as technical terms, and both rather more common in Japanese writing and speaking than their translation-equivalents arc in English—an example, if one were wished for, of Japanese vocabulary and usage outstripping those of English for dealing with the same topics. These two terms are *seiritsu* (development) and *keitō* (genetic relationship).

Like *kigen,* the word *seiritsu* may be used of many things. In general contexts, it means "formation, establishment," but as a specialized term in the treatment of historical linguistic questions, it covers more or less the same range of ideas as English "historical development" does when applied to the history of a language. In other words, *seiritsu* is concerned with how a language has come to be the language that it is, how it changes, and how it develops throughout its history. This is an extremely important set of problems, and quite relevant to any discussion of historical linguistics; but it is not at all the same thing as *kigen,* or the same as "origins."

The word *keitō* is something different. In general contexts this word originally meant "bloodline, pedigree, lineage," but now one most often finds it in contexts where the history of the Japanese language is being discussed. In such contexts the word *keitō* is a specialized technical term, and exactly equivalent to the English technical term "genetic relationship" when referring to the historical connections between different languages.

Both "development" *(seiritsu)* and "genetic relationship" *(keitō),* in either English or Japanese, are terms that are relatively easy to deal with, because in one way or another both are technical terms and hence have clearly agreed-upon limits and dimensions of meaning. Unfortunately, the same is not true of English "origin," much less of "origins," nor of the Japanese word *kigen* that can serve for either of these terms. To use any of these last terms for the purposes of serious discussion, we must first set some reasonable bounds on the area of meaning in which we agree to employ them.

It is perhaps easiest to begin by making clear what we do not mean here by "origins" when we talk about the Japanese language, or about any language, for that matter. We do not mean that we will attempt to find out how the Japanese language actually began, in the sense of studying how this particular language arose as a specialized human activity. Speculation about the "origin" of one human language or another in this sense—sometimes about the beginning of all human languages—was popular about a century ago. Many interesting and ingenious theories were set forth about how language may have managed to come into being: some of these speculations ascribed it to the imitation of natural sounds (the "bow wow" school), others to more sophisticated patterns of behavioral genesis; and one group ascribed its "origin" to the need for lying and deception in gradually evolving economic situations, on the grounds that economic transactions were the only human affairs that could not be conducted conveniently without the availability of a linguistic medium, and its attendant possibilities of prevarication.

Some of these speculations of the last century still make interesting reading today, but for the modern linguist most of them have only curiosity value. For some years the question of the origin of language in this sense was an issue that had ceased to be discussed seriously among linguists, mainly because it was felt that this was an area in which we lack not only concrete evidence on which to base our theories but also any methodology for evaluating such theories. Without evidence, and without the possibility of verifying a hypothesis, speculation is limited only by the inventiveness of the individuals who like to think about this sort of thing.

More recently, there have been signs of a cautious revival of interest in this subject. In 1975 the New York Academy of Sciences organized a conference (a critic has described it as being of "Wagnerian proportions") at which linguists met with philosophers, psychologists, biologists, anthropologists, and neurologists, in an attempt to renew a serious consideration of this area of speculation. But this revival of scholarship in the area of the origin of language properly so-called is still at a very early stage; and speculation about how people first began to speak, or theories about how human language first came into being, is definitely not what we are concerned about here when we set ourselves the task of studying the origin (or even the origins) of the Japanese language.

[11]

What, then, do we mean to consider under the topic of the "origins" of the Japanese language? Most simply, what we mean by "origins" in the present context—and also what "origins" (or *kigen*) implies when employed correctly as a technical term in historical linguistics—is the pursuit of the history of the language in question. Our goal is to pursue this history as far back into the past as possible. Thanks to the assumptions and methodology of linguistic science, particularly of that branch of linguistic science that is known as the comparative method, we are able to push this inquiry far beyond the limited chronological barriers that would be imposed on our study if we were confined to those materials that happen to have been preserved for us by early written records.

It is this application of the comparative method that adds an entirely new dimension to our studies of linguistic origins. Without it, we would be limited to the resources of the earliest written records. As we have seen, the earliest of these documents, in the case of Japanese, is really quite recent in terms of the over-all history of man and his civilization. Japanese scholarship today, almost a century after its first opportunity to become acquainted with this methodology, still generally hesitates to apply it to the study of Japanese linguistic origins. Hence our Japanese colleagues remain limited by the chronological span of the earliest written records. This is also the chief reason why, despite all the scholarly activities undertaken in Japan in this field over three postwar decades of academic freedom, no substantial progress has been made in the study of Japanese linguistic origins. In the West, while we do not claim to be any more perspicacious than our Japanese colleagues, and certainly cannot pretend to be any more diligent, we must admit in this single respect at least to having been more fortunate: not hesitating to apply the comparative method to the study of Japanese linguistic origins, as we would to the study of the origins of any other language, we have been able to push the pursuit of its history far beyond those narrow chronological limits imposed by the simple inspection of written records.

In other words, the study of the "origins" of Japanese, or of any other language, is simply a special aspect of the study of the history of that language. Language is a human institution, in the sense that it is a set of highly specialized human behavioral

[12]

patterns. Other sets of highly specialized human behavioral patterns include marriage customs, kinship systems, political institutions, and taxation arrangements, among many others. But of all such institutions, language is the most highly involved phenomenon, and the most highly specialized, of any that can easily be isolated for identification and study. It surely is also the oldest, as old as the species *Homo sapiens* itself. All systems of human behavior have their histories, just as individuals, families, nations, and countries have theirs. We could and do study the history of marriage customs, or of kinship systems, just as we can and do study the history of nations and states. And we can and do study the history of language, that most involved, most complex, and most highly specialized of all systems of human behavior.

Starting with the language as we have it today, we are able to go further and further back toward its earlier stages; when we pursue this study of a given language as far back as the materials and the methodology available to us permit—when we have taken the history of a language back as far in time as we can—then we are able to speak of the "origins," or the *kigen,* of that language. This, then, is what we are concerned with: how far back can we, at the present state of our knowledge, and at the present state of the science of historical linguistics, pursue the history of the Japanese language? And what do we find when we get back to that most remote past that our materials and methodology will allow us to uncover?

Perhaps this definition and delimitation of "origins" or *kigen* will at first seem a little disappointing, if we have been hoping that our study would indeed reveal to us some of the ways in which human beings first began to evolve their utilization of articulate speech. But most of us will probably agree that the study of linguistic origins as here defined and delimited is, in the long run, far more exciting and productive than any amount of unfounded speculation about whether people first began to speak by "bow wow" imitation or in order to tell one another lies about things they were buying and selling, or any other pure and simple speculation. As linguists, of course, we must leave all such speculation to the realm of creative writing and belles-lettres, where it belongs; we will concern ourselves instead with establishing, investigating, and pursuing history itself.

[13]

To some this may seem to run counter to "common sense." There appears to be a considerable body of opinion that in the investigation of language, particularly the history of language, all usual rules of scientific inquiry are somehow automatically suspended—apparently for no other reason than because the subject of the investigation is language.

It goes without saying that we cannot accept this "common sense" assumption. No one would suggest that it is possible to study the historical events in France at the time of Napoleon simply by speculating about what might have happened; no one would try to fix the date of the birth or death of a historical figure by guessing when it would have been possible, convenient, or likely that he might have been born or died. To determine these things we must find out what can be known from the surviving evidence. The study of the history of language is in no way different from the study of any other kind of history.

If we define our terms of investigation as we now agree to do here, we will be able to distinguish between what we do know about the remote past of this language, and what—for the present at least—we do not know. For most of us, that is a much more satisfactory state of affairs than the alternative of unrestricted speculation limited only by how inventive we may be in thinking up new "possibilities."

Viewed in this fashion, the "origins" of any language will be seen to be directly related to the "development" *(seiritsu)* and "genetic relationship" *(keitō)* of that language. We have now agreed that by studying the origins of the Japanese language, we mean pursuing the investigation of the history of that language back into the remote past, going as far back in time as our materials and methods will permit. This is closely related to the concept of linguistic study reflected in the term "development." We might think of the study of the "development" of a language as advancing from the past down toward the present, while the study of the "origins" of a language covers more or less the same things but in the opposite order.

When we have taken the history of the language, and the course of its development, as far back into the past as our materials and methods permit, we reach the question of "genetic relationship." This is because the linguistic concept of genetic

[14]

relationship *(keitō)* has direct reference to the most remote historical stage of any language to which we can approach in our research, that stage at which a given language is no longer the language we are studying but actually some other language, to which we generally refer to it as being "related." In the study of Japanese linguistic origins, this most remote historical stage, the stage in our inquiry when we encounter the question of the genetic relationship of Japanese to other languages, is in many ways the most important, and surely for most of us the most interesting, stage of all.

Having clarified what we *are* going to study, it will probably not be out of place to stress a few matters that we are *not* going to be concerned with. Actually, these "nonconcerns" can be summed up in a single statement: we are studying the history of language, not the history of race or the history of human genetic stocks or the history of anything else. But since the "common sense" approach to all these issues is often clouded by well-intentioned but extremely dangerous confusion between a number of terms and concepts (a confusion that most schools and universities in both Japan and the West do almost nothing to clear up, when indeed they do not actually increase it), we should give some attention to the problem.

Language is, as we have already emphasized, a complex set, the most complex set possible, of human behavioral patterns. But language is not the same thing as race, it is not the same as genetic stock, it surely is not nationality, and it is not material culture. As the single most complex set of behavioral patterns, it has a vital role in civilization; it participates intimately in every possible aspect of human endeavor; and it is difficult, if not impossible, to imagine divorcing language from the operation of any significant level or facet of human life.

But we do not have any evidence that language is essentially associated with human genetics, or with the history or development of any given human racial characteristic or bloodline. Languages have their histories; so do races and peoples, as well as smaller groups such as tribes and families. But there is no essential or causal connection between language and human genetic groupings. The study of linguistic origins, as here defined, will tell us a great deal about language, but it will never tell us anything

[15]

about human genetics. In the same way, evidence from the history of human genetics, in particular evidence from physical anthropology, cannot be taken over and applied to the study of linguistic origins: such evidence is important in its own field but is irrelevant to ours.

This necessity for a strict separation of linguistic evidence, and of linguistic studies based on this evidence, from the evidence for other varieties of human experience, and in particular from what we know, or would like to know, about the racial and genetic origins of the human stock, often comes as a surprise to persons interested in these topics. Many persons suppose— again, it is a natural enough, quite "common sense" assumption— that language somehow correlates closely with race or genetic background, and that in studying the one we are necessarily studying the other. This assumption is quite false, as a consideration of its theoretical basis and further implications will make clear.

Not only do languages change in the course of time, they also may be changed by their speakers—in the sense of being replaced. A person often grows up speaking one language, learns to speak others later in life, and eventually stops speaking—or even understanding—the first language. One is tempted to think of this as total or complete linguistic change—that is, the complete replacement of one language by another. If it were total or complete linguistic change, it would be particularly interesting, because unlike the other varieties of historical linguistic change, it would have taken place quite rapidly—within a few years in the lifetime of a single individual. But we know from experience that total or complete linguistic change of this variety is rare. If it takes place at all, it happens before the age of seven or eight, but hardly ever later. Beyond that age many speakers change their language, and many become extraordinarily proficient in the newly acquired language, but the change is rarely total or complete.

At any rate, if language had any essential or one-to-one link with race or genetic make-up, this entire process of language-learning and language-replacement by any individual would be impossible, since obviously no one can alter his or her racial background or genetic make-up. Language, like all aspects of human behavior, is acquired. It is acquired by imitation, either over a long period of time (the way an infant gradually learns a language while growing up), or over a comparatively short length of time (with later, artificial, or adult, language-learning). Language is a set of behavior patterns that can be relearned, altered, changed, abandoned, and replaced. None of these operations are possible for race or genetics.

For all these reasons, it is necessary to stress that even when we have finally managed to learn something about the "origins" of the Japanese language, we will not have discovered anything significant about the origin of the Japanese racial stock, or about how the Japanese people or race came into being, or even about where they came from—as a race, people, or genetic entity.

Many will find this disappointing. The reasons for their disappointment can be understood, but they do not alter the facts, nor do they justify violating the rules of scientific inquiry and trying to arrive at conclusions that will tell us something about certain fields—physical anthropology, human genetics, racial origins—on the basis of evidence and findings that are only valid for another field. Among the reasons why many persons, particularly in Japan, find this necessity for strict separation of linguistic history and linguistic investigation from questions of racial, national, and genetic origins extremely disappointing, probably the most important is the current search for national identity that is such a visible phenomenon today on so many levels of Japanese life. There is hardly any segment of Japanese society that is not concerned with what the Japanese themselves call the *Nihonjinron*—a concise term that is difficult to translate but easy to explain. It refers to the entire question of the identity crisis that modern Japanese society is experiencing.

More than half the present population of Japan was not born when the Pacific War ended. Still fewer persons in Japan today have any direct recollection of its disasters. With the horrors of the war thus rapidly receding, and propelled upon the world stage by the vigor of Japanese economic penetration into the markets of other countries, Japanese of all ages and from all walks of life, particularly since the early 1970s, have had both leisure and the strong motivation to ponder the *Nihonjinron,* and in the process to give serious consideration to their national identity:

[17]

Who are we? Where did we come from? How did we get to be the way we are? Where are we all going?

Most of these are queries that other people in the world first put to the Japanese, largely in response to the Japanese advance in the world economy. Initially, the Japanese were too busy with gaining and holding onto their new foothold in foreign markets to bother much about providing answers to these questions—questions that they were at first totally uninterested in, and questions for which there did not appear to be any answers. The older Japanese, of course, knew the set answers that the old fascist-nationalistic orthodoxy had provided for these questions, but clearly such answers would not do today. The younger Japanese had no answers at hand, and were not at first interested in the question.

With the coming of the 1970s, the situation reversed itself. No new answers were forthcoming; but now these same questions were being asked by the Japanese of themselves. Furthermore, they were being asked with an immediacy and urgency as remarkable for their intensity as for their permeation throughout all levels of Japanese society. As a result, Japanese scholarship, along with Japanese popular writing and journalism, has seized on these issues, and is busily approaching them from all possible avenues of inquiry—often, in the process, violating the most elementary rules of scientific investigation, in its eagerness to come up with easily understood and quickly available answers. It is this eagerness that more than anything else explains why so much of the writing—both scholarly and popular—on these problems in Japan makes the elementary methodological error of mixing up data from physical anthropology and genetics with data from linguistic history, and attempts to employ findings from one of these fields to answer questions that can only be treated in the other.

In Japan one can scarcely pick up a daily newspaper or weekly magazine without finding some article—often by a university scholar of surprisingly orthodox credentials—"announcing" the "discovery" that the Japanese language is genetically related to this or that language, generally some language whose geographical position from Japan is quite as remote as is the probability that it has anything to do with Japanese.

And always involved in these sensational accounts, sometimes simply by implication but often also by overt claim, is the further statement that since it has now been proved that Japanese (the language) is related to language X, then the Japanese (the people) are also related genetically, racially, anthropologically, to the speakers of that language. Even if the former claim were justified (which is hardly ever the case), the second statement would still not follow, either logically or necessarily. Unfortunately, it is always the second, the more unfounded and least supportable, of the two claims that attracts the most journalistic attention. This is because it is this second claim that comes closest to answering the identity-crisis demands of the *Nihonjinron*— seeming, as it does, to tell the Japanese who they are and where they came from, even if it has little to add about where they might be going.

In this way, most of the lively interest in questions of the history of the Japanese language for which one finds evidence in contemporary Japan—evidence in the form of countless articles in daily newspapers, sensational headlines in weekly magazines, and piles of books with equally sensational titles in every book-store—itself suffers from something of an identity crisis. It purports to be an interest in the language and its origins; but it is not so much that as an interest in the Japanese race, its origins, and its make-up. The confusion between language on the one hand and race and genetic background on the other is so deeply ingrained in modern Japanese thought that readers by the hundreds of thousands eagerly devour articles and books about the language and every aspect of its history, confident that in the process they will find out what they really want to know: who are we, and where did we come from? Their confidence is based in the usual, common-sense equation of language with race; and because this equation is false, their confidence is misplaced.

If we go to the trouble of pointing out in such detail the problems that the erroneous equation of race and language causes for others, it is only because we must always be on guard against its pitfalls ourselves. On the face of the matter, nothing could be simpler to keep in mind than the separation of linguistic data, and of conclusions based on their study, from anthropological, racial, or genetic data and conclusions. Even a society as remarkably homogeneous with respect to both race and language as modern Japan has plenty of opportunities every day to remind its members that language is not the same thing as race, and that learning about one does not necessarily reveal anything about the other. If, like the author, a person grew up speaking one language (German) and then all-but-totally replaced it with another (English), and meanwhile struggled hard to be able to deliver these lectures in a third (Japanese), he lives every day with the most concrete evidence of the essential nonconnection of language and race. After all, neither my race nor my genes changed when I stopped being able to use German and thereafter found I could only use English, nor do either my race or genes alter in the least, I suspect, when I gird my linguistic loins to deliver lectures in Japanese. But common-sense attitudes and approaches, sometimes even those that we know intellectually to be quite erroneous, can still prove to be extremely stubborn elements in our thought processes. It is better to run the risk of overemphasizing their erroneous nature than it is to find that we ourselves have fallen victim to their built-in fallacies.

The necessity for keeping linguistics, and linguistic data, separate from other kinds of data and investigation is not only the most important single problem that confronts the contemporary *Nihonjinron,* at least in the majority of its popular, journalistic representations as we encounter them in Japan today. The same necessity is one of the essential tasks—and apparently one of the most difficult problems—for all linguistic study, regardless of time, place, or the identity of the particular language in question. The great American linguistic scientist Leonard Bloomfield often remarked that the most difficult single thing about the entire field of linguistics is to make the decision to study language (which is, after all, the subject matter of linguistics) and then stick to that decision—in other words, not to neglect the study of language itself for extraneous, nonlinguistic considerations such as thought patterns, intellectual currents, sociological trends, and the multitude of other interesting red herrings that are so easily hauled in and dragged around once the study of language is mentioned. Sometimes anything, or everything, seems easier, or more rewarding, than the scientific study of language, that is, than linguistics. The difficulty that modern Japanese intellectual life is having today, and that it has been having since the early 1970s, if not earlier, in keeping its interest in the Japanese language and its origins separate from its interest in the Japanese race and its beginnings, is a specific illustration of what Bloomfield was talking about.

Now that we have a clearer idea of what we are going to be concerned with in this book, one final introductory question remains to be asked. Apart from the very special intellectual stimulus exerted by the *Nihonjinron,* is there really any good or considerable reason for us in the West to be concerned about the origins of the Japanese language at all?

If we think about this problem for a moment, we will see that it is a major one. The *Nihonjinron* is by definition something that can only involve a Japanese—and properly so: it arises in response to the stimulation of the modern Japanese identity crisis, and we in the West do not share in that crisis. The modern Japanese, in his search for an identity in which to clothe himself as he sets forth into the world's markets with his Aladdin's bag of magic transistors and tiny TVs, is in a state of identity crisis. But his crisis will only be increased if he is mistakenly led by those who should know better into believing that some clue to his identity as a world citizen will be found lurking within his language. We can all sympathize with this, but we do not all share his crisis; and so we must ask if there is any point at all to our involvement, as non-Japanese, with these questions in the first place—especially since we have already gone out of our way to point out that whatever we may learn about the origin of the language, we will still not be in a position to tell our friends from Japan very much about where, as individuals or as members of the human race, they "came from."

Fortunately, the answer to this final and most important of our introductory questions is an unqualified yes. There is a real, and important, question to be localized in the problem of the origins of the Japanese language; moreover, it is a question that is far more important than any association, real or misleading, that might possibly be made between it and the *Nihonjinron.* The question of the origins of the Japanese language is a genuine, intellectually important one, and it is worth our serious consideration, whether we are Japanese or not. As we approach its solution, we will not, to be sure, find ourselves learning concrete information about "where the Japanese came from," at least not in the confident, identity-crisis-answering fashion that the *Nihonjinron* would like to see. But that kind of an answer is important, if it is important at all, only for Japanese. For us, as non-Japanese scholars who are engaged in the study of this topic, the question of the origins of the Japanese language is a matter of great interest and importance. But this interest expresses itself differently from that of our Japanese colleagues. For that reason, it will be worthwhile to explore the subject here, if only briefly.

The question of the origins of the Japanese language poses a valid scientific and intellectual problem for world scholarship—not simply Japanese scholarship—for the simple but profound reason that the Japanese language exists where it does, in the Japanese islands, and for the related fact that it has been there for at least a thousand years, and probably much longer. Where did it come from? The only way we can answer that question, in this context, is to study the origins of the language, in the sense of pursuing its history back as far as possible.

The Japanese language is in Japan today; and it must have come there from somewhere. This is a simple and plain but extremely important fact, which like many of the basic facts of human life, follows upon what are again simple but extremely important matters of physical geography. The Japanese islands are largely volcanic in geological origin. The home islands, as well as the much longer chain of smaller bits of land that stretches on toward the south, are in fact the surfacing tips of a vast volcanic ridge. The Japanese islands are the tops of volcanoes, now mostly extinct, but not all or totally. In recent years merchant ships or coastal patrol vessels in Japanese waters have from time to time reported the awesome sight of underwater volcanic activity so intense that it begins to break through to the surface, and on occasion even begins to form the land mass of a new island, thus giving us an on-the-scene example of how the majority of the islands were formed in the extremely remote past.

In this sense, then, the Japanese islands are not only isolated from the land mass of Asia but are largely the products of late geological activity. This means that everything that is found on them now, and everything that has been on them in historical times, must have come from somewhere else—unless we are to assume that it evolved independently on these islands. And there simply is not enough time in the geological scheme to accommodate the long process of evolution for any of the higher plants or animals of the Japanese island chains. Everything found on these islands had to come from somewhere: the plants, the animals, the people, the language.

Since few would seriously attempt to argue for an independent Japanese evolution of thousands of species of plants and animals, not to mention *Homo sapiens*—that most complex and slowest to evolve of all the higher animals—only one other possibility is worthy of consideration: all these things had to come from somewhere else. They cannot be native to the Japanese islands, in the sense that they did not evolve there from other forms. (Even that would leave us with the question of where these other forms came from, but the point is valid even without that additional complication.)

Man is the highest animal, distinguished from other higher animals chiefly by possessing language, that most elaborate set of behavioral patterns, more complex than any other system of communication employed by any other of his subhuman relatives. We still know too little about the history of human evolution to answer the question of how many different times in history (or the equally difficult question of at how many different places in the world) man—*Homo sapiens*—may have evolved.

Certainly the process of the evolution of man from the lower animals was involved enough, and something that took such a very long time, that the chances of it having happened often under totally independent circumstances of time and place appear to be extremely remote. All myths incorporate hard kernels of truth; the greater the myth, the greater the truth on which it ultimately rests. The tremendously impressive myth of a unique creation of man, at a single time and place, to be found, for example, in the pages of the Old Testament as well as in the creation myths of more than one other ancient religion, may very well represent, *mutatis mutandis,* a fairly faithful narrative of the way the entire thing happened: once, and at one place, and only once for all mankind.

But for the purpose of our present consideration, it does

not very much matter whether man evolved only once or several different times. Either way, no reputable scholar would seriously argue that the evolution of *Homo sapiens* took place in the Japanese islands. Neither the substance nor the spirit of the Japanese myth, with its folk-wisdom interpretation of the oldest memories of the race, as recorded much later in such texts as the *Kojiki* and the *Nihon shoki,* points in any such direction.

It is the nature as well as the function of myth to provide an understandable and rational framework within which the essential, and often awesome, observed facts of life can be accommodated--a framework that for the formulators as well as the believers of the myth brings order and reason to what would otherwise be the baffling evidence of everyday life. The Japanese myth is full of arrivals and advents: gods coming down from heaven, gods coming to the islands, gods sending their semidivine relations throughout the islands on missions of conquest. The Japanese myth is, of course, not to be confused with history; but like all true myths, it is also not antihistorical. The Japanese myth served its essential mythic ends by explaining the "meaning" of all the arrivals, journeys, and dangerous advents in new, unfamiliar, and surely often hostile territory, that were the common, well-remembered experiences of the entire Japanese race from its earliest days—whoever they were and wherever they came from. And whoever they were, they surely came from somewhere.

The language of this island race also had to come from somewhere. If we must define the point at which one of the higher animals became *Homo sapiens,* surely few would hesitate to correlate that point with the development of articulate human language. It does not really matter that language, by its very nature, leaves no tangible evidence for paleontology, archaeology, or any of the allied sciences. Language does not begin to leave visible, tangible evidence until the invention of writing systems, and we know that all of them, even the oldest in the ancient Middle East, are much more recent that the development of language itself. But our species is called *Homo sapiens* for only one obvious reason: the term refers of course to language; and one can hardly believe that human language evolved independently in the Japanese islands any more than one can believe that man himself did.

Thus the Japanese language had to come to the Japanese islands from somewhere: that we have now established. But does the question of where that somewhere was, or how this all happened, matter for anyone who is not a Japanese, or for anyone who is not caught up in the identity crisis of modern Japan and its *Nihonjinron?* This question is a little more difficult to answer than the first, but only a little; and the answer here too is a strongly affirmative one.

The question does matter, for the again quite simple reason that Japanese is the language of Japan, one of the five or six major nations that determine the course of modern life and history for all of us, no matter who we are or where we live. But among the languages of these five or six major nations, it is the language of Japan and of Japan alone that remains obscure, as far as its linguistic origins are concerned.

This is true of the language of no other major nation in the world today. We know a great deal about the origins of English, German, and Russian, and about all the Romance languages such as French, Italian, and Portuguese. We are able to pursue the history of these languages back into the extremely remote past, and to relate all of them, in various ways and along extremely different paths of descent, to an original linguistic unity that linguists call Indo-European.

With Chinese the situation is a little different. No one has yet presented convincing linguistic evidence for the historical relationship of Chinese to any other linguistic family or stock, but that does not mean we are ignorant of Chinese linguistic origins. This apparent paradox is explained by the fact that when we speak of Chinese, we are in fact already speaking of an enormous family of related languages. The many different languages of the different parts of China—the varieties of speech that are, in the West, often but most incorrectly and misleadingly referred to as dialects—are all genetically related to each other. Having recognized this fact, linguists have been able to pursue the study of Chinese linguistic origins totally within the Chinese linguistic domain itself. In the process, they have learned a great deal about the earlier stages of the Chinese language, even about the language in those remote periods in its history that predate the use of writing in China. In this sense, we are well informed about the origins of Chinese.

[25]

This means that only one language of one major nation remains today without clarification of its origins—Japanese. As long as this remains true about Japanese, all the rest of the world, along with the Japanese themselves, will be in the dark about something that is essential for a fuller understanding of Japan and its role in the modern world.

The Japanese themselves want to know these things for different reasons—reasons that are very important for them. The Japanese are increasingly faced by the stimulus to know themselves, as they take on the full role of international responsibility that Japan has at last begun to assume in the modern world. Their needs in this connection are different from ours: but we are faced with a similar need to know much the same things, if for different reasons. We in the West simply cannot afford to remain ignorant about Japan and its culture; and the language of any country is without question one of the most important facets of the culture and the civilization of that country.

Japan is, and will surely remain, an important member of the family of nations. It is one of the world's leading industrial and economic powers. In a sense, the fortunes and destinies of us all are controlled to some measure by Japan, as they are controlled by all the modern, highly developed countries of the world. Simple self-interest, and a concern for our own lives, means that none of us can afford to live in ignorance of this nation, its culture, and its civilization. Knowledge of the language, and of the origins of that language, must undergird all our understanding. Otherwise such understanding as does exist will continue to be what it has too often been in the past—superficial and trivial.

But even having said this, we still have not directly answered the question why non-Japanese scholars of linguistic science should find it necessary to become involved in these studies. Why is it not possible for us in the West simply to inform ourselves on these issues, important as we now recognize them to be, by studying the research and conclusions of Japanese scholars? Again, it would seem to be only "common sense" to assume that Japanese linguistic scholarship either had already reached a considerable body of opinion concerning these questions or was well on its way toward achieving such a position. Once more,

[26]

the "common sense" approach to the issue turns out to be totally misleading.

The simple fact is that the question of the origins of the Japanese language turns out to be something about which contemporary Japanese scholarship can tell us almost nothing. So if we in the West are agreed that there is a genuine need for us to know about this subject, we must find out about it largely on our own. Surprisingly enough, this is an area of investigation in which we can count on little assistance from our Japanese academic colleagues.

For all who are familiar with the rapid proliferation of higher education, and of facilities for every sort of advanced scientific research in Japan, ever since the introduction of a system of modern education from Europe and America some hundred years ago, the extremely flat and negative statement just made will no doubt come as something of a surprise, and may indeed be greeted with disbelief. Is it possible that this country, with its thousands of colleges and hundreds of universities, this highly developed industrial power whose engineers, technicians, and designers are able to produce scientific and mechanical devices of every variety, and often of the most surprising precision and capability, has lagged so far behind in the study of its own linguistic heritage? Is it possible, given the large numbers of Japanese in all educational fields who go abroad to study each year in Europe and America, that there can remain anything about this subject that has not been discovered by the Japanese themselves?

In each case, the "common-sense" answer would be negative. Surely we would expect that this highly advanced country had settled this question once and for all, long ago. And certainly this is a topic on which our Japanese colleagues might justly be expected to have come up with satisfactory, and fairly conclusive, answers. But again, in each case, the facts are different. Japanese scholarship has not come up with any satisfactory explanation for the origins of the Japanese language, nor does it appear to be any closer to achieving such a position than it was fifty or even a hundred years ago.

All this is a most surprising paradox. Like any paradox, this situation itself is worthy of investigation, since its study would have much to teach us about Japanese civilization, and in

[27]

particular about Japanese academia and intellectual circles (the last two being no more congruent in Japan than they are anywhere else in the world). Near the end of this book we shall consider some of the major reasons why contemporary Japanese linguistic scholarship finds itself at this stalemate. At present, it is sufficient to record that the stalemate does exist, and to note that it is not only a very real one but also has become an almost total block that stands squarely in the way of almost all Japanese scholarship in this area of investigation.

Japanese academia likes to work, and to think as well as to talk, in terms of what it calls a *teisetsu*. This is a word very commonly met in Japanese writing (and in college and university lecturing), but like many words that are extremely common in Japanese, it turns out to be harder to translate into English than one might expect. It can be approximately rendered in English as "established theory, accepted opinion, settled conviction"; but all these translations more or less miss the real point of a *teisetsu*. The word refers, in effect, to a theory or hypothesis (and Japanese scholarship does not, in this connection at least, generally distinguish between the two) that is sufficiently well established, and accepted sufficiently large numbers of Japanese scholars, to be safely employed as the "right answer" for questions set on university entrance examinations.

Since in America we have nothing resembling that remarkable system of university entrance examinations that distinguishes Japanese academic life, at the same time that it so sharply affects every facet of Japanese society, we do not generally have to worry about having a *teisetsu* on any given topic. But in Japanese life and society, the university entrance examinations are matters of tremendous importance to everyone. The futures of many lives hang on getting the "right answers" in these examinations. Each of many different fields of knowledge must somehow arrive at a *teisetsu* if it is to be represented in the examination procedures. For the origins of the Japanese language, there is at present no *teisetsu* in Japanese academic circles. If the question of its origins were to be raised on university entrance examinations, the only "right answer" possible would be to state that, concerning this problem, there is no *teisetsu*. (To avoid using the Japanese term further, we shall render it below with the

English word "consensus," even though consensus is hardly an exact equivalent for *teisetsu,* lacking in particular the adumbrations of orthodoxy that are a necessary part of a *teisetsu;* still, consensus is about the best that we can do for this difficult term in English.)

Not only does Japanese linguistic scholarship today in this way universally admit that it has arrived at no consensus concerning the origins of the Japanese language, but this lack of a consensus on the subject itself become almost a matter of pride in some of the academic circles that have taken a special interest in the question. Most Japanese scholars who write on this topic content themselves with repeating over and over (and often at what strikes us as surprising length, considering the essentially negative content of their views) that there is no consensus in Japan today on where the Japanese language came from, or what other languages it is related to. Since this approach tells us nothing we did not already know, its usefulness is quite limited; but at least it is to be preferred to another approach, also not difficult to document, in which the very lack of a consensus concerning its origins is treated as if it were a distinguishing or remarkable characteristic of the Japanese language itself—and, in the hands of a few scholars, even as if this were a characteristic of the language about which there was some reason to feel proud.

In these hands, the very lack of a consensus on this question has almost become a scholarly fetish. Not only do some scholars repeat over and over that nothing is known about the subject, but they also stress their equally strong belief that the very lack of knowledge is itself something of importance, and indeed, a matter for Japanese racial pride. This curious reversal of scholarship sometimes goes so far that we find Japanese scholars who not only claim that nothing is known about the subject today but who also confidently predict that the situation will never change: nothing can ever possibly be found out about this subject by anyone, themselves included.

At this point, the serious student of historical linguistics will cease to be interested in their views, which are no longer as much his concern as they are now the special province of the sociological pathologist. To attempt to make a virtue out of what is known, and to claim that what is not known now will always remain obscure, represents a behavioral pattern that can hardly be accommodated within the usual canons of scholarship. Fortunately, many avenues exist for the further investigation of such highly deviant patterns of behavior, but, equally fortunately, none of those avenues are the immediate concern of the linguist, and so we gladly and gratefully leave to others the burden of pursuing these curious deviations from scholarly norms.

The essence of all scholarship, and of all academic inquiry, is the wish, as well as the will, to know. Both are predicated on the conviction that at least some important and significant facts can be found out about everything that exists in the world in which we live, if only we study and try hard enough. To assume that the problem of the origins of the Japanese language is an exception to this rule—and that by definition it is a subject about which we will never be able to learn anything worthwhile—is to abandon scholarship and academic inquiry totally. At the same time, it must be noted that these prophets of ignorance do merchandise a completely reliable self-fulfilling prophecy. Nothing is more certain than the fact that if one works on such assumptions of nihilism and academic agnosticism, nothing worthwhile will ever be found out about this or any other subject in the world.

In other words, Japanese scholarship has achieved no consensus on the origins of the Japanese language. We cannot, therefore, simply turn to Japanese scholarship on this question and thus spare ourselves the considerable labor of investigating this difficult but important subject ourselves, for the simple reason that Japanese scholarship has—by its own admission, if not by its own proud claim—so far discovered nothing useful to tell us about the matter.

So much for the East: what then about the West? When we turn to Western scholarship on the origins of the Japanese language, we find a situation that is quite the opposite of what we have just described for Japanese scholarship. In the West, there is a consensus on this question. (Here, of course, we are using the term "consensus" somewhat less in the rather special meaning of Japanese *teisetsu* than we have above, but hope in the process to bridge at least a part of the semantic gap between these two terms, as well as between the two concepts that lie behind them.)

Western scholarship does have a consensus, a general agreement of opinion on the part of those in a position to speak with more or less authority—the authority of original scholarship and scholarly investigation—on the question of where the Japanese language came from.

This alone is fairly surprising. Equally surprising is the fact that the consensus of Western scholarship on this question is almost unknown in Japan, where it has received little notice or general attention, despite the tremendous interest currently being taken by all levels of the Japanese public in these questions. The failure of these findings by foreign scholarship to permeate the Japanese mass media, and through those channels to reach the broad horizon of the Japanese reading public, is not difficult to explain. Largely it has to do with the fact that these findings have been more often than not published in a number of European languages, particularly German and Russian, that are less widely read and studied in Japan today than English is. Still, this does not explain why findings that have been published in English have also generally been ignored in Japan. And certainly it cannot explain the most surprising fact of all, namely that these findings have failed to achieve any wide distribution even in the specialized scholarly circles of Japanese academia that are most deeply involved in the study of this very question, and with professional research and study of the Japanese language itself. If scholars, particularly scholars in the same field, are not motivated to follow and digest the world literature related to their specialities, no matter what language it may be published in, is it any wonder that newspapers and cheap weekly magazines do not?

This is, indeed, a strange paradox. On the one hand, we have Japanese scholarship, busily proclaiming its own inability to achieve a consensus about where the Japanese language came from, and in some quarters even boasting that it will be impossible for anyone ever to find out more than it knows about this subject at present, which is to say, nothing. On the other, we have Western linguistic scholarship, which believes it has been able to reach a consensus on this issue. Furthermore, the paradox is complicated by the fact that academic and intellectual traffic between these two camps is almost entirely one-way. Western

[31]

scholarship closely monitors the work of its Japanese colleagues for whatever it may pick up that will be useful or informative, but Japanese scholarship almost totally ignores Western findings, and so it stands today almost totally unacquainted even with the existence of a consensus on this important question among most non-Japanese scholars, much less achieving a firsthand familiarity with the scholarly works in question.

This is the curious, and frustrating, situation to which I would like particularly to address myself, not only because it is obviously by taking on the task of informing one of these branches of scholarship about the findings and views of the other that I can be most useful, but also because I am quite sure that it was largely with this in mind that I was asked to deliver these lectures in the first place. And that invitation itself shows quite plainly— if such demonstration were at all necessary—that certain Japanese scholars themselves are by and large no more satisfied with the present sharp isolation of their work from that of their Western colleagues than we are. There can be no doubt that many Japanese scholars are as anxious as we in the West to bring the present unnecessary and frustrating separation between these two different camps of scholarly inquiry to an end as quickly as possible.

2. The Comparative Method

Before summarizing the current consensus of Western scholarship on the origins of the Japanese language, it may be both interesting and useful to note that the study of this question in the West has had a somewhat longer history than it has had in Japan. This is an important fact neither widely known nor generally understood in Japan, hence not without its own value for our present discussion.

The first serious scholarly work on this question in Japanese academic circles did not appear until 1908, in a paper published by Fujioka Katsuji (1872-1935). Fujioka had studied comparative and historical linguistics in Europe, mainly in Germany, during the period 1901-5, and after his return to Japan he became a professor at the so-called Tokyo Imperial University. Fujioka and his new post, as well as the Imperial University itself, were all significant expressions of the tremendous strides that Japan, following the Meiji Restoration of 1868, had almost immediately begun to take in order to introduce modern facilities for education, research, and technology from Europe and America. Fujioka's paper in 1908 on the probable origins of the Japanese language was the first such contribution to appear from Japanese academic circles for the simple reason that before his time there were no Japanese academic circles.

But almost two decades before Fujioka was born, and eleven years before the Meiji Restoration was finally to set modern Japan on its course of participation in the world community, a Viennese scholar named Anton Boller had already published a lengthy monograph on the question of the origins of the Japanese language. His study, of course, has many defects and inadequacies, which are only to be expected considering when it appeared (1857). Many of Boller's linguistic materials were incomplete or inaccurate, both those he drew from Japanese and many of the forms he cited from other Asian languages, and his conclusions could hardly rise above the level of his sources. Nevertheless, in 1857—the year after the landing of the first American consular official, Townsend Harris, in the miserable rural fishing village of Shimoda—Boller in Vienna was able to achieve a number of concrete results in his study of the origins of the Japanese language, and to document a number of facts that even today must command both our attention and our respect. Given this impressive running start that Western linguistic science has had ever since Boller's pioneering efforts, it becomes somewhat easier to understand why Japanese studies of the question have tended to lag behind.

The essential directions for the origins of the Japanese language in which Boller's studies pointed in 1857 are still, in the main, those to which the consensus of Western scholarship looks today, though naturally in the more than 120 years since Boller's time, we have found out much more than he was able to, and are able to present arguments and evidence based on far more reliable data from all the linguistic areas concerned than he had available to him at the time he did his pioneering work.

Boller concluded, in 1857, that Japanese was genetically related to the family of languages that he called Ural-Altaic.

By the term Ural-Altaic, the Viennese scholar meant a large family of languages, embracing Finnish, Hungarian, and other Uralic languages at the one extreme, and Turkish, Mongolian, and other Altaic languages at the other. Today the consensus of Western scholarship would somewhat modify his position and identify Japanese simply as one of the Altaic languages—in other words, as a language genetically related to the same original, but now lost, language of an extremely remote period (Altaic or Proto-Altaic) to which are also related such languages as Turkish, Mongolian, Manchu, and most likely also Korean. (We shall see below more of what is meant by the Altaic languages, and also some of the further implications of the term and concept "genetic relationship.")

Boller, for his part, was very certain of his results; in fact, his monograph was entitled *Nachweis,* or "Proof," since he believed that he had completely demonstrated the relationship of Japanese to the other languages with which he attempted to associate it historically. Today we have a somewhat different, and somewhat more carefully defined, view of the entire nature of historical relationships between languages, no matter what type of grammar or syntax they may display structurally or where in the world they may be spoken. We understand better than Boller did some of the ways in which languages stand in historical relationship to one another. Given our present understanding of these problems, few historical linguists would attempt today to speak or write of "proof" in connection with such questions. We now understand that the historical relationship of one language to another—in other words, the entire question of the existence of genetic relationships between various languages, and hence also the issue that we have here termed the origins of a language— is not actually something that is susceptible to proof, if by "proof" we understand the word in its generally accepted sense of a final, positive demonstration of evidence so totally conclusive that no one can challenge or question it.

The existence of a historical relationship between two or more languages, is, we now understand, not something that we can ever prove. What we can do is continue to collect more and more convincing evidence, materials that carry more and more power of conviction, data that more and more point in the direc-

[35]

tion of such a conclusion. The genetic relationship of one language to another cannot be proved and it cannot be disproved. The same is true of the origin of any given language since by origin we simply mean the genetic relationship of the language we are talking about, pursued as far back into the past as we can manage.

But even though proof, positive and final, is impossible here, that does not really matter very much. In questions of this sort, we are dealing, first of all, with the establishment of a reasonable hypothesis and, second, with the possibility of supporting it by evidence. As the evidence grows, the hypothesis, if it is correct, becomes more and more convincing. If not, it must be abandoned or replaced by a new or revised hypothesis. When sufficient data have been brought together, studied, sifted, and analyzed, then they will carry conviction among scholars who are equipped, by their training in the science of historical linguistics on the one hand and their knowledge of the languages concerned on the other, to evaluate such matters.

Thus, instead of the "proof" of which Boller wrote, we would rather speak today of collecting more and more convincing evidence on the historical origins of the Japanese language; and rather than finding such origins in the Ural-Altaic language family, we would today look instead to the Altaic language family alone. But with these two largely technical revisions of terminology, Boller's scholarly achievements of 1857 still have surprising validity. There is no question that this Viennese scholar of over a century ago, not very well known today even in Europe, and all but unknown in Japan, deserves credit for the first significant, modern contribution to the question of the origins of the Japanese language.

In order to evaluate Boller's tremendous contribution, and especially to understand somewhat better the significance of the presently held consensus of Western scholarship on the Altaic origins of the Japanese language, we must first make clear some of the essential facts about the other Altaic languages, and also comment briefly on the nature and concept of "genetic relationship" between languages. Once these questions have been treated, we will be in a much better position to understand how Japanese goes together historically with these languages, and also, in a larger sense, what is meant by the deceptively simple statement that Japanese is one of the Altaic languages.

To begin with, it is important to understand that the word Altaic as employed in this book is not the name of any single language. There is no living language today that we can point to as the Altaic language, and while we identify a very special kind of linguistic entity of the remote past as Altaic, this does not mean that we know or believe that there ever was a group of speakers who called themselves, or their language, Altaic. Rather, the word Altaic in the special sense employed here is a technical term, coined by historical linguists, as a convenient label to designate the family of languages of which Japanese, along with many other languages, is now generally thought to be a member.

The word Altaic was originally a geographical not a linguistic designation. It is an adjective that refers to the Altai Mountains of Central Asia, a major range that stretches across southwest Mongolia, runs between Mongolia and Sinkiang Province of the Chinese People's Republic, and extends deep into the present territory of the Soviet Union. We do not know precisely where the oldest, most original form of the Altaic language family was employed as a language (any more than we know what name, if any, its speakers called themselves, or their language), but since from the available evidence it has long seemed likely to many students of this problem that this original location—the "original home" *(Urheimat)* of the earliest Altaic speakers—was somewhere in the Altai mountain range (or rather more likely, as we shall see below, in its southern foothills), scholars have long used this adjective Altaic as a convenient designation for the entire family of languages with which we are here concerned. It is also this same Altaic family of languages to which most of us who are concerned with this question in the West now believe Japanese to be historically related.

The Altaic language family is enormously large, and extremely important for an understanding of the distribution, history, and probable early movements of populations throughout the vast land mass of Asia. It may be divided into three principal subbranches, consisting of the Turkic, Mongolian, and Tungusic languages. Each of these three branches in turn embraces

[37]

a large number of different but genetically related languages—languages genetically related to one another within each of these three principal subbranches, but also genetically related to one another, since they are all later, changed forms of an original—*the* original—language of the earliest Altaic sociolinguistic community, wherever in Asia this may have been located.

Among the many important languages in the world today that belong historically to this Altaic family are such languages as the modern Turkish of Turkey, the modern Mongolian of the Mongolian People's Republic, and—belonging to the third of these principal subbranches, the one of the three least familiar to nonspecialists in the West—the so-called Tungusic languages (such languages as Lamut, Evenki, and Goldi, all still employed in parts of the Far Eastern regions of the USSR, where they are the languages of small racial minority groups who still apparently manage to preserve a certain amount of their original cultural and linguistic identity).

Among these generally little-known Tungusic languages, one stands out in particular because of its importance for the history of China in premodern times. This is Manchu, or Manchurian, a Tungusic language that today is all but extinct, but which in the seventeenth century was the language of the Manchu tribes who overran China at the end of the Ming dynasty, replacing the Ming line of rulers with their own, and ruling China as the Ch'ing dynasty for some three centuries, down to the establishment of the Chinese Republic in 1912. In the early part of the Ch'ing period, the original Manchu language of these foreign rulers of China was employed, together with Chinese, in all matters of state and administration, although as the Ch'ing period continued, Chinese was used more and more frequently and the Manchu language was increasingly neglected.

Even from this brief description we see one of the most important things about the Altaic languages: the enormous scope of their geographical distribution. They reach all the way across Asia, from Turkey to the northern coastal regions of "Manchuria," the original homeland of the Manchus (today the province of Kirin in the Chinese People's Republic). And this tremendous geographical range grows even more impressive when, following the consensus of most Western scholarship, we add to these principal languages, as noted above, Korean—also most likely one of the Altaic languages—and Japanese. With these additions to the more traditional inventory of the Altaic languages, the geographical distribution of the family is extended even beyond the furthest limits of the Asian land mass, to embrace the islands of the Japanese archipelago, as well as the Korean peninsula.

All the Altaic languages mentioned above—with the possible exception of Manchu, which is either already a dead language or well on its way to extinction—are living languages, in use today, hence available for scientific observation, either directly (going to the country, learning the language, etc.) or indirectly (through studying grammars and dictionaries produced by scholars who are able to study them directly, or working with native speakers of the languages). This second kind of indirect study is necessary, for example, for most of the Tungusic languages, and also for many of the Turkic ones that are found in their modern, living forms only in areas of the USSR, where generally only Soviet scholars are permitted access for purposes of study. So we must generally rely on the grammars and dictionaries that these scholars prepare for our information about such languages. But many other varieties of the modern Turkic languages, and even Mongolian—plus, of course, Japanese and Korean—are much more easily available for direct study and observation.

In any investigation of the possible historical relationship between languages, however, we will not only concern ourselves with the modern, living forms of the languages, but we will also wish, whenever possible, to consult any written documentation that may exist for the earlier forms of the languages in question. In studying the historical connections between the various Romance languages, for example, we do not limit ourselves to modern French, modern Italian, modern Spanish, and so on, but also study the earlier written records, including early written forms of French, Italian, and Spanish, and particularly the early written records of Latin, since in one sense or another all the Romance languages are later, changed forms of one variety or another of Latin, even though this was not precisely, nor necessarily, the classical, literary Latin of our written records.

In the case of the various branches of the Altaic languages, we will be disappointed if we insist on looking for early written records of any significant antiquity. Here nothing is to be found that is anywhere as remote in time as are, for example, the earliest written records for some of the languages of the ancient Middle East, or for Chinese, or for some of the early Indo-European languages, such as Sanskrit, many of which go back thousands of years. Among the Altaic languages the earliest written records that we have are, as it happens, a relatively few from the easternmost branch of the family, Turkic, and a large number from Japanese, at the westernmost geographical extremity of the vast area of Eurasia that finally came to be dominated by Altaic speakers.

For Turkic, these oldest written records are a number of inscriptions found along the Orkhon River and deciphered by European scholars in the last century, inscriptions written in an early form of one of the Turkic languages that scholars now call Old Turkish. This name is used because these monumental inscriptions from the Orkhon are the oldest form of any of the Turkic languages for which surviving written records preserve substantial linguistic evidence. In the terminology of historical linguistics, "Old" is a relative, not an absolute term; it is used to refer to the oldest form of a given language for which there is documentary evidence. In the case of Old Indic (Sanskrit), the language in question is recorded in a form that was used millennia ago, while on the other hand the language we call Old English is as recent as the twelfth century.

Contemporary with these records of Old Turkish are the written records for the earliest stage of Japanese, the language of the Nara period which we have already noted above under the designation Old Japanese. There were certainly also old written records for the Korean language dating from this period, or perhaps even from some centuries prior to the time of both Old Turkish and Old Japanese. Unfortunately, most of these early written records for Korean were destroyed in the course of the troubled political and social history that has over the centuries characterized life on the Korean peninsula. And even for the few precious Old Korean texts that we do have left to us by history, the unfortunate fact is that not enough is understood about the language that underlies most of them to make these documents, old though they surely are, genuinely useful for historical linguistic studies

[40]

With Old Korean, apart from a few fragments, thus effectively removed from the picture, we are left, in the Altaic language family, with old written records existing only for Old Turkish at the one geographical extreme and Old Japanese at the other. And neither of these is particularly old, certainly not in terms of the antiquity of the peoples who spoke these languages, and especially not when viewed against the evidence we have for the antiquity of the original Altaic linguistic entity itself.

Otherwise, and again with the exception of a few fragmentary records, the oldest written evidence for most of the Altaic languages does not go back very far. For Mongolian, the bulk of the old written materials are not earlier than the quasi-historical, quasi-mythological text known to Western scholars as the *Secret History of the Mongols.* (The word "secret" in this curious title actually means "private" or "intimate." It refers to the fact that this text, which was orally transmitted long before it was committed to writing, contains ancient mythic materials of the early Mongols, along with the genealogies of their rulers and other ethnic lore which they preferred to keep secret from their neighbors, including the Chinese, with whom they were generally at war.) But the language of this text, while extremely important for the history of the many different later Mongolian languages, and also for the history of Altaic languages in general, is neither representative of nor close in its linguistic features to the earliest forms of the Mongolian language, and so we call its language Middle Mongolian.

For the many Tungusic languages, we have almost no earlier evidence from written records. The peoples who have spoken, and who today speak, the Tungusic languages live in some of the most unhospitable terrain on the face of the globe. The harsh circumstances of their economic and social life, resulting from the unfavorable economic and ecological situation in which they find themselves, have seldom allowed them the luxury of developing systems of writing. In most cases, scripts have been fitted to the Tungusic languages only in modern times, usually by Soviet linguists working with the speakers of these minority languages subsequent to their political incorporation into the USSR.

The only notable exception is, again, the Manchu language, which was first written in a script borrowed from the Mongols

[41]

in the latter part of the sixteenth century. (The Mongols in turn had borrowed this script from others: writing, almost like language itself, has had relatively few totally independent discoveries in the long course of human history.) Technically speaking, the earliest written records of Manchu might be called Old Manchu, or even Old Tungusic, but since they are actually so very recent in date, these terms are hardly ever used. Slightly earlier than these earliest Manchu written records is a corpus of important, though difficult to interpret, written records for another older form of a Tungusic language, the language of the Jurchens. The Manchus considered the Jurchens to be their ancestors, and their language shows itself to be closely related to, though linguistically slightly older than, the Manchu language. Otherwise, the entire Tungusic subbranch of Altaic is totally lacking in old written records; here we must depend entirely on the evidence of the modern, living languages.

If the methodology by means of which the science of historical linguistics collects its data, and through which it is able to assemble the increasingly convincing evidence that finally leads to significant statements concerning the historical connections between various languages, were totally or even principally dependent on the testimony of old written records, then obviously, from what we have just seen of the Altaic languages, this methodology could not find useful application in the study of the genetic relationship of these languages. Particularly in the case of the many Tungusic languages, and also in the case of Korean, where early written materials are almost totally lacking, any kind of historical linguistic study that depended wholly or in major part on the existence of old written documents, or on any variety of ancient written documents, would have to be ruled out. Our studies simply could not proceed.

Even in the case of such languages as Turkish and Japanese, the earliest written records that we do have for the older forms of these languages—in other words, the texts that document those stages of these languages that we have been calling Old Turkish and Old Japanese—are relatively recent in time. The time span between Old Turkish, or Old Japanese, and the present, is such a mere moment in history, compared with the interval between each of these languages and the origins of the language itself,

[42]

that even these written records, old though they are and precious though they may well prove to be for our study, really do not take us very far back into the history of these languages.

If our pursuit of the history of Japanese, or of any other Altaic language, were to depend solely on written records, we would find out very little about its origins. Fortunately, this is not the case. Important and valuable though they are, early written records are not essential for the historical study of linguistic origins. And even when they are available, and are far older and more abundant, they do not provide us with a major method-ological tool for the pursuit of the history of each individual language in the group back as far as it is possible, as well as neces-sary, to go—in other words, back far enough to become involved in the study of the origins of each individual language, Japanese included.

Fortunately, our chief tool for this study is not the inspec-tion of older written records, even in the case of languages that do have them. Rather, our most important tool is the comparison of the languages with one another. Such comparison, when carried out according to a rather involved procedure that unfortunately can be described here only in outline, soon shows us which ele-ments these languages have in common because they have inherited them from an original, common ancestor.

In this way, the technique of linguistic comparison itself provides us with information about extremely remote stages in the history of the languages concerned—stages so remote that no written records could possibly be expected to have existed then. This comparison should always "keep one eye," as it were, on the data of early records, if such data are available. But even in the fortunate cases where this happens to be true, the history of a language must always be based on the comparison of data obtained from observed, attested, living languages, if such lin-guistic history is to achieve any significant time depth in its treat-ment of the subject matter.

It is this methodology of comparison—the specialized scholarly technique of linguistic study that is generally called the comparative method or sometimes comparative grammar—that makes it possible for us to pursue linguistic origins back into time, much further back than those periods in the past for which

[43]

we do have written records for any human language, even for those languages of the ancient Middle East that are attested in writing long before any other languages in different parts of the world, China and the rest of the Far East included.

By applying the techniques of this comparative method, which was first discovered and then refined to a high point of precision largely by the efforts of German scholars in the nineteenth and early twentieth centuries, who were working with the languages of Europe, India, and Persia (the so-called Indo-European family of languages), we are able to learn a great deal about the remote history of the Altaic languages. It is also by applying the techniques of this method that we are able to arrive at reliable information concerning the probable membership of Japanese in this linguistic family—information that is reflected in the current scholarly consensus among Western students of this question. This is, in essence, the same method Boller used in 1857, in his original monograph on this subject, though of course much has been learned and many refinements have been added since his day.

Unfortunately, the comparative method has been little used in modern Japan. Even when it has been investigated and taught in the Japanese university system, it has almost always been treated as a kind of foreign academic novelty, suited only for the study of European languages and their history, as if it were without application to the problems of the origins of Japanese. Nothing could be further from the truth. The comparative method, although originally worked out by linguists who were studying the history of European languages—but also deeply involved with Sanskrit, a language of Asia—has been applied with equal success to languages throughout the rest of the world, including native Indian languages of North and South America, Tibetan, Chinese, and the Semitic languages. If the method is applied, and if the languages are related, the method works, no matter what the languages are, and no matter what type of languages they may be.

The failure of Japanese academia to familiarize itself sufficiently with this technique of historical linguistics, and the reluctance of Japanese scholars to apply it to their own language, remain the two greatest obstacles in the way of clarifying the question of the origins of Japanese by Japanese scholars in Japan. On this score in particular, scholars in the West can count themselves fortunate indeed, since they labor under neither of these self-imposed disabilities.

The comparative method, or comparative grammar, combines the principle of a working hypothesis with a technique for demonstrating that hypothesis. This demonstration is presented in the form of the increasingly convincing evidence that is the outcome of the application of the method itself to the materials with which it works. These materials are, most simply put, all the forms, or words, of the languages concerned, including their sounds, their inflections, the orders in which they appear in phrases, clauses, and also in sentences, their meanings, and all other essential parts of any language. The method itself has many involved technicalities; but fortunately the essential principles in terms of which it operates are neither difficult to explain nor especially hard to understand.

What is most important about the comparative method is the two theorems or assumptions on which it is based. These two assumptions are exactly comparable to the theorems of geometry, such as, "A straight line is the shortest distance between two points." They must be assumed to be true, since no one has yet come up with a way to "prove" their truth; at the same time, they are perfectly self-evident, and no one has ever seriously suggested that they might not be true, even though they cannot be demonstrated or proved directly.

The two essential assumptions of the comparative method are (1) that languages change, and (2) that linguistic change—the same phenomenon of change that is assumed in the first assumption—is regular. From these two assumptions follow all the findings and conclusions of historical linguistics.

Neither assumption can be proved or directly demonstrated by attested evidence. Still, no one would seriously question the fact that language undergoes change over time, even though our life spans are hardly sufficient to test or demonstrate this assumption. About the second assumption, there may be less "common sense" appeal. But this second assumption is also based on sound theoretical grounds, even though they are too elaborate to permit summation here. This assumption too is essential to the science of historical linguistics. If linguistic change is not regular, we cannot make historical statements of any kind about the earlier stages of a language. We cannot prove that it is regular (any more than we can demonstrate or prove that language changes, or that a straight line is the shortest distance between two points), but there is substantial experimental evidence, deriving from the study of hundreds of languages, that points convincingly to the conclusion that this second assumption is correct, and that linguistic change indeed is regular. Those instances which appear to be sporadic or unpredictable are the exceptions, not the rule.

These two basic assumptions of the science of historical linguistics are not only the theoretical basis on which one language may be compared with another (first always making the assumption, and also assuming that one is correct in so assuming, that the two languages being compared are historically related to one another). They also provide the necessary theoretical framework in terms of which we can now explain, simply and concretely, what we mean by the historical relationship, or genetic relationship, of one language to another. In other words, it is in terms of these two basic assumptions of the methodology of linguistic comparison that we are able to explain what Western scholarship has in mind when it arrives at its present consensus concerning the Altaic origins of the Japanese language.

3. The Altaic Languages

Thanks to a large amount of painstaking scholarship, mostly carried out by a few European scholars over the past half-century, it is possible to sketch, in fairly broad but clear outline, the earliest history of the speakers of that original Altaic language to which all the other Altaic languages for which we have later, historical evidence—including Japanese—stand in the historical relationship of being what we are, throughout this book, calling "later, changed forms." This last expression is simply another way of referring to what we have already explained as the historical phenomenon of the genetic relationship of one language to another.

The evidence that underlies the following general sketch of the earliest stages in the history of the Altaic languages is, by its very nature, extremely complex. An enormous amount of scholarly labor has been expended, and a tremendous mass of evidence, both from textual sources and from archaeological findings, as well as from the comparative method, has had to be exhaustively investigated and analyzed, before our present understanding of these earliest stages in the history of the Altaic speakers was achieved; and of course, future discoveries, both from archaeological materials and from linguistic evidence, will surely amplify, as well as alter, the consensus of scholars on many of these points. In the meantime, the complex nature of the evidence that underlies almost all the general historical statements below makes it all but impossible, in a presentation of this kind, to substantiate our general statements with specific references to the evidence on which these conclusions are based.

This is unfortunate, because a summary statement concerning any variety of historical experience, whether related to the extremely remote past or concerned with more recent events, is always sure to be more convincing when it can be offered with at least some elementary indication of the types and varieties of concrete evidence on which it is based. Such specific references are of course available in a large number of technical archaeological and linguistic studies, where anyone interested in following up, or verifying, the account that follows may do so—indeed, is invited to do so, because in the process he or she will find that there is a great deal more known about these topics than the summary that follows has been able to incorporate.

One further point remains for brief discussion before we can continue with this summary of the present consensus of Western scholarship concerning the earliest history of the Altaic languages and their speakers. We shall often use such expressions as the "original Altaic language," "speakers of the original Altaic language," and so forth. Indeed, it is the earliest history of this language, and its speakers, that concerns us at this point. But as is often the case in discussions of linguistic problems, particularly questions of linguistic history, a brief amount of time spent in the definition of these terms, with a view to pinpointing the concepts behind them, will be a wise investment.

When we speak or write of the "original Altaic language," we are using the word "language" in the same way, and with the same implications, that we would for a modern living language, or for a language with early historical records. As we have already emphasized, no human language is completely uniform in all its various aspects—pronunciation, vocabulary, grammar, and so forth—at any time in its history. Different people often use different words for the same things, different expressions, and different pronunciations, even though both they, and the linguist, would agree that they are still using the same language, and when it is obvious from the evidence of their successful social interaction with one another that they are still communicating with one another within the same social group (a possible, and useful, definition of what is meant by the "same language"). Concrete examples of the phenomenon of linguistic diversity within what we will still wish to identify and define as the "same language" or a "single language" are close at hand for all of us, no matter what language we speak or where we live. In older, more elaborate cultures, and more or less rigidly stratified societies such as the Japanese, these differences are often especially striking, particularly since in such circumstances they often correlate rather impressively with socioeconomic and cultural diversities within the population involved.

Furthermore, every human language is constantly in a state of change, or flux, even though it is clear that such change takes place extremely slowly. But in these two ways, which we might classify as "synchronic" (referring to a specific time) and "diachronic" (taking place through time, or resulting from the comparison of evidence from one period with that from a later period), language is never a completely unitary or a totally uniform phenomenon. This is true of modern Japanese; it was certainly true of Old Japanese; and it was also true of what we are here calling the "original Altaic language."

The fact of linguistic diversity—diversity which does not, however, interfere with the successful operation of the language in question as a medium for social cooperation—may readily be verified in the case of living languages. Languages with substantial earlier written records (such as Old Japanese) also generously document the same diversity for earlier periods. But when we come to something as remote as the earliest stages of the Altaic language, we certainly cannot verify this phenomenon of internal diversity firsthand. And of course we have no written records for the language: none ever existed.

Our linguistic evidence for this earliest stage of Altaic, or for the earliest stage of any other language family, comes solely from the comparative method. This means that we have available only that evidence which points to earlier common origins for inherited elements that have survived in the later, changed languages, together with those techniques, based on the assumptions of regular linguistic change, that make it possible to recover, or "reconstruct," many of the features of that earlier but now lost language for which we have no direct historical or documentary evidence.

For the phenomenon of linguistic diversity within that original language, however, since we can rely in this case on neither direct observation nor earlier written records, we must rely on theory and methodology. But we assume the existence of such diversity for the original language, since we assume that the original language was in no particular way substantially different from any other form of human language. Hence it, too, was internally diverse. It was not uniform at any point in its history, and it was constantly in a state of change—again, like any other language.

This is particularly important because the later history of the original Altaic language is a history of separation and division, eventually resulting in the proliferation of what later become separate, distinct languages. Mongolian is different from Turkish, not only today but as far back as we can trace the history of either subgroup within the Altaic language family. A speaker of Turkish cannot successfully operate with only that linguistic equipment in a Mongolian linguistic situation; one or the other of the two must change languages if there is to be linguistic communication. Because of the assumptions of the comparative method, and because of the findings growing out of the comparisons that can be made between these languages, together with similar evidence from the other branches of Altaic, we do know that this was not always true. At some time, very long ago in the history of these languages, the remote ancestors of the speakers of Turkish and the remote ancestors of the speakers of Mongolian—together with the remote ancestors of the modern speakers of Japanese, and of the modern Tungusic speakers, and probably also of the speakers of Korean—did function together in a common linguistic community. And it is this common linguistic community to which we are referring when we write or speak of the "original Altaic language."

Within this original linguistic community—in other words, within the original Altaic language—linguistic diversity surely existed. Not everyone always used the same words in this original Altaic language for the same things, or precisely the same pronunciations, or the same expressions and grammatical forms. There were differences within this language; but it was nevertheless a single language. Like all other human language, it had internal diversity and was constantly changing. We do not know just how this internal diversity related to the development of the subgroups that much later became so different from one another that they finally became separate languages (Turkish, Mongolian, the various Tungusic languages, etc.); nor do we understand as well as we would like to all the details of historical change by which these later languages were established.

But somehow and somewhere in the history of all these languages, what began simply as instances of internal linguistic diversity—differences in words, their meanings, pronunciations, and the like—grew to such an extent that they finally began to interfere with communication. From this point on, it was no longer a case of internal diversity within a single, complex language, but now rather, one of different languages.

It seems almost certain that within the original Altaic linguistic community—in other words, in the original Altaic language—there were subgroups that differed from one another in various aspects of their overall linguistic usage; it is also clear that these original subgroups were, by and large, the ancestors of what later became the earliest speakers of the different, and later separated, individual languages such as Turkish, Mongolian, and the like. But the linguistic evidence also points to the existence of an extremely early stage, which lasted for a very long time, at which all these differences were still on the level of internal diversity.

It is for this reason, and in the sense of the concepts and terms just explained, that we speak and write of an original

[51]

Altaic language—that original language of which Japanese is a very much later and very much changed form, but to which it is nevertheless genetically related. Whatever can be discovered concerning the earliest history of this original Altaic language is, in a very direct and real sense, a concrete answer to the question of the origins of Japanese; indeed, such history *is* the history of the origins of Japanese.

HOMELANDS AND MIGRATIONS

Just as we can, and do, speak of an original Altaic language, so also is it possible, as well as useful, to speak of an original homeland for the speakers of that language. By this homeland we mean the earliest geographical location to which we can trace the speakers of the original language; of course, still earlier they may have come to that place from somewhere else. Indeed, they probably did just that, unless they evolved into the condition of *Homo sapiens* in the very same home in which our combination of archaeological and comparative-linguistic research locates them, a conclusion that does not seem likely, particularly in the case of the Altaic language. But even though there may have been still earlier homes, the "original homeland," in the sense in which we shall use this term and the concept below, is the earliest geographical point to which we can trace the speakers of a given linguistic community.

Here we are reminded that the pursuit of linguistic origins further and further back into the remote past does not eventually confront us with abrupt beginnings or sudden interruptions in the chronicle. We do not come to a point, in any of this research, where we can say with confidence, "This is where it all began; beyond this point, there was nothing." All that we are doing, in the pursuit of linguistic origins, is going back further and further. Perhaps one day soon, thanks to new findings and more carefully conducted research, we will be able to go back still further. In the meantime, we shall describe what is, for the present, the most remote point in geography as well as in time to which the history of the speakers of the original Altaic language may be traced, thus describing at the same time the most remote location to which the origins of the Japanese language may presently be traced.

[52]

The history of the Altaic speakers and their original language begins in the Transcaspian steppe, some six or seven thousand years before the Christian era. How long the Altaic speakers lived in this area, or where they had come from, we do not know. It does seem quite certain, however, that in the long period during which they inhabited this region, which stretches out northeast from the Caspian Sea, and reaches in the west from the basin of the Volga River and the southern stretches of the Ural Mountains eastward in the general direction of the T'ien-shan Mountains, they came into contacts with speakers of other, unrelated languages.

Most important among these early linguistic contacts of the Altaic speakers was their apparently close association at one time or another with speakers of the Uralic family of languages (later, changed forms of which include such present-day languages as Finnish and Hungarian). In the course of these contacts, the speakers of the original Altaic language imitated or borrowed certain linguistic items (words, grammatical elements, etc.) from the speakers of the Uralic language, who in turn probably borrowed from the Altaic speakers. It is always difficult to distinguish the kind of linguistic evidence that points to this kind of early mutual borrowing from the kind of linguistic evidence that points to genetic relationship between languages. Some scholars believe that Altaic and Uralic are themselves genetically related, and that the similarities to be observed between the two are not, as here explained, due to early linguistic contacts and consequent borrowing back and forth between the two early languages. These were, we will recall, the terms in which Boller wrote in 1857 when he attempted his pioneering demonstration of the genetic relationship of the Japanese language, which he believed to be a later, changed form, not simply of Altaic but of Uralic-Altaic, that is, a still larger (and, by implication, still earlier) linguistic community.

It is difficult, at the present stage of our studies, to be sure that Boller was not right about this. Still, the current consensus is that a safer interpretation of the available data consists in separating Uralic from Altaic, as an example of the kind of apparent linguistic relationship that results from early contacts and mutual borrowing rather than from genetic relationship,

[53]

and to talk in terms simply of an original Altaic language, and of an original Altaic homeland in the Transcaspian steppe country, when we study the origins of Japanese.

Sometime before about 2000 B.C., the original Altaic speakers undertook the first of a long series of migrations that would distribute the Altaic languages across the Asian continent, from Turkey in the west to the Pacific coast in the east. These migrations would eventually take them to the Japanese archipelago: the much later movements of Altaic peoples into the Japanese islands, in the course of which the Japanese language was brought into this region, may be viewed as nothing more or less than still another chapter in the immensely long history of migration and movement by the Altaic speakers. From their original homeland in the Transcaspian steppe area, the Altaic speakers first appear to have moved more or less as a group, and also probably as a socially functioning linguistic community, to a second homeland. Here they began another long period of habitation as a unified linguistic community, no doubt once more displaying a large amount of internal linguistic diversity, but at first, at least, still justifying the designation of a language. It was from this second homeland, and in the course of the variously timed migratory movements that took them away from this second geographical focus of their community life, that the Altaic speakers later split up in the process of the formation of what would become the principal subgroups (Turkic, Mongolian, Tungusic, etc.) of this linguistic family. It was out of this second homeland, therefore, that the different Altaic languages eventually took shape.

The reasons for the original migration away from the first Altaic homeland are fairly clear. Around the second millennium before our era, the human geography of all Eurasia was drastically altered, thanks to the tremendous changes brought about by the sudden expansion and migrations of the Indo-Europeans. These were the speakers of yet another extremely early language, which linguists call Indo-European; later, changed forms of this original language include most of the modern languages of Europe, such as German, English, French, and the Romance languages, as well as Persian (the language of Iran), and most of the languages of the Indian subcontinent, ranging in time all the way from the ancient language of the Indian civilization that we call Sanskrit (which in one of its many forms was also the original language of the Buddhist religion) down to such modern languages as Hindi and the many other contemporary languages of India, Pakistan, and Bangladesh.

The Indo-Europeans, at about this time, began a vigorous series of migrations and travels of conquest that worked lasting changes on the population map of the world, and that account for many of the subsequent movements of their early neighbors. These neighbors, like the Altaic community, were usually speakers of different and unrelated languages, who undertook their own migratory movements in an understandable effort to flee from this sudden outburst of energetic conquest upon which the Indo-Europeans had embarked.

There were different responses to the Indo-European advances, depending on the area and the time involved. For the speakers of the original Altaic language, their response took the form of a shift in their homeland, away from the first homeland in the Transcaspian steppe region, and out into the direction of the southernmost extent of the Altai Mountains in Central Asia. Here they established their second homeland; and it is, as already noted, from this region and in particular from the name of the Altai Mountains that linguists have borrowed the term by which this original language and its earliest speakers are known to scholars today.

Again, we are able, with a considerable degree of confidence, to correlate the eventual dispersement of the Altaic speakers from their second Central Asian homeland with outside stimulus in the form of the movements of other early peoples and groups. A vigorous and important people known to history as the Huns start to disturb the map of Eurasia from about the third century B.C., and it was eventually, in a kind of domino-relay response to the various movements of the Huns, as well as to the earlier population shifts that anticipated these movements, that the Altaic speakers began the series of migrations from their second homeland. We do not know much of consequence about the linguistic origins of the Huns, even though they were one of the most important of all the ancient peoples whose activities deeply affected the history of Eurasia. That they have nothing to do, at least linguistically, with the modern Hungarians, does, however, seem certain. (For centuries after the fact, the name of the Huns was a synonym in Europe for a fierce, warlike, nomadic people; and the designation was later given to the Hungarians by their enemies—not, of course, in a complimentary sense—when they appeared on the scene of European history.)

The Altaic speakers did not leave their second homeland solely to get out of the path of the Huns, in the way that they seem to have left the first, original homeland largely to get out of the way of the encroaching Indo-Europeans. This time the history of Eurasia was rendered rather more complex by the effective military activities of the Chinese Empire of the Han dynasty, which climaxed a long history of military action related to the movements of the Huns by smashing Hun forces in the territories bordering on China, and forcing them to flee the Far East, sending many in the general direction of Western Europe. Once more, a kind of domino effect in migrations was operative at this point. With the power of the Huns destroyed, the Altaic peoples once more began to move, this time partly in order to occupy some of the areas that had been depopulated as a result of Chinese military action and the eastward flight of the Hunnic peoples.

LINGUISTIC DIVERSITY

It was not only in stimulus and motivation that the second great Altaic migration differed from the first; it also had important linguistic differences, which of course interest us even more. When the Altaic speakers left their original homeland, they apparently all moved at about the same time, and more or less as a single, unitary linguistic community. When they arrived at and began to inhabit their second, Central Asian homeland, the internal linguistic situation was at first not greatly different from that of their first, Transcaspian steppe homeland. There were surely internal differences within the language employed in both, but in neither instance did these differences interfere with social communication—that is, with the operation of the linguistic unity in question as a social entity. The Altaic speakers began as a linguistic unity, and as a cooperating social group, in the first homeland; they moved to the second homeland as the same kind of group; and for a time after their arrival at that second homeland, they continued in that fashion. But shortly thereafter, something important happened.

What happened was a series of linguistic changes that completely altered both the linguistic and the social nature of the Altaic community. We do not know when these changes first began, nor do we know why they began. But there is little question that they did take place, and they resulted eventually in the separation of the original Altaic linguistic community and its dispersal into the earliest versions of what later became the principal subgroups of the Altaic language family. These subgroups developed in turn into the historically attested Altaic languages of the earliest written records and from these came the languages of this family that we know as living languages today.

What must have happened at this point in the history of the Altaic people and their language was something along the following lines. We have already stressed that at no time was the original Altaic language completely uniform in all respects: no real human language ever is. Within the original linguistic community, both during the period when the Altaic speakers still lived in their first, original homeland, and during the first part of their residence in their new, second homeland, different persons within the community spoke slightly differently from each other, even though such differences were not sufficient to interfere with communication within the group. In other words, these differences were not great enough to break up the intrinsic unity of the linguistic entity that the Altaic speakers constituted. This was also the linguistic situation of the Altaic speakers during the period of their great trek from the Transcaspian steppes to their new Central Asian site. But once they had arrived at that new site, more and more of the linguistic differences that until then had been internal differences within a single language began to occur often enough and with sufficiently striking linguistic effect so as first to hinder, next to interfere with, and finally to render completely impossible that very communication within the entire group that had until this point distinguished the Altaic linguistic community.

This was the critical process that operated to transform the original Altaic language into what eventually became the

[57]

Altaic languages. And if we are looking for a time and a place to point to as the birthday and birthplace of the Japanese language, this is it—the place is the second Altaic homeland in Central Asia, the historical point is the time at which the internal differences within the Altaic linguistic community ceased to be simply internal differences and began instead to cluster together into bundles or blocks of significant differences in the language—bundles or blocks that finally became substantial enough to interfere with social cooperation, that is, with communication, within the original linguistic community. To these events in Central Asia, then, we may point as representing the origins of the Japanese language.

These linguistic events are of such tremendous importance, not only for Japanese but also for all the Altaic languages, that it will be useful to explore in a little more detail the probable process of the changes that they represented. Up until this point, there were differences in words, in their meanings, their pronunciations, and the way in which they were used together with each other, in order to build phrases, sentences, and even longer sequences, even though all the speakers concerned were speaking the same language; but these differences, while obvious and apparent to all concerned, were not great enough to interfere with communication. Everyone always still knew what the other person was talking about, and what he or she meant, even if something was not always said in exactly the same way or with exactly the same words by everyone.

On the basis of later linguistic evidence, and by application of the comparative method, we can even recover some of these early linguistic differences that existed within the Altaic linguistic community in the first homeland, later during the period of their first great trek out of the Transcaspian steppes, and then during the first portion of their residence in their second homeland.

For the number "one" at least three different words were used within the Altaic linguistic community. Some speakers used the word *bīr, others the word *niken, still others the word *ämün. All these words were quite different from one another; they were pronounced differently and were indeed different words, surely of different origins. We cannot, at least at the present time, suggest how it came about that three different words were used for the number "one" in the Altaic community; but we do know that these three were employed by various speakers within the community. The same general situation was true of some of the other numbers. The word "four," for example, was *tȫrt* for some speakers, *dȫrben* for others, and *dügin* for still others. This was a little different from the situation with the number "one," where different speakers used what were obviously totally different words, words not connected or associated with one another in any way. In the case of the words used for the number "four," different speakers used different words, but the words themselves were not totally different; there was some phonetic similarity between them (e.g., the *t-* initial of *tȫrt* sounded somewhat like the *d-* initial of the other two words; the first two words have the same vowel in the first syllable, *-ȫ-*, and this vowel must have sounded, in pronunciation, much like the first-syllable vowel in the third word, *-ü-*, etc.). To express this in another way, the various original Altaic words for "four" were not completely different from one another, as were the words for "one."

In neither case did the differences in these and similar words interfere with communication within the linguistic community. This was true both of the cases (of which there must have been a great many) like "four," where only relatively minor differences in pronunciation marked the distinction between one form and another, as well of the cases (of which there were most likely relatively few) like "one," where different speakers used totally different words for the same thing.

At the historical stage represented by this variety of linguistic evidence, we must assume that two different phenomena were operative within the language. We have stressed the first of these two phenomena, that of linguistic diversity: the same thing is expressed by different words, or different pronunciations of what is apparently the same word, by individual speakers. The other phenomenon is equally important in explaining how the various Altaic languages arose out of the original Altaic linguistic unity. In the second phenomenon, one speaker uses more than one word for the same thing, or more than one pronunciation for the same word, or what is nearly the same word, depending on different situations, his or her mood or emotional feeling, or still other factors which are difficult to estimate or recover.

In other words, not only were there some speakers who said *bīr* for "one," while others said *niken* and still others said *āmün*. There were still other speakers who sometimes said *bīr*, sometimes said *niken*, and sometimes said *āmün*, meanwhile employing all these words in the same general area of lexical meaning that we identify when we translate these forms, as here, with the English gloss "one." But it is important to remember that even though we identify all these words with a single gloss, the speakers of the language in question most likely used each of these words with slightly different nuances of meaning, or with different sociolinguistic connotations, depending on which form they selected for use in any given linguistic situation. Just because we translate each of these forms in the same way does not indicate that their meanings were all the same.

In historical linguistic study, it is always necessary to distinguish carefully between the meaning of a given word in any language and the usually quite brief translation into English or German or any other language that we may attach to this same word, simply to serve our own convenience in identifying this word when we talk about it, or otherwise discuss its role in the language in question. The two are not at all the same.

The meaning of any linguistic form is a vast and extremely subtle and difficult entity, something that we still by and large lack the necessary tools and techniques for describing or expressing in a useful fashion. Meaning is the sum total of all the significant contexts in which a form or a word or any other linguistic entity is employed by the speakers of the language in which it is found. Meaning is particularly difficult to pin down for earlier stages of a language. When we say that Altaic *niken* or *āmün* or *bīr* meant "one," we are not really referring to or directly expressing the meaning that these forms had in the original Altaic language. All that we are doing is attaching a handy identification tag to these forms—an identification tag that takes the form, in the present case, of a translation into English. The comparative method generally provides us with enough evidence to permit us to attach these handy—and very necessary—identification tags to earlier linguistic forms, as a part of the data that it supplies for the reconstruction of these earlier forms themselves; but it only rarely permits us to reconstruct actual meanings. Too often unexperienced investigators of the history of language mistake these translation identification tags for the meanings of the linguistic forms with which they are working. When they do this, they also often reach erroneous and oversimplified conclusions about many of the questions that they are attempting to study.

At any rate, it was the existence of this second variety of Altaic speakers—those who sometimes used one form or another—that made possible the functioning of the linguistic unity as such. It was the ability of these speakers to bridge the communication gap that must have existed among the other, more limited speakers, some of whom only used *bīr, or some of whom only used *niken, or others of whom only used *ämün, that in turn made possible the reality of effective, functioning communication among all the speakers concerned.

What specific stimulus leads an original linguistic community to fragment in this fashion? Why does it split up into later, smaller groups? If we were able to pinpoint specific reasons for such changes in the make-up of a historical linguistic community, we would be well on our way to understanding some of the most fundamental questions that underlie the nature of human language, as well as its existence as a historical entity. Unfortunately, hardly any of the concrete causes that we have reason to suspect underlie these changes, or splits, can be identified in a rigorous or scientific fashion at the present state of historical linguistics.

Just as is true of many other factors that surely played a part in the history of human language, here also we can do little more than speculate about these reasons and stimuli. We can suggest what appear to be plausible reasons for the initial stages of such splits, and we can often identify the principal linguistic mechanisms by means of which those changes that we actually know did take place may most likely have been facilitated. But as in all scientific inquiry, it is important to keep in mind that what we are doing is actually only assembling a carefully ordered series of calculated guesses. We always try to keep our speculations

[61]

within the range of the plausible. In any given case where two or more different causes may be suggested, we will of course always choose the probable over the merely possible. But neither of these methodological safeguards should tempt us into forgetting that what we are doing is simply speculation—speculation that we try to keep as well informed and as realistic as we can.

Most modern students of these problems tend today to identify the principal stimulus for such splits or separation of original linguistic communities in the socioeconomic sphere, or as somehow associated with the problems encountered by the speakers of the community in question in coping with new and different problems of ecological control and adjustment, most often brought on by their advancement into new and different terrain. There is much to be said for such a view. As any linguistic community was forced to develop new and different methods for coping with the daily social, economic, and especially ecological realities of existence, new and different linguistic devices necessarily had to be worked out, if only to permit the continued sociolinguistic functioning of the group as a group.

Viewed in this fashion, it is more than plausible to identify the principal stimulus for the separation of linguistic communities with the socioeconomic necessities imposed by ecological change. Still, we must always keep in mind that for the earliest periods—which are unfortunately the most critical for our understanding of this entire issue—we have very little evidence for any of this change, whether ecological or socioeconomic, apart from what is provided by the linguistic evidence itself; and so our analysis at once runs the risk of becoming circular if we insist on asking too many detailed questions about *why* early linguistic communities fragmented. There is nothing wrong with asking the questions; the problems arise only when we attempt to make our answers too specific.

The historical-linguistic mechanism involved is itself somewhat clearer than any picture that we are able to evolve of initial or principal stimuli underlying such changes. With these socioeconomic changes, and with differences in ecological conditions, most often brought about by advances into new and different terrain, the original linguistic community soon found itself confronted with a new and significantly different phenomenon.

[62]

This phenomenon was the virtual dropping out, and the subsequent sociolinguistic loss to the linguistic community, of this second group of speakers.

In the process of such change, the linguistic community also now found itself deprived of a sociolinguistic resource upon which it had placed tremendous dependence. This was the facility of this second group of speakers to switch back and forth from one linguistic form to another. And as this loss accelerated, the dispersal of the original Altaic linguistic community into the later, separate, and no longer mutually cooperating subgroups and individual languages accelerated as well, thanks to the same combination of socioeconomic and sociolinguistic stimuli.

At some point after the move to the second homeland, those speakers who had until then switched back and forth from one form to another (e.g., from *bīr* to *niken* to *ämün*), or back and forth between different pronunciations (from *tȫrt* to *dȫrben* to *dǖgin),* now altered their linguistic behavior in an important way. They settled on the use of one form or the other, and stopped treating different forms or different pronunciations in their speech as equivalent to each other. From this point on, they either went along, in their linguistic behavior, with those other speakers who had always used only *bīr* to mean "one," or else with those who had always used only *niken,* or else with the exclusive users of the word *ämün.*

This process might be described as a variety of linguistic, or lexical, polarization. As it progressed, rigid lines of demarcation in usage replaced the former fairly free interchange between many forms that earlier had characterized these same speakers. With the loss of this free interchange, and with the linguistic polarization of the speakers who had until this point felt free to use different forms, or different pronunciations, the course of historical development was set out of which the Altaic subgroups (Turkic, Mongolian, Tungusic, etc.) developed, and out of which in turn the later, historically attested languages grew (Old Turkish, modern Turkish, Middle Mongolian, Old Japanese, etc.).

From this point on, there were—to continue to use these same two examples, which are, however, representative of hundreds, even thousands, of other words in the language—no longer speakers who sometimes used *bīr,* sometimes *niken,* or sometimes *ämün* for "one," or who sometimes pronounced "four" as *tört*, sometimes as *dörben*, or sometimes as *dügin*. These speakers had now been replaced—or they had replaced themselves—by increasingly rigidly polarized groups, one of which only used *bīr*, another only used *niken,* and another only used *ämün.* As such groups became more and more strictly polarized in their linguistic usage, the free linguistic communication within the social community that had distinguished the life of the Altaic speakers came to an end. No longer can we, from this point on, speak of an Altaic community or of an original Altaic language; from here on, we must speak of the major Altaic subgroups, or of the various individual languages that grew out of each of them.

Those speakers who polarized their linguistic usage so that they now used only *bīr* for "one" were the earliest representatives of the subgroup called Turkic, or as linguists often refer to it, Proto-Turkic. Those who settled exclusively on the word *niken* for "one" are now to be identified with the Mongolian subgroup, or Proto-Mongolian, and those who employed *ämün* are the earliest representatives of the Tungusic subgroup of Altaic, or Proto-Tungusic.

It is important to note that in all these linguistic expressions involving the prefix Proto-, the intent behind the terminology is to stress two different aspects of the forms thus identified: recognition of the extremely remote historical period to which they, by definition, go back; and the equally important fact that we know about these forms, and the groups of speakers with which we identify them, solely through the rigorous application of the comparative method. When we employ the prefix Proto- in such terms as Proto-Turkic, Proto-Mongolian, or even Proto-Altaic, we never use it to imply in any way that the language we are identifying was primitive, underdeveloped, or incomplete.

These so-called proto-languages, we have every reason to believe, were languages that were just as developed, and just as complicated and complex, as any language always is at any point in history. The only thing incomplete, or underdeveloped, or in any sense primitive, about such linguistic entities as Proto-Turkic or Proto-Altaic is our knowledge of them; because of the special circumstances under which we are able to learn about these languages, our control of them as sets and systems of linguistic data is necessarily fragmentary. But we must always keep in mind that it is our knowledge that is lacking and incomplete; the languages themselves were total, complete, and satisfactorily functioning linguistic systems. The application of the comparative method does *not* (as was sometimes thought, but mistakenly, a century ago) take us back to any primitive, or formative, stage in the development of human language.

We have stressed the rigid quality of this linguistic polarization, since an understanding of that aspect of the phenomenon is necessary in order to explain the kinds of changes that resulted in the separation of the original Altaic language into different subgroups, and the development of the later languages. But this does not mean that absolutely rigid, watertight divisions ever existed to separate any one of these early subgroups totally and completely from all the others. Even after the polarization had made considerable progress, and to some extent even after it had advanced sufficiently to interfere with linguistic communication within the group, traces of the earlier, freer linguistic situation still could be found in one subgroup or another. This may be effectively illustrated by noting the Japanese evidence for the words for "one" in the original Altaic language.

Of the three different words cited above, the first and the third have survived (in later, changed forms of course) in Japanese. Original Altaic *bīr*, after undergoing many changes (which are, however, neither sporadic nor ad hoc, but may be related to other, regular patterns of change between Altaic and Japanese), became the ordinary Japanese word for "one," the element *hito-* in the word *hitotsu;* original Altaic *ämün* became Japanese *omo,* meaning "chief, principal, main." This second word thus provides an example of a change, over the course of time, not only in the form of a word but also in its meaning. Not only did the form *ämün* change to *omo,* but the meaning of the word also underwent change.

We have already stressed, of course, that the meaning of any of these linguistic forms is not the same as the translation identification tag we attach to it; nevertheless, we may still conveniently indicate the principal direction of the changes in mean-

[65]

ing that we are able to establish for these words by making appropriate, if not directly corresponding, changes in our translations. In this particular case, we may indicate the change in meaning through the difference between our translation "one" in the first instance and "chief, principal, main" in the second. Even though we lack effective techniques for dealing directly with meaning, these translation identification tags serve as convenient indicators for the larger, comprehensive, but elusive entities of semantic content that we would otherwise not even be able to identify, much less describe or express.

Changes in the meanings of words in the course of history, like the changes in the sounds and shapes of the forms themselves, are an important aspect of the overall phenomenon of linguistic change. In the present case, we have a change of meaning that we may symbolize as a change from a sense of "one" to a sense of "chief, principal, main," but always remembering that these English words are nothing more than shorthand translation tags and not in any way the actual or basic meanings of the linguistic forms concerned.

But even these simplified identification tags give us some idea of the semantic changes that took place in the segment of linguistic history with which we are dealing; and in this case, at least, probably most students of historical linguistics will agree that a shift in sense from "one" to "chief, principal, main" is a semantic change that is neither very difficult to understand nor hard to explain. After all, "one" is the chief, principal, or main number in any system of counting. Furthermore, we could easily find parallel examples of similar semantic change, involving words meaning "one" as well as "chief, principal, main" in many other languages. Exactly how relevant parallel cases of similar semantic change from other, unrelated languages are for understanding or explaining changes in meaning in a given language is a question on which linguists are not at all in general agreement. At the very least, such parallels are often reassuring to us as we go about our work of trying to sort out the various things that apparently happened to the meanings of linguistic forms in the course of history. The most important thing to keep in mind is that no matter how we choose to express the details of semantic changes, it is clear that these changes, like the parallel changes in pronunciation that are so much easier to study and categorize, took place over a long period of time, surely in most cases thousands of years.

In this particular case, Japanese has preserved evidence for its Altaic linguistic inheritance that goes back to two of the three different principal historical subgroups of the Altaic family— Turkic (*bīr* and *hitotsu* "one") and Tungusic *(*ämün* and *omo)*— but at the same time, it lacks any trace of the third form for "one" that was also current in the earliest stages of the Altaic linguistic community, a form that soon after the founding of the second Altaic homeland in Central Asia became polarized as the word for "one" among those speakers who later became the ancestors of the Mongolian subgroup.

As we study more and more examples of this kind, we discover that this particular pattern is fairly frequent. Japanese quite often shows that it has inherited lexical materials (word forms with specific meanings, though both forms and meanings will generally have changed in the course of time) from these two particular branches of Altaic, Turkic and Tungusic, at the same time that it apparently refrained from continuing, in any form, no matter how changed, the lexical materials that were polarized for later specific employment in the Mongolian subgroup. The bulk of the evidence that has been studied to date with respect to the Altaic word stock as it has been inherited by Japanese shows a fairly impressive pattern of common inheritance by Japanese along with the Tungusic subgroup, and also, though to a somewhat lesser extent, by Japanese along with the Turkic subgroup. On the other hand, evidence for common inheritance by Japanese along with the Mongolian subgroup is rather less striking, though it does exist.

Presenting the detailed linguistic evidence upon which the above rather sweeping generalization is based is of course not possible here. Such evidence can only be exhibited effectively in specialized papers and monographs, and only in such form can it receive the detailed study and scrutiny that it requires if it is to be both effective as data and convincing as evidence. All that we can do here is to present the conclusions of and the consensus resulting from such studies, to the degree and extent to which they have been carried out.

[67]

The description of the historical-linguistic mechanisms of change that were most likely involved with the different forms for words meaning "one" and "four" must be understood as being what it is—only a somewhat simplified sample case, selected largely because of the obvious, concrete nature of the meanings involved, from among an extremely large number of parallel cases that might have been selected instead and used to illustrate the same point.

The process of change and specialization of usage just described did not happen only with the words for the numbers; it happened throughout every level of the vocabulary, or lexical stock, of the original linguistic community. We have chosen here to illustrate it with examples chosen from among the number words because such words are easy to identify and to gloss, and also of course because they are important to the socioeconomic functioning of any and all language—but for that matter, so are the other words in any language. It is not methodologically advisable to stress the particular importance of the numbers, or of any other segment of the lexical stock. In this sense—and it is an important one—*all* words are equally important.

A further example of the kind of internal diversity that originally existed within the Altaic linguistic community—one that at the same time illustrates both the polarization of this diversity among the various later subgroups and the way in which this same internal diversity was inherited by Japanese—will provide a useful illustration of the kind of evidence that the comparative method can bring to bear upon the entire question of linguistic origins. It will also show how this same method can clarify the operation of historical change in language and its usage, even in periods of the remote past.

This example illustrates a case of internal linguistic diversity within Altaic that, in effect, combines both the kind of diversity we saw above for the word for "one" (different words for the same thing) and the kind of diversity seen for the word for "four" (different but rather similar pronunciations of the same word).

The words that illustrate this second example all have the same general meaning of "a stone, a rock," and this is the English-language identification tag that we will attach to these Altaic forms in the discussion that follows, particularly when we are identifying extremely early stages in the history of the Altaic languages. We also understand that these identification tags are not themselves really the "meanings" of the forms but simply a convenient way to pin down the major semantic dimensions of the words in question.

In this general semantic area of "a stone, a rock" then, the Altaic linguistic community originally employed two quite different and unrelated words, in the earliest historical stages of their sociolinguistic life in the first Altaic homeland and probably for some time thereafter. One of these words we may reconstruct as Proto-Altaic *görö, the other as Proto-Altaic *tyāl₂. Before continuing the discussion, we must first comment briefly on these words, in connection both with their overt forms and with their meanings.

As far as the forms of these reconstructed words are concerned, we understand that each symbol used in writing them indicates an original and significant sound (phoneme) in the original Altaic language, reconstructed according to the techniques of the comparative method. These sounds are written with phonetic symbols that as closely as possible indicate what we can ascertain, with reasonable certainty, about the pronunciations these words received in the original language. The symbol * that begins each form indicates that the word is a reconstruction, not a word attested in just that form in written records (though very early written records, when such are available, may sometimes be old enough to preserve forms very close to some of our reconstructions). The only other symbol that has been used in writing these two particular forms that requires special comment is the combination l_2. Historians of the Altaic languages use this writing to indicate a significant unitary sound (phoneme) that we know, from the evidence of correspondences established by comparisons among the later, historically attested languages, must have existed in the original Altaic language.

We know that this phoneme was some kind of an *l* sound, but we also know that it must have been somehow different from another—and probably more usual—*l* sound that also existed in the language, and which we write simply as *l*. Since we do not know precisely how these two original sounds in the earliest stages of the Altaic language differed in pronunciation, but only that they were significantly different—that is, two words could mean quite different things, depending solely on whether one of them had $*l$ or $*l_2$, all other phonemes in both instances being the same—we write the second one with the subscript numeral 2, as $*l_2$, simply as a convenient notation that will help us remember this difference.

We are also fairly well informed about some important details concerning the meanings of these forms in the earliest Altaic language. The evidence drawn from comparisons among the later, attested languages shows us that the word that we are reconstructing and writing as $*g\ddot{o}r\ddot{o}$ generally was used to indicate small, pebblelike rocks, or sometimes small rocks and pebbles that were recognized, by the early Altaic speakers, to have some special mineral content, especially iron or some other metallic ore. The form written here as $*ty\bar{a}l_2$ was, by way of contrast, apparently a more general term, one used of rocks and stones without significant semantic differentiation, though sometimes this word appears to have been employed to distinguish a large rock from a smaller one.

But since our information about earlier meanings, like our information about earlier linguistic forms, comes only from the evidence drawn from comparison of the later, attested languages, we would be guilty of overprecision if we attempted to carry this same semantic differentiation back into the earliest stages of Altaic with which we are now dealing. We shall therefore continue instead to refer to the "meanings" of both these early forms simply as "a stone, a rock," meanwhile of course also keeping in mind this evidence for an early semantic differentiation between the two, or at least that they were apparently used to express rather different nuances of meaning at an early period in the history of the Altaic languages.

Of these two forms, it was the second that was affected by the most sweeping phonological changes in the course of the history of the Altaic languages. Sometime early in their history, either during or at the end of their trek into Central Asia—or perhaps during the early period of their inhabitation of the new, second homeland—some Altaic speakers began to use a slightly different pronunciation for this second word for "a stone, a rock," a new pronunciation in which the final $*l_2$ of $*ty\bar{a}l_2$ began to be pronounced like the *sh-* in English "ship," a sound that we will write here with the symbol *š*.

From this point on, there were not just two but three different forms, all generally meaning much the same thing (a stone, a rock) in the Altaic linguistic community: $*g\ddot{o}r\ddot{o}$, $*ty\bar{a}l_2$, and $*ty\bar{a}š$. Before the linguistic polarization that came soon after they reached their second homeland began to set in, some speakers used the first of these forms (a totally different word from the other two), while other speakers used the second, and still others used the third (the second and third being slightly different pronunciations of the same word). We do not know if any significant difference in semantic nuances accompanied the development and spread of this change in pronunciation; as always, meaning remains the sector of linguistic history that finds us least well equipped, hence least well informed.

After this polarization had become firmly fixed, speakers of what later became the Mongolian subgroup of Altaic continued to use later, changed forms originating in the first of these three words for "a stone, a rock." Still later, these same forms, now even further changed in both form and meaning, are finally attested in such words in historical Altaic languages as Written Mongolian *gürü,* and Khalkha and Kalmuck Mongolian *gür,* in the meanings "pebble" or "ironstone." At the same time, speakers of what later became the Turkic subgroup of the Altaic languages continued to use a later, changed form of the last of the three, which eventually became Old Turkish *tāš,* modern Turkish *taş,* and so on, all meaning "stone," with many other similar forms in the other Turkic languages.

But this was not all that happened with respect to the history of these words in the later Altaic languages. At the same time that it continued the use of the form $*g\ddot{o}r\ddot{o}$, the early Mongolian subgroup also continued to use the second of these three original forms as well. This usage eventually resulted in the Written Mongolian word *čilaγun* "a stone, a rock," a form in which the final syllable -γ*un* is a suffix, and a later addition that does not go back to the original Altaic language, but in which the first two syllables, *čila-,* are nothing more or less than another later, changed form of Altaic $*ty\bar{a}l_2$, with the $*ty$ changing to *č-,*

[71]

the original Altaic $*l_2$ changing to Mongolian -*l*-, and so on. (We emphasize the consonants because they are relatively easy to account for historically; the vowels, of course, are of equal interest and importance for the history of these words, and similar regular statements of their phonetic change can also be made for these sounds.)

The Tungusic subgroup also polarized its lexical usage around the second of these three original forms. The word did not survive in Manchu, but all the other Tungusic languages have it, in such forms as Lamut *jol* and Evenki, Goldi, and Oroch *jolo,* and so also in a surprisingly large number of other modern languages and dialects. A recent dictionary of the Tungusic language family compiled by Soviet scholars lists some fifty-seven different variations and forms of this same word appearing in different dialects of nine major Tungusic languages.

What is particularly interesting to us about this word is that, in one way or another, both Japanese and Korean have also inherited several different forms that clearly go back to one or another of the three members in this early set of diverse forms that the original Altaic language had in the sense of "a stone, a rock," and that later became polarized among each of the principal subgroups of this language family. Most important among the surviving Japanese and Korean evidence for their inheritance of these Altaic words are the modern Japanese words *ishi* and *koro,* together with the modern Korean word *tol,* which goes back to Middle Korean *tolh.*

In the modern languages, and in earlier times also, according to the evidence of the available written records, both Japanese *ishi* and Korean *tol* mean "a stone." In modern Japanese the word *koro* is not used by itself, but it appears in the compound noun *ishikoro,* which means "a stone, a pebble," and in which, of course, the first element is the same word *ishi* "a stone, a rock," that we have already noted. Among these words, the -*koro* of Japanese *ishikoro* is a later, changed form of the same original Altaic **görö* that also, and separately, changed into such words as Written Mongolian *gürü* and Khalkha and Kalmuck *gür.* Here the changes in form have been very slight, and the changes in meaning, as far as we can study and discuss meaning, almost negligible. This is particularly demonstrated by the interesting fact that Japanese in its form of this word continues the nuance of meaning (small stone, pebble) that we earlier assumed for this particular form in the earliest stages of the Altaic linguistic community.

It is also significant to note that the modern Japanese compound *ishikoro* provides a number of exact parallels with a compound in Written Mongolian that joins together both the Mongolian inheritances of these earliest Altaic forms, the compound being Mongolian *gürüčilaɣu* "pebble." We are now able to understand how this Mongolian compound employs the two Mongolian inheritances from Proto-Altaic, in just the same way that the Japanese compound *ishikoro* employs the two Japanese inheritances of these same forms. The only difference is that the elements that were inherited from Altaic, and that go together to make up each of these compounds, appear in reversed order in the two languages.

But Japanese *ishi* and Korean *tol* are another story. Again, the changes in meaning are slight, and hardly significant, at least to the degree to which we are able to study and trace them. But the changes in form between the original Altaic language and these languages for the words in question are important and striking.

We know, from other evidence too complicated to illustrate here, that modern Japanese *ishi* was pronounced *isi* in the Old Japanese period, and furthermore that earlier than this form, which we find in Old Japanese written records, there was a still earlier form, in the state of the language that we call pre-Old Japanese—a form that we can write with the symbols **yisi*. This is the earlier, pre-Old Japanese form that is most immediately relevant for our comparison of Japanese, and of the Japanese word for "stone," *ishi,* with words of similar meaning, and with what we now have reason to believe are also related forms, in the other Altaic languages.

But this is not the only Old Japanese, or even the only pre-Old Japanese form that is relevant to the question. The Old Japanese language had several slightly different forms for the word that meant "stone"—forms that were related to each other, but each of which was somewhat different in pronunciation depending on the circumstances in which it appeared in the language. When the word in question appeared in Old Japanese

[73]

in isolation, as an independent word in its own right, it was Old Japanese *isi,* for which we have also reconstructed the slightly earlier form **yisi.* But in compounds with other linguistic forms, this same Old Japanese word sometimes appears with the vowel *-ŏ(-)* at the end, and sometimes with the vowel *-a(-)* in this position, instead of the vowel *-i* with which the form Old Japanese *isi* ends when found simply and in isolation.

Examples include such expressions as the place name *isŏ nö kamĭ,* which seems originally to have meant something like "above (or upon, *kamĭ*) the rock," a designation for the region around the modern city of Tenri, near Nara, which interestingly enough also appears once in an Old Japanese poetic text as *isu* rather than as *isŏ.* With the vowel *-a(-)* we have the Old Japanese word *isagŏ* "sand, pebbles," and semantically this in turn reminds us of still another related Old Japanese word, *isŏ,* which in the older language refers particularly to rocks or stones at the shoreline on a beach, and shows the final vowel *-ŏ(-)* even when it is employed in isolation and not as part of a compound expression or larger syntactic structure.

Particularly when we recall that the Tungusic words for "stone" generally have the vowel *-o-* not only in the first syllable but also in the second (in those cases where the forms in question are polysyllabic), and also if we keep in mind that the Turkic forms that we believe to be related here all have a vowel *-a-,* we will at once understand why not only Old Japanese *isi* but also the other Old Japanese forms for this word that end in *-ŏ(-)* and *-a(-)* are also historically relevant here. (The relevance of the *-o-* vowel with respect to the Korean forms already cited, as well as for the Tungusic words, will also be noted.)

Leaving aside at this point the still quite complicated question of the further connections on the etymological level between all the vowels in these words from various languages, with respect to the initial consonant of the Old Japanese forms, whether we study Old Japanese *isi* or *isŏ(-)* or *isa-,* it is in each case the initial **y-* that we must reconstruct—thus, **yisi, *yiso(-), *yisa-*—which is a later, changed form of the initial **ty-* of the Altaic original word involved with the history of Japanese *ishi;* and this Altaic original word is of course itself the third alternate form cited above, **tyās,* since Japanese, in this case, went along with the Turkic subgroup in using the variant pronunciation that had the sound $\breve{s}$ and not the one that had the *l*-like sound that is represented by the symbol $*l_2$, the second of the three variant forms cited above.

But at the same time it was this second of the three variants that was inherited, changed but still easily recognizable, by Korean and also by the many Tungusic languages. Korean *tol* is a later, changed form of $*ty\bar{a}l_2$, as are such Tungusic forms as Evenki, Goldi, and Oroch *jolo,* along with Mongolian *čila-* in *čilaγun.* This case is a particularly useful illustration of linguistic evidence and the role that it can play, thanks to the methodology of linguistic comparison, in our recovery of the earliest stages of the history and development of individual languages. We note that Japanese has inherited two different words for "a stone, a rock" from Altaic, just as Mongolian has. Furthermore, in the case of one of these words, Japanese *ishi*—a later, changed form of original Altaic $*ty\bar{a}\breve{s}$—Japanese inherited the same original variant form from Altaic that Turkic did, while Korean, on the other hand, inherited another original variant, the same one $(*ty\bar{a}l_2)$ that the Tungusic languages did. But we must not forget the further important complicating fact, namely that these last two original Altaic variants, $*ty\bar{a}l_2$ and $*ty\bar{a}\breve{s}$, were themselves simply earlier variations in pronunciation—variations that somehow came about at a still earlier stage within the Altaic linguistic community, and at the same time variations that eventually go back to a single original form.

In this manner, then, thanks to the findings of the comparative method, we are able to pursue the history of individual linguistic items far back into the remote past, even in the absence of written records of any great antiquity. We are also able, by following up the implications of the concepts and assumptions of historical linguistics—particularly as embodied in the terms explained earlier, as well as in the definitions for these terms that we have agreed on—to push our search for linguistic origins equally far back in time.

The period in the history of the Altaic linguistic unity at which there were three different variant forms for "a stone, a rock" was surely in the extremely remote past. Sometime after the trek to the second homeland, and after settling down

[75]

in that area, each of these three variant forms was selected by one or another of the internal groups that later became the nuclei for the major subgroups into which this family thereafter divided—one by Mongolian, another by Tungusic (and also by Mongolian and Korean), and the third by Turkic (and also by Japanese). The first of these three variant forms for this word had nothing to do with the second two; but the second two were themselves later, changed versions of a still earlier linguistic form.

In this way, we are able to achieve even further historical insight into the origins of forms that we know only from our recovery (reconstructions) of what is itself an extremely ancient original language. The differentiation in the pronunciation of the second two variants for this word must go far back into Altaic history, at least to the earliest period of residence in the first homeland, if not before. Against the background of this kind of historical time-depth, we can appreciate all the more the important difference that separates historical linguistic findings based solely on the evidence of written records from those based on the comparative method.

Nowhere in the Far East, even in the Chinese area, can written records take us back as far as the comparative method can. Apart from China, there is no linguistic sector of the Far East with written records of any notable antiquity. If we were to rely solely on the testimony of written records for our study of the history of Japanese and the other Altaic languages, we would not be able to learn anything significant about the history of these languages earlier than ca. A.D. 700. This is far too recent to tell us anything about the origins of any of these languages. But when we apply the comparative method, and follow up the implications of its assumptions to their logical conclusions, we find that enormous historical vistas are opened.

In the case of these words for "a stone, a rock," we have seen that Japanese happens to go along with Turkic in selecting, from among the three competing variants that existed in the original language, the variant with the final consonant $\breve{-s}$. This is the variant that we know also goes back to an earlier form that was itself historically related to the second variant as we have listed them above, that is, the one with $*\text{-}l_2$. This second variant is the one that was selected, from among these three competing forms, by Mongolian and also by Tungusic. In other words, here Japanese did not go along with Tungusic, but rather with Turkic (and also Mongolian, in the fact of also inheriting the first of these three variants).

VERB FORMS AND CATEGORIES

As we consider the bulk of the evidence, however, we shall see that in many other cases, Japanese does go along with Tungusic in terms of the particular selections that its earliest speakers made from among the variants available to them in the original Altaic linguistic community. This communality of historical linguistic selection between Japanese and Tungusic is clearly marked, and also of particular significance for the history of both languages, in the verb morphology. By verb morphology is meant the various changes and inflections by means of which the verb is made to express various shades of meaning, usually having to do with the way or manner in which an action is performed, especially with whether the action to which the verb refers is or was carried out completely or whether it is incomplete, and at least potentially is therefore still going on.

It is clear that in the original Altaic language the verb was inflected to express all these delicate nuances of meaning, along with a great many others. Not all of these differences that were so important for the Altaic verb will be familiar to those of us accustomed only to the categories for which verbs are inflected in the more usually studied European languages, such as English, French, German, or even Russian. We are most often accustomed to thinking of the verb as something essentially concerned with expressing the time at which an action takes place; time in this sense is the grammatical category which is generally called "tense." But even in many modern European languages (which are later, changed forms of the original Indo-European language), the verb is more often than not employed not simply to indicate the time at which an action was performed or took place. In other words, it is not only inflected for tense but it also often indicates either the manner in which an action was carried out or—and this last category is extremely important, for example, in Russian and the other Slavonic languages—

[77]

whether or not an action has been carried out completely, and is now over, or whether it is still incomplete, incompleted, and hence potentially continuing. This last category, having to do with whether an action was or is complete or not, is generally referred to by linguists as "aspect."

We are accustomed to an additional grammatical category of "voice" from our experience with European languages, referring to the distinction between active ("I killed the bear") and passive ("I was killed by the bear"). Voice was also an important morphological category of the verb in the original Altaic language. But in the Altaic languages, along with this kind of contrast of voice, we more often encounter a somewhat different, but equally important one, in which the verb is inflected to express ideas having to do with whether an action was performed at the wish or volition of the person undertaking it or whether that person was forced, or caused, to do the action by someone else. This is the grammatical category that linguists call the "causative." We can, of course, express the same idea as the Altaic causative in English or the other European languages, if we wish to. The difference between passive and causative would roughly be that between "I was killed by the bear" (passive) and "I was made to kill the bear" (causative)—both expressions further contrasting with the simple active, "I killed the bear." But in the Altaic languages, these causative verb forms were a distinct morphological category of great importance. They covered many shades of meanings that are not commonly employed in English; and they were expressed, not by stringing together different words into phrases, as in the English examples just given, but by adding to, or altering in some way or another, the form of the verb itself.

Anyone familiar with modern Japanese has of course by this time recognized the Japanese inheritances of these causatives, and will also require no further comment on how important these causative verbs, in the wide variety of semantic situations in which they occur, are for the Japanese language. One has only to recall such characteristic modern Japanese verb forms as the often-heard *nomaserareta* "I was made to drink" (that is, someone plied me with drinks and I could not refuse out of politeness until finally I was made to get drunk in the process).

Together with its characteristic Altaic meaning, this modern

Japanese verb also shows exactly the kind of verb formations that existed in the original Altaic language. It consists of a verb root *nom-* "drink," to which a number of smaller suffixes have been added, making up the long string of forms *-a-se-rar-e-ta,* a sequence in which each individual part, as here written separated by hyphens, plays its own role in conveying the total semantic message of the entire form. This verb form is also quite typical of all Altaic verbs in that although it is extremely involved morphologically (that is, it consists of many different and separate smaller parts that go together to form a single word), the categories of meaning with which it is concerned have to do almost entirely with the manner in which the action of the verb—in this case that of drinking—is or was performed, and hardly at all with the time this action took place or is taking place. In this particular example, *-se-* indicates that the verb is a causative (expressing an action that someone has caused, or forced, another person to do or undertake); the *-rar-* indicates that the action is passive, not active; and the *-ta* shows that the action is past and completed, not current or continuing. (The vowels *-a-* and *-e-* also play their part in the formation of the whole, but the role of such elements in the formation of the Japanese verb is too involved to be explained simply.)

All these semantic and grammatical categories, as well as the general type of verb inflection or formation to be seen in a modern Japanese verb such as *nomaserareta,* were also important in the original Altaic language. Like everything else in that language, most of these verb inflections existed in several variant forms; and as the languages split up into separate entities after the trek to the second homeland, individual choices were made in this area of linguistic resources also, just as was done with many of the nouns, especially the words for numbers, as illustrated by the examples above.

Taken as a whole, the most convincing body of evidence for the genetic relationship of Japanese to other languages is that provided by the details of the structure of the Japanese verb, both in its morphology (word formation) and in its inflections. This body of evidence is convincing because it involves correspondences in a large number of interlocking details of forms and their meanings that may be shown to exist, and to correspond

[79]

in a regular fashion with each other, in a large number of Altaic languages, including Japanese. The quantity of items involved, as well as their correspondence in details of forms and meanings, all but rule out the possibility that the observed similarities are due either to chance or borrowings. The possibility of borrowing is further reduced by the history and the geographical distribution of the languages involved (how, for example, could Old Japanese possibly have borrowed anything from Old Turkish, thousands of miles away across the continent of Asia?). This leaves only the explanation of a real, if remote, genetic relationship among all these languages, a relationship for which the data in question, for the reasons just explained, provide extremely convincing evidence.

In its morphology, the original Altaic language used a number of suffixes to form verbs from nouns (denominal verbs), as well as to form more complicated (secondary derived) verbs from other, simpler verbs (deverbal verbs). The most important of these suffixes used for forming secondary verb stems in the original Altaic language were the following ones: *-k-, added to a noun to form a verb that then expressed an action that directly employed the noun, or an action otherwise closely related in meaning to that noun; *-g-, similarly used with nouns, but with an added semantic feature of transitivity (when forming complex verbs, this same suffix made new causatives); *-t-, used with both nouns and verbs, to form transitive derivative verbs indicating that an action relating to the original noun or verb was performed in a sudden, jolting, or otherwise conclusive manner; *-r-, used with both nouns and verbs, to form verbs for actions transpiring naturally, without external causation (often translated "to become . . ."); *-l-, used with both nouns and verbs, for transitive verbs in which an action is performed by an external agent (often translated "does . . ." or "makes . . ."); and a large number of secondary verbs, particularly in the Tungusic languages, with suffixed *-p-, indicating in part a passive or other secondarily caused action, and in part a continuous, durative state or act, often one resulting from such a passive action.

All these secondary verb-stem suffixes are sufficiently well attested in the various Altaic languages, including the many Mongolian, Turkic, and Tungusic languages, to permit us to assume that they were part of the original Altaic language; most of them may also be observed, though generally in considerably altered forms and meanings, in the morphology of the Korean verb.

The hypothesis of a historical relationship between all the Altaic languages—the same hypothesis that is the only tenable explanation for the numerous formal and semantic parallels in linguistic data revealed by comparison among these languages—also presupposes an enormous time depth separating the original Altaic language from the later languages for which we have documentary attestation, even those few Altaic languages having relatively old written records. The oldest Altaic written records, those for Old Turkish, go back only to the early decades of the eighth century, which interestingly enough also happens to be the period of the bulk of the written records for Old Japanese, the language of the court of Nara. In the course of the long period of historical change that separates each of the later languages from the original Altaic language, some languages will have preserved certain features of, for example, this system of secondary verb-stem derivation, while others will have kept others; it would be unrealistic, and not in keeping with our hypothesis concerning the nature of historical change in language, to expect to find the entire original Altaic system surviving intact in each and every later language.

Nevertheless, impressive segments of this original system for deriving complex verbs, as it must originally have existed in the oldest form of the Altaic language, do survive in all the later languages; and the evidence that may be cited for the survival of important portions of this same original system in Japanese is also the most convincing of all the arguments that may be advanced for the genetic relationship of Japanese to the other Altaic languages.

To demonstrate how this system of verb derivation operated in the original Altaic language, it is necessary to cite a few forms from some of the later languages. The *-k-* used to form verbs from nouns is seen, for example, in Tk. *taγyq-* "to climb up," where *-(y)q-* has been added to the noun *taγ* "mountain"; *ičik-* "go inside" from *iči* "inside"; *tašyq-* "depart" from *taš* "outside"; and *birik-* "unite" from *bir* "one." The same suffix, but meaning "become . . . ," is seen in Tk. *jazyq-* "become spring" from *jaz* "spring," and *sūq-* "become wet" from *sū, sub* "water." The original semantic and formal distinctions between the suffixes *-r-* and *-l-* in the Altaic language are well illustrated by the following Mongolian examples, three secondary verbs derived from the adverbial noun Mo. *suɣu* "out, off" ("aus einem Inneren heraus"): *suɣul-* "pull off," *suɣura-* "slip, fall off by itself," and *suɣuči-* "pluck out." The last verb shows the original suffix *-t-*, changed to Mo. *-či-*, in its characteristic Altaic sense of a sudden, determined, transitive action. The first of these three Mongolian secondary verbs happens to have an exact Japanese parallel in the verb *sugur-* "pluck off, strip (rice ears)." From the evidence, we may assume that this Japanese verb, like Mo. *suɣul-*, to which it corresponds in both form and meaning, goes back to an older formation in the original Altaic language, in which an underlying noun was made into a verb by the suffixation of *-l-*. Early in its prehistory, Japanese lost the original phonological distinction between *r* and *l,* which were separate sounds in Altaic; but in this and many other cases in the morphology of the Japanese verb we may still determine whether a Japanese *r* goes back to original *r* or *l,* partly on the basis of meaning (as in the example above), and partly by other evidence, to which we shall return below.

Japanese denominal verbs showing the inheritance of the original Altaic suffixes *-k-* and *-g-* are numerous and striking. The formation is seen in such words as *wanak-* "throttle, strangle" from the noun *wana* "noose, snare"; *sitak-* "tread underfoot" from *sita* "bottom"; *makurak-* "use something as a pillow" from *makura* "a pillow"; *kabuk-* "bow, incline the head" from *kabu* "head"; and *miduk-* "soak, steep" from *midu* "water." This last example is particularly important, since a parallel formation, also inherited from Altaic, appears in Korean *mulk-* "be watery, thin" from *mul* "water," and we have also seen above yet another genetically related formation in Tk. *sūq-* "become wet."

In Japanese deverbal verbs, a related *-k-* suffix, also of Altaic origin, has a causative function: *haruk-* "cause something to be opened wide" from *har-* "open up, esp. new land"; *matak-* "be made to wait upon" from *mat-* "wait for, on." Similarly, Japanese *sir-* "know" underlies the secondary formations *sirak-ë-* "wake up, sober up" and *siragah-* "do something in such a way that it is noticed," in exact parallel to formations, similarly inherited from Altaic, to be seen in Mo. *sere-* "to awaken" and *serge-* "sober (oneself) up." The original Altaic language also employed **-g-* in analogous factitive formations, exhibited by such Japanese verbs as *matag-* "straddle" from *mata* "crotch"; *hag-* "make an arrow by fitting a feather to a shaft" from *ha* "feather"; *hutag-* "close up tightly" from *huta* "lid"; *tunag-* "pursue quarry in the hunt" from *tuna* "rope, bast hawser," and *unag-* "wear at the throat or neck" from *una* "nape of the neck."

The way in which Japanese inherited both forms and functions of the three original verb-stem suffixes **-r-*, **-l-*, and **-t-* from the original Altaic language is particularly well attested. Original Altaic formations in **-r-* in the sense of "become . . ." are seen in such words as Japanese *akar-* "become bright, colored" from *aka* "red, brightness"; *takar-* "become, be high" from *taka* "high"; *masar-* "excel" from *masa* "correct"; and *sakar-* "defy, run counter to" from *saka* "incline." Original Altaic **-l-* meaning "do" or "perform" also appear as Japanese *-r-*, but with the critical difference that a voiceless stop in the underlying Japanese noun becomes voiced in these forms. This makes it possible, even in Japanese, to distinguish original formations in Altaic **-l-* from those in **-r-*. Japanese *tugar-*, "attach, connect" from *tuka* "haft," *modor-* "return" from *moto* "origin," *kagir-*, "set limits" from *kaki* "a fence," and *sagar-* "droop down, hang" from *saka,* "incline" all illustrate this old inherited principle of Altaic word formation as operative in Japanese. A morphological pattern such as this, with *-g-* for **-k-*, and also *-d-* for **-t-*, in Japanese secondary verbs depending on the original suffix being Altaic **-l-* and not Altaic **-r-*, even though both these suffixes later merged into undifferentiated Japanese *r,* is the most convincing kind of evidence for demonstrating the genetic relationship of the language, that is, its Altaic origin.

Also notable for the power of conviction that it carries in any discussion of Japanese linguistic origins is the evidence that the language preserves for its inheritance of the original Altaic suffix **-t-* for sudden or deliberate transitive actions, particularly when this suffix contrasts both in form and meaning with other parallel **-r-* and **-l-* formations. Thus, from the simplex verb *wak-* "be set apart, separate" Japanese has two different secondary formations, both inherited from Altaic, *wakar-* "become separate," with original *-r-, and *wakat-* "break apart, split, rip open," this last form showing the distinctive sense, as well as the form, of the inherited suffix *-t- quite clearly. Similarly, Japanese *sak-* "split into two" underlies both *sakar-* "be split apart" and *sakat-* "butcher, kill," again demonstrating the semantic force of this Altaic suffix as it was inherited in Japanese. Other words similarly formed include *hagat-* "destroy, tear completely out" from *hag-* "flay," and *hanat-* "let fly, as an arrow from a bow" from *han-* "bound, spring up." Parallel Japanese denominal formations with this suffix are *awat-* "cleanse, rinse" from *awa* "foam"; *irat-* "be agitated, excited" from *ira* "thorn, pain"; and *tagit-* "(water) rushes, boils up" from *taki* "rapids, cascade." (The *-g-* in *tagit-* was analogically carried over from another inherited Altaic deverbal formation on *taki*, the verb *tagir-* "boil, churn up," where the *-g-* is regular because the Japanese suffixed *-r-* goes back to original Altaic *-l-.)

The Altaic verb-stem suffixes were also extensively employed in the original language in compounds containing two or more such suffixes, of the pattern *-kar-*, *-gal-*, and so on. The Tungusic languages in particular later developed this morphological device extensively, employing it to form large numbers of secondary verbs. Japanese and Korean both go closely together with Tungusic in this feature, and both make considerable use of such compound suffixes in verb morphology throughout their history. Since these compound suffixes are longer in form, and more involved in their meanings, than are the single elements of which they are made up, they provide even more convincing evidence for genetic relationship when, as often, they may be identified in many different and now widely separated languages. Space precludes even a sample of the evidence, but to the Altaicist such Japanese secondary verb formations, employing several compound suffixes, as *tukarakas-* "make to be exhausted," with the compound suffix *-kas-* added to *tukar-* "be exhausted," a word that is itself a secondary formation with suffixed *-r-* from a stem *tuk-* "be exhausted," immediately reveal their Altaic origins (cf. Tk. *tükä-* "exhaust," also in Turkic with suffixed *-t-* as *tükät-* "exhaust," and with *-n-* as *tükän-* "become exhausted").

Japanese particularly drew upon its Tungusic connections

for its many verbs in stem-final -h- having a durative or continuative meaning; this Japanese suffix is a later, changed form of Altaic and Tungusic *-p- in the same sense and function. In Japanese it characteristically appears as the second consonant in a compound suffix, such as the -gah- in sita-gah- "follow upon" from sita "bottom, below." Also of Altaic origin is the Japanese transitive-intransitive contrast seen in verb-stem final -r- and -s- pairs, for example, tar- "be sufficient" contrasting with tas- "fill up, make full." The original Altaic language had exactly parallel, and historically related forms, cf. Tk. tol- "be full, sufficient" and toš- "fill up." The existence of such sets of detailed parallels in linguistic forms and their meanings in different languages can only be explained by the genetic relationship of all the languages in question to one another, that is, by the hypothesis of their descent from a common, though long lost, original language.

"Basic Vocabulary"

Data involving details of word formation, along the lines of those above, are the most convincing evidence in any discussion of linguistic origins; but this of course does not mean that regular parallels in forms and meanings from other levels of the languages, including uninflected forms such as nouns and grammatical particles, are by any means to be neglected. Such evidence, which makes possible the recovery of much of the common vocabulary of the earlier linguistic unity (in this case, the original Altaic language), is also available from Japanese in impressive quantities.

In studying uninflected forms such as nouns in particular, many well-meaning amateurs of linguistics—and even a surprisingly large number of supposedly trained historians of language— often make the assumption that there are certain forms in all languages that are more resistant to historical change than others, because these forms refer to ideas or concepts or things that are somehow "basic" to human existence. Upon this unfounded assumption they further argue, also erroneously, that the identification of common items of supposedly "basic vocabulary" in different languages is a necessary part of establishing convincing evidence for the genetic relationship of the languages concerned.

[85]

For the historical linguist, the entire proposition of "basic vocabulary," including both the idea that some words in a language are, or should be, more resistant to historical change than others, and the idea that certain kinds of words are of special importance in helping to demonstrate the genetic relationship of languages in a convincing fashion, is unsupported, undemonstrable, and unscientific. Mainly, this fallacy of basic vocabulary as a critical issue in historical linguistics is rooted in an old, and difficult to eradicate, confusion between words and the things they mean: no one would question that eating, and drinking, and sexual intercourse are basic human functions, in the sense that if any or all of these activities were long interrupted, human life would soon cease.

But it is one thing to recognize that such activities, and the parts of the body that make them possible—in other words, the real-world referents of the words involved—are in this fashion and in this very practical sense "basic." It is quite another to conclude from this that the words that arbitrarily indicate these activities, or that go with the body parts that make the activities possible, are themselves also basic; and it is particularly misleading to assume that, for these reasons, such words tell us more than other kinds of words do about the history of a language. It is eating, drinking, reproduction, and related activities that are basic to human life, not the words that people use when they refer to such things. The damage that has been done to historical linguistics because of the mistaken application of the essentially erroneous thesis of "basic vocabulary," particularly when some scholars have attempted to employ it for quasi-statistical purposes ("glottochronology" or "lexico-statistics"), has been immense.

Nevertheless, because questions of the genetic relationship of different languages are matters to be considered in terms of the accumulation of more or less convincing bodies of evidence, rather than in terms of "proof," it cannot be denied that correspondences between words having their immediate semantic referents in simple, everyday, "basic" items, such as terms for parts of the body and essential bodily functions, are for obvious psychological reasons somehow more convincing than correspondences between words that refer to ideas and concepts that are less concrete, and also sometimes more difficult to identify and specify. In this sense, and in this sense alone, the consideration of so-called basic vocabulary can add conviction to our demonstrations of historical-linguistic evidence; and when we compare Japanese with the other Altaic languages, we find no lack of such "basic vocabulary" correspondences, connecting all the languages involved.

In the brief sample list that follows, only one Japanese lexical item has been cited, together with one (or at the most two) from other Altaic languages, out of considerations of space.* It is important to keep in mind that the comparisons made here are not between the two or three words actually cited but rather between the Japanese word, on the one hand, and all the other Altaic forms that could be cited in every instance, if space allowed. The examples selected for this short sample list have been chosen because they refer to easily identified, and important, if not necessarily "basic," items of vocabulary in all the languages involved: Japanese *ago* "chin, jaw," Tk. *aγyz* "mouth"; *hara* "belly," Tk. *bäl* "midsection of the body"; *wi-* "to be," Ma. *bi-*, Mo. *bü-* "to be"; *iro* "face" (Old Japanese) "color" (later), Tk. *jüz* "face," Mo. *düri* "appearance"; *tab-* "eat," Ma. *jef-* "eat"; *kir-* "cut," Tk. *qyr-q-* "scrape," Mo. *kir-ga-* "clip"; *kokoro* "heart," Tk. *kököz*, Mo. *kökür* "breasts"; *kuri* "chestnut," Ma. *kuri* "spotted, dapple"; *natu* "summer," Tk. *jaz* "spring," MKo. *nyŏl-* "summer"; *heta* "stem of a fruit," *heso* "navel," MMo. *hesi* "haft, handle"; *hokuro* "mole," Ma. *fuhu* "wart"; *huru* "old," MMo. *hurtu*, Tk. *uzu-* "long"; Old Japanese *Fötö* "vulva," MMo. *hütügün* "id.," Ma. *fontoho* "small hole"; *sik(k)o* "urine," *sik-* "dampen, moisten," Tk. *sig-* "urinate," Ma. *sike* "urine"; *siri* "buttocks," Mo. *sili* "nape, back"; *ketu* "rump," Tk. *käd* "behind, end"; *sigure* "autumn or winter drizzle," Mo. *siγurgan*

---

* The abbreviations "Tk." for Turkic and "Mo." for Mongolian are used here as general identifications for the linguistic forms cited, without specifying which particular Turkic or Mongolian language is at question; specifics of language identification may be found in the other literature cited. Manchu ("Ma."), Evenki ("Ev.") and Goldi ("Gl.")—also called Nanai—are the names of Tungusic languages. The abbreviation "M" means "Middle," in the name of an earlier stage of a language—that is, earlier than the modern language but not as old as the oldest written records.

"snowstorm," Ev. *sigir* "rain with wind, a storm"; *simo* "frost," Gl. *semata* "id."

Surely a listing of this sort—which, it is again to be stressed, includes only a sample of the evidence available—provides a remarkably wide representation of vocabulary items that relate to every possible variety of "basic" human activities, needs, and circumstances, including body parts, bodily functions, and climatic and seasonal phenomena. Further and equally convincing evidence could be cited from the comparative study of grammatical items such as post-positions and other syntactic markers, including an inherited indicator for plural number (Japanese *-ra,* from Altaic, and particularly Tungusic *-la),* as well as the distinctively varied paradigms that the inherited personal pronouns and interrogatives display in Old Japanese (though here especially the modern language has lost almost all traces of the forms involved).

Tungusic and Japanese

In the selection of possible variant forms for the verb inflections, the evidence for identical choices by Japanese and the various Tungusic languages is particularly striking. It can only point to a considerable period of intimate contact, in the second homeland, between the earliest ancestors of those who later became the speakers of Japanese and the earliest ancestors of those who later became the speakers of the Tungusic languages. Much of the evidence that directly relates to this common sharing of a number of features between Tungusic and Japanese as far as the morphology of the verb is concerned has only recently been discovered, and the bulk of it still awaits publication. In the meantime, our awareness of the existence of such evidence means that if we are interested in the origins of Japanese, we will also be extremely interested in the origins of the Tungusic languages, since it is clear that the earliest speakers of both Japanese and the Tungusic languages shared a long period of close symbiosis, somewhere in the Altaic linguistic community and at some time in the remote history of that group.

Another rather more obvious reason exists for associating the origins of the Tungusic languages with the study of the origins of Japanese. This is the· evidence provided by the geographical location of these languages today. If we look at a map of the Far East, and focus our attention on the region between the Asian mainland and the Japanese archipelago that appears on most maps as the Sea of Japan, we will see why, even without this substantial linguistic evidence from the verb inflections and morphology, we might well expect that Tungusic and Japanese would have a close connection. The reason is, of course, to be found in their present-day geographical proximity (see figure 1).

The Japanese archipelago lies in an easy curve off the coast of Asia, and approaches closest to it at two points—Korea in the south, and the general Tungusic-speaking area of Asia in the north. The distance between the Japanese islands and those regions of mainland Asia in which the Tungusic languages are still employed is greater, to be sure, than the distance between Japan and Korea, but it is still extremely small, particularly as we go farther north on the map, and consider the narrow expanse of sea that separates the northernmost islands such as Sakhalin, USSR, from the continent. Little wonder that major attention must be paid not only to Korean but also to the Tungusic languages in our pursuit of the origins of Japanese.

The original Tungusic language employed two different (though probably mutually related) suffixes for the formation of two types of deverbal nouns that were of great frequency and importance in the language. (In dealing with Tungusic, and indeed with all the Altaic languages including Japanese, we must always keep in mind that the employment of such grammatical terms as "verb" and "noun" is simply a convention of scholarly convenience, and that it is not based on any rigorously established descriptive categories; here we follow these conventions of the scholarly literature in employing such terms, even though they are largely based upon translation equivalents in Indo-European languages, and hence essentially irrelevant to the structures of the languages with which we are dealing.)

The first of these suffixes, which may be reconstructed as Proto-Tungusic *-ra-*, was used to form a variety of tenseless verbal noun, one that indicated that the act or action of the verb involved was of a repeated, habitual, or customary nature.

[89]

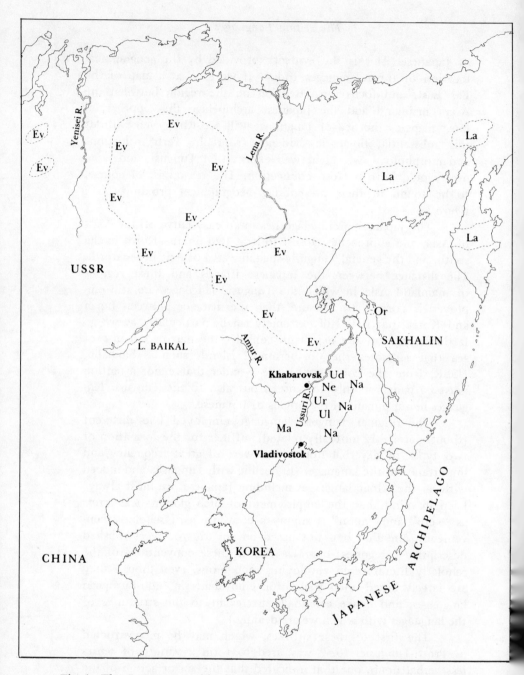

Fig. 1. The Japanese archipelago and the Tungusic areas. The Tungusic
language groups are: Ev = Evenki, La = Lamut, Na = Nanai, Ma =
Manchu, Or = Orok, Ud = Udehei, Or = Oroci, Ul = Ulci, Ne = Negidal.

The acts or actions indicated by this, the so-called Tungusic *nomen usus,* have the particularly important semantic dimension of being "incomplete" or "imperfect," in the sense that they are not tied to any particular chronological time (this of course follows from their earlier definition as repeated, habitual, or customary); hence they might as well happen in the past, the present, or—as often is the case in many of the languages that inherited these forms—the future. For this reason they often find their employment, especially in Japanese, in expressions for conditionals or negatives, where again, by definition, the time of the act or action is of no consequence.

The second of these suffixes may be reconstructed as Proto-Tungusic *-rĭ-.* This suffix was employed to form another, contrasting variety of verbal noun, distinguished from the first variety in *-ra-* mainly because it was specialized to indicate acts or actions taking place in the present, or at least having some concept of present time as an important constituent in its semantic make-up (these are the forms of the so-called Tungusic *nomen praesens*).

Both these distinctive Tungusic verb formations may be traced in Japanese, where their inheritance from the original Tungusic linguistic unity provides a historical explanation for forms and their meanings that cannot be arrived at solely in terms of Japanese itself. For example, the original Altaic verb *ā-* "exist" appears in Japanese in forms that are actually, and historically, deverbal nouns displaying both these inherited suffixes; with the second of these two suffixes, *ā-rĭ-* gave Japanese *ari,* literally a deverbal noun meaning "existing." Meanwhile, and with the same verb root, *ā-ra-* gave Japanese *ara-,* a form of the verb that in Japanese is specialized for employment with quasi-conditional hypotheticals *(araba),* negatives *(arazu),* and a few other special formations. Just as Japanese *ari* continues the Tungusic deverbal *nomen praesens,* so also does Japanese *ara*—the so-called *mizenkei* of Japanese grammarians—continue the Tungusic *nomen usus.*

Sometimes a single verb root has yielded two different *nomen usus* forms in Japanese, because of different patterns of assimilation between the *-r-* of the suffix *-ra-* and the final consonant of the verb root; thus, for the verb root *sak-* "bloom," we find both the noun *sakura* "cherry blossoms" and the dependent verb form *saka-* (as in *sakazu* "does not bloom," etc.). Both *sakura* and *saka-* involve the inheritance of Tungusic **-ra-*, but two different sets of phonetic changes have resulted in the suffix surviving in a more obvious form in *sakura* than it does in the verb form *saka-*, where earlier **sak-ra-* was subsequently simplified to become *saka-*. The same relationship exists between the two words *makura* "a pillow" and the verb form *maka-*, in their relation to the verb root *mak-* "spread out." Sometimes both Japanese inheritances of these Tungusic **-ra-* deverbal nouns have fallen together into what would appear to be the same word; but they are actually different forms both in grammatical use and meaning. Thus *nar-* "make a noise" has both the dependent verb form *nara-*, from **nar-ra-*, and the simple deverbal noun *nara*, which means "a fart." Interesting also are Old Japanese *Fuguri* "scrotum" and *Fukura* "anything distended, plumped up," both related through these two inherited Tungusic deverbal noun suffixes to the verb root *Fuk-* "inflate, blow up."

In the light of such data, it is particularly important to note that even without the linguistic evidence of the Japanese verb morphology and its Altaic origins, scholars have other, independent reasons for believing that after the Altaic linguistic community arrived at its second homeland in Central Asia, it was those internal linguistic groups that later became the first Tungusic speakers who undertook the initial steps in the great second wave of Altaic migrations. In fact, it is believed that these first migrations of those who later became the Tungusic speakers took place even before the disruptions of the ethnological map of ancient Central Asia that resulted from the Hunnic movements, and to which we have related the later Altaic dispersal from the second homeland.

This means that the Tungusic speakers—or, more accurately, the immediate ancestors of the Tungusic speakers—were the first of the Altaic subgroups to leave this second homeland. (Of course, as we shall stress shortly in somewhat more detail, the fact that they were the first to leave does not imply that they left once and for all; subsequent splitting off, and gradual moving away, by remnants of the same or closely related groups may very well have followed after them.) And not only were they the first to leave, but their migration eventually took them farther away from their original starting point than any of the other Altaic groups were to go—always with the possible, and important, exceptions of the ancestors of the Japanese and Koreans, important elements of whom most likely left the second Altaic homeland together with this first wave of Tungusic dispersal, but who eventually settled for good in sites even more remote from that second homeland than those areas in which the Tungusic speakers domiciled themselves.

Once the ancestors of the later Tungusic speakers—and any others who accompanied them along the way—had broken off from the remainder of the Altaic linguistic community, whom they now left behind in the second Altaic homeland, the trek upon which these people set forth was no simple matter; nor was it a journey that could have been completed within the lifetimes of those individuals who began it. Many would die and be replaced by others born along the way. Surely several generations would intervene between the time of the earliest leave-takings and the final arrival of these speakers in their new homes, far up in northern Asia and scattered along the shores and islands of the Pacific Ocean.

The length of time required for this, the first of the great Altaic migrations from the second Central Asian homeland, is an important factor for us to keep in mind. Linguistic change takes place very slowly, but nevertheless it does take place across the dimension of historical time. The more time that elapsed during this enormous migratory trek, the greater was the likelihood of the language of the persons involved also changing enormously. When these speakers first split off from the Altaic linguistic community, they had already, in one way or another, agreed among themselves to favor certain internal variants that existed in the common Altaic language. This habit of selecting one variant rather than another had already began to set them off, linguistically, from their Altaic neighbors and kin.

What next happened might, with slight but probably pardonable exaggeration, be termed an irreversible voyage of migration. Once the Tungusic speakers had set out upon their trek, and once they were totally isolated from the rest of the Altaic community, there was no need for them to make any further

[93]

effort to conform to community norms of linguistic usage. The necessity for social cooperation with other Altaic speakers had ceased. It no longer mattered what words they chose to use or which of a number of different possible pronunciations they employed for a given word. As long as their Tungusic fellow travelers on the trek understood what was being said, that was enough.

As the trek away from the second homeland took longer and longer, the linguistic differences that earlier had already set this group off from the rest of their Altaic relations now became more and more pronounced. Entire generations came into existence along the route of march whose members had never lived in the Altaic homeland. They had never faced the problem of communicating with other Altaic speakers who used different words or favored other variant forms or pronunciations. The only linguistic world that these new members of the community knew, since they had come to linguistic maturity in the course of the great trek that took the Tungusic speakers out of Central Asia and eventually up into the northeast coastal regions of the Asian mainland, was the linguistic world of the group with which they were traveling. Under such circumstances of language and society, it is not difficult to see why and how this group soon came to use a variety of the once common and original Altaic language that became very different indeed from the language of the people they had left behind in the second homeland. (And needless to add, the word "soon" here is to be understood only in a relative sense; in absolute chronological terms, the process must have taken a very long time, probably as long as the trek itself.)

As this Proto-Tungusic linguistic community—as we may now designate these early groups who first moved away from the second Altaic homeland—removed themselves from their Altaic kin and neighbors, they passed through an extremely varied landscape. For a long period in their history, this Proto-Tungusic linguistic community appears to have lived as nomads in the Siberian area that is called the *taiga*. The term *taiga* is a Russian word for the swampy, coniferous forests of Siberia that intervene between the steppes and the *tundra*, another Russian word that refers to the level, gently undulating treeless plains of the northern arctic regions.

As residents of the *taiga*, the members of the Proto-Tungusic

[94]

linguistic community were now able to support themselves by engaging in several new economic pursuits made possible by the physical environment and ecology of the area, particularly hunting, fishing, and reindeer breeding. It is believed that they first became engaged in these livelihoods during the period in which they mostly lived in the region that stretches from the shores of Lake Baikal up to the Amur River basin, and that they continued to use these skills when once again they set out on the final stages of their migration, which eventually brought them all the way to the Pacific coast of Asia.

Life-supporting activities such as the hunting and fishing that were possible in the *taiga,* with its spruce and fir forests and enormous swampy regions, were in sharp contrast to the ways of sustaining life that these Altaic speakers had been familiar with in their homeland. This is particularly true of reindeer breeding, which the Tungusic speakers eventually brought to a high degree of development, and upon which they eventually focused not only their economic but also their social life.

In this Tungusic migration, two aspects of the physical geography are clearly of major importance, since they not only determined the course of much of the linguistic development within this newly separated subgroup of the larger Altaic family but they also help us understand why the Tungusic subgroup of Altaic does not have the same kind of historical relationship to the original Altaic community that the other subgroups—particularly Turkic and Mongolian—do. The differences in this relationship are matters of the degree, not of the type, of historical relationship involved; and to a large extent the fact that they arose in the first place has to do with the conditions of physical geography and ecology encountered by the Tungusic community in the course of their travels.

The first of these two aspects of geography has to do with the enormous differences in physical conditions, weather, and climate that were encountered by these people in the terrain through which they gradually moved, hence also with the necessity for evolving strikingly different ways of providing for their economic livelihood—a stimulus to which, it must be added, they responded exceptionally well, particularly in the development of complex socioeconomic behavior patterns that came

[95]

to focus on the breeding, care, and exploitation of the precious reindeer herds. The way in which this stimulus would promote important and lasting linguistic changes in the newly separated community is certainly easy to understand. New words, terms, and expressions necessarily found their way into the daily linguistic life of the group as they came to focus more and more on the constantly evolving techniques for sustaining life in northeast Asia, particularly ways for nurturing and protecting the reindeer herds that had become the source of so much of their livelihood.

From what we understand of the detailed processes of linguistic development in the case of languages whose history is better documented, we may usefully speculate that here two different processes were at work. One was the internal development of new linguistic combinations, and sometimes even of new linguistic forms, in order to handle new developments in the material culture. The other was linguistic borrowing, a different and tremendously important variety of linguistic change that plays a role in linguistic history everywhere in the world, and to which we must give further consideration later. In its essence, linguistic borrowing is a special case of linguistic imitation, in which new terms and expressions are taken over by mimicry of the languages of those nearby groups in whose sociolinguistic culture these terms and expressions are already present. It is not always a simple matter to distinguish cases of linguistic borrowing from cases of the genetic inheritance of etymologically connected common linguistic items, particularly when such borrowing took place at early periods and in the absence of early written records, which are most useful for tracing the precise course of such take-overs, through mimicry, of ready-made linguistic materials from others.

The tremendous differences that all this would make in the language of the group can easily be imagined. One has only to think, for example, of the great number of new words and expressions that had to be introduced into the English language in order to accommodate the invention and general public use of the automobile a generation ago, or of the flood of new words from many sources that were introduced into Japanese during the period of rapid modernization following the Meiji Restoration.

[96]

What difficulties would we encounter, for example, if we were placed in the position of holding a conversation with someone from our grandparents' generation, or before, who was unfamiliar with the automobile, not to mention the airplane and space travel? How puzzled a pre-Meiji *samurai* or Kyoto court noble would surely be if he were able to listen to two modern Japanese converse in Japanese. One might also speculate about how much of a typical Japanese conversation such a figure from the fairly recent past would even be able to understand, given the enormous number of new words, terms, and expressions that have come into the Japanese language in the past few decades as a concomitant of modernization and the increasingly marked focus of the society on technology.

These close-at-hand parallels help us understand both how and why the language of the Proto-Tungusic migrant community soon developed into something quite different from the original, common Altaic language spoken in the community from which this group had taken its departure. The socioeconomic culture of the reindeer herds, their care and exploitation, was only one—though it remains the most impressive and perhaps the most important—of a large number of totally new situations of daily life, each of which had to be responded to by developing new linguistic forms and usages. As such new linguistic forms and usages gradually grew in number, and became more and more a major portion of the language of the Tungusic community, the net effect of this accumulative process of linguistic change was eventually to push the Tungusic linguistic community further and further away from its Altaic heritage.

The process, it should be emphasized, was gradual and accumulative. We cannot specify just how much new lexicon is necessary to sever a language from its parent linguistic community; and the problem is further complicated because the introduction of new lexical items—whether generated from within the community or borrowed from outside—is never an isolated process. It is always accompanied by other kinds of linguistic change. Somewhere in the course of this involved process of linguistic change, the addition of a single straw, in the form of one more new lexical development, or one more item of some other variety of linguistic change, apparently breaks the linguistic community's

[97]

camel's back. And with that, what was one language is now two—still related but now different. In this way, and as the result of a long accumulative process, and the accretion of multiple layers of linguistic change, the language of the Tungusic linguistic community after a time ceased to be mutually intelligible to the other Altaic speakers who had been left behind in the second homeland.

The Tungusic language of this new, separated group was still Altaic, in the sense that it was genetically related to the Altaic common language of the community left behind—that is, it was a later, changed form of that language. But the changes soon went so far, and were so complicated, that they grew to the point where they began to interfere with communication within the social group, and finally interrupted such communication entirely. From this point on, the relation of Tungusic to Altaic had become solely a historical matter, something that concerned only the origins of the Tungusic languages.

The second of the two aspects of ecology that are of major importance in connection with the early separation of the Tungusic speakers from the main body of the Altaic community may be described as the irreversibility of the terrain across which the Tungusic group traveled. The physical geography of the northeastern trek differed in important essentials from the physical conditions of much of the territory that the other major subgroups, particularly Turkic and Mongolian, would make their own when they in their turn, somewhat later, left the second homeland in Central Asia. "Irreversibility" in this connection means that the physical conditions of the terrain in which the Tungusic speakers found themselves were such as to render all but impossible any significant subsequent communication with their Altaic kin whom they had left behind in the second homeland.

The mountains, forests, and vast swamps into which their trek took the Tungusic speakers were more than simply a difficult terrain of a most demanding nature. Negotiating the journey itself took a great toll in lives and economic resources. Only a madman would have dared entertain the idea of returning, even part of the way. In this sense, the terrain and its physical conditions made the trek irreversible; once the Proto-Tungusic speakers had moved on, they had moved on for good, and the possibility of return, or of frequent trips back and forth, even for a small segment of the route of march, was almost nonexistent. Again, one does not have to go far afield or far back into history to find close parallels. The pioneers who left the eastern settlements of the United States to trek west encountered a similarly demanding terrain. For them, too, the mountains, forests, and other natural features they encountered were tremendous barriers—something to be overcome, if possible, but surely never to be undertaken more than once.

The linguistic implications of this one-way migration that was imposed on the Tungusic speakers by the facts of the physical geography of northeast Asia are obviously of a high order of importance. Had these Altaic speakers been able to remain in close, or even fairly close, communication with the speakers whom they had left behind in the homeland—or if such communication could, for example, have been reopened by trips back and forth, even if only at times separated by generations—linguistic changes in the Tungusic languages, when viewed from the point of the other Altaic languages, would have been kept to a minimum. In such a case, the Tungusic languages would still have been rather special within Altaic, but they would not have ended up being as different from the other Altaic languages as they are.

Later, when the ancestors of the linguistic subgroups that we now identify as Turkic and Mongolian themselves also moved away from the second homeland, they set out in different directions. In their treks they did not encounter physical conditions nearly as forbidding as those met by the Tungusic speakers. Moving in the general direction of the west, or southwest, or in other directions away from the homeland, the Turkic and Mongolian subgroups still generally found themselves in terrain that was familiar, and by no means as demanding or as formidable as that to the northeast. For these groups, as a result, the migratory movements, once undertaken, were anything but irreversible.

The rich lexical evidence that survives attesting to the existence of a pair (doublet) of related words meaning "to nomadize" in the earliest stages of the original Altaic language not only provides materials showing how these words changed in their meanings and forms in the various later languages but

also throws semantic light on the nature of the earliest Altaic
migratory movements.

Two original roots are involved here, Proto-Altaic *negü̈-
and Proto-Altaic *nug-, the second of the two roots generally
appearing in the later languages with a variety of secondary
verb-stem derivative suffixes, which sometimes unvoice its final
*-g-, giving forms like nuktę-, or interchange positions with it
(metathesize), giving forms like nulgī-. Both these original roots
had semantic reference to trekking, migrating, and moving resi-
dences from place to place. In the various languages, one or the
other of these forms has given Mongolian negü- "to nomadize;
change pasture grounds," Manchu neo- "roam, wander away
from home," and in Tungusic, such forms as Ev. nulgī- "move
residence," nulgīktęję- "to nomadize," and nuktę- "to nomadize."
In Turkic, corresponding forms are to be identified in such words
as MTk. jok- "rise, ascend," and the modern Turkish noun yokuş
"a rise, an ascent."

But it is the development of these original roots in Korean
and Japanese that is of particular semantic interest. Here we
find two different Japanese forms, one going with each of the
original Altaic roots: Japanese nig-e- "escape from the power
or influence of an opponent," and also Japanese nog-e- "flee,
escape"; while Korean has as cognate to the second original Altaic
root the verb noh- "release, let go, set free," a verb of particular
relevance to this entire question when we also find it employed
in the modern compound verb Korean noh.a mŏk.i- "graze,
pasture, keep (animals) running loose," with Korean mŏk.i-
"keep, feed (animals)."

There is much for us to learn in all this lexical evidence
relating to trekking and migrations. The movements of the Altaic
peoples must often have involved fleeing from powerful enemies
and escaping from the immediate vicinity of dangerous foes
(as the Japanese cognates stress), as well as simply shifting residence and changing pasture grounds (which is the principal meaning that we would recover for the original Altaic linguistic unity
if we did not have the Japanese evidence at hand). But the Turkic
evidence also emphasizes how often this fleeing and escaping
must have involved running away from enemies encountered
on the lowland, and how often the problem was solved by taking

refuge in higher, more mountainous terrain—places where the physical geography itself provided the fleeing groups with an added measure of security. And to this already fairly detailed scenario of flight and migration the Korean evidence adds yet another important semantic dimension, stressing as it does the factor that must always have been one of the main concerns motivating all such migrations—the search for a place where the animals of the group could be let loose and set out to pasture in comparative security and peace. Already, with the Korean developments, we are in the presence of groups that either had managed the transition to a settled agricultural economy or were well on their way toward accomplishing that goal—the quiet pasturing and feeding of domesticated animals, who may at last graze safely, without fear of the intrusion of enemies.

Meanwhile, a few speakers sometimes managed to return and live among the Altaic inhabitants of the second homeland, so long as it was still a homeland, and so long as it was still inhabited by any Altaic speakers who were not, unlike themselves, more or less constantly on the move. These sporadic back-and-forth movements, even if they were repeated only with the interval of a generation or more between each trek, kept other subgroups such as Turkic and Mongolian speakers in closer linguistic contact than was ever possible for the Tungusic speakers.

We can do little more than speculate on the reasons for such oscillation, which must have required enormous effort and consumed valuable resources, not the least of which would have been the carefully hoarded remnants of the community's precious food supply. Some cyclical ritual requirements calling for periodic returns to earlier inhabited areas come to mind in this connection, but such matters remain on the level of speculation. Someday, when we have more reliable data concerning the ethnography and ethnology of all Altaic peoples, other, more specific reasons may suggest themselves.

At any rate, and whatever the reasons behind these costly treks back and forth, these closer linguistic contacts meant that new words and expressions, necessarily developed on the march and representing linguistic responses to new sociolinguistic, socioeconomic, and ecological circumstances encountered along the way, were also in turn communicated back to the speakers who had been left behind in the course of all this trekking.

Eventually, of course, what happened linguistically to the Tungusic subgroup also happened to the Mongolian and Turkic subgroups. In the long run, and after many generations, linguistic cooperation between these subgroups themselves, as well as between these subgroups and any remnants of the Altaic speakers who had not yet moved away, became so difficult that eventually it was interrupted. But the possibility of a certain amount of continued coming and going between the later dispersed groups and the second homeland—a possibility that was enhanced by the physical features of the terrain over which the Turkic and Mongolian migrations took their speakers—delayed this eventual interruption of communication for a long time. Even after this interruption, Turkic and Mongolian continued to be closer to one another, and to share more features in common than either of them shared with Tungusic. Consideration of the circumstances of the migratory movements involved in each instance makes it clear why this is so; and these circumstances were largely imposed by the physical geography of various parts of the Asiatic continent.

In this fashion, we are able to postulate many of the conditions and circumstances out of which arose the special nature of the later Tungusic languages, and in particular the characteristic nature of the genetic relationship that exists between these languages and the other Altaic languages, both now and in the past. We are able to see quite clearly just how the development of the Tungusic languages was affected by the physical conditions of the new terrain into which their speakers advanced, and to whose stimulus they found it necessary to evolve not only a socioeconomic and a cultural but also a linguistic response. The nature of this response to a large measure determined the internal changes that resulted in the emergence of many of the special words, expressions, and other distinctive features of these languages, and at the same time it shaped the nature of their ultimate historical relationship to the original Altaic language itself. Taken together, these factors, which we have sketched in general outline, determined that while these languages would retain impressive evidence for their genetic relationship with Altaic, the nature of that relationship would always be somewhat different, both in degree and in extent, from that existing between Altaic and such other major subgroups as Turkic and Mongolian.

All these formulations are of particular interest to us, of course, because of the special bearing they have on the origins of the Japanese language. Geographical considerations alone, even in the absence of linguistic data, would make it incumbent on us to give special consideration to the earlier history of the Tungusic languages. But in this case we do not work in the absence of linguistic data, which here point in the same direction as do the facts of geography—toward an especially important relationship, within Altaic, of Japanese to the Tungusic languages. Most important, it is against the background of the understanding of the major historical steps in the evolution of the Tungusic languages out of the original Altaic linguistic unity that we may most meaningfully interpret the evidence that we now have for the earliest introduction of human civilization into the islands of the Japanese archipelago. With this civilization, some early form— even though it was one that was already "later, and changed"— of the Altaic language also most likely found its way into the archipelago.

PREHISTORY AND ARCHAEOLOGY

The first and most striking thing we learn from a survey of the Japanese archaeological evidence that appears to bear on the chronology concerning the earliest introduction of *Homo sapiens* and his language to the Japanese islands is that it will most likely be necessary to push further and further back into the past the entire system of dates that has been developed in order to accommodate this variety of data. The more we learn in this field, the stronger is our impression that almost all datings, not only for Japan but also for the rest of Asia—particularly those for Korea and the Tungusic-speaking regions of the northeast Asiatic continent—have consistently been underestimated.

In the special case of Japan, it is not difficult to identify a proximate cause for this persistent tendency to underestimate the remoteness of early periods. Before scholars in Japan began to enjoy the privilege of working under conditions of academic freedom, following the defeat in the Pacific War in 1945, it was impossible for them to take proper cognizance of archaeological evidence, or indeed any kind of evidence indicating a chronological pattern for the evolution of early Japanese civilization that did not fit the rigid outlines of the totally unrealistic and artificial system of dates that had earlier been fitted to the annalistic portions of the *Nihon shoki.*

The materials available from this text, together with even more difficult data from the *Kojiki,* appeared to make no provision for anything happening in a Japanese context before 660 B.C. Today we realize that by 660 B.C. Japan had been inhabited by *Homo sapiens* for millennia, and also that Japanese culture and civilization had by that time already gone through many important periods of growth, development, and evolution. These facts were also, for that matter, quite apparent to a considerable number of perspicacious Japanese scholars of the 1930s and early 1940s. These scholars had been sufficiently trained in Western methods of text-criticism, and were sufficiently informed concerning the course that the investigation of similar historical questions had taken in the West, to realize that neither the materials available from Japanese archaeology—few though they were at the time—nor the evidence preserved in the early Japanese historical texts, when read with a critical, unprejudiced, and scholarly eye, could possibly be accommodated within such a narrow chronological scheme. But once the official policy of the fascist, militaristic rulers of the Japanese superstate had settled on this official chronology, these scholars gave open expression to their views only at the risk of their employment, family reputations, and personal liberty. To suggest openly, before 1945, that all Japanese history did not literally begin in 660 B.C. was to court charges of disloyalty, disrespect to the imperial line, and even treason to the state.

Little wonder, then, that under these circumstances of rigid thought control, and in the absence of academic freedom, Japanese scholars became so accustomed to constricting all data related to early periods in the development of the Japanese nation and its civilization into an unrealistically narrow time span that even after these restraints on free investigation were removed by the Allied occupation of Japan in 1945, there was a continuing tendency to think and work along much the same lines. We are all creatures of habit; and grateful though we may be for newly achieved freedoms, it is not always easy to learn to exercise them. Even after it no longer meant that a scholar was courting personal disaster to suggest that important stages in the development of Japanese civilization had taken place thousands of years before 660 B.C., the rigid thought control of the fascist-nationalistic rulers who had led Japan to her defeat in the war proved to be the most durable of their many unlamented concoctions.

For a long time after such restraints on thought and research had ceased to be anything to be concerned about, Japanese scholars still tended to underestimate the chronology of early Japan, and still largely attempted to fit the postwar flood of new archaeological evidence—together with the evidence that soon became available from new, critical readings of the early texts—into an extremely shallow time scheme. This was not, to be sure, as limited as that set by the 660 B.C. dating of the prewar official orthodoxy, but in its own way it was almost as restrictive. At the very least, it did not make nearly sufficient allowance for the extremely long period of time that the actual evidence, from all sources, clearly calls for.

Today, after three decades of academic freedom, and with the coming to age of a new generation of Japanese scholars who have grown up with no personal memories of the fascist-nationalistic period of Japanese history, much of this is finally beginning to change for the better. Japanese scholars have, on this particular question at least, begun to free themselves from the lingering psychological barriers that in one way or another continued to hamper the freedom of their investigation, long after the actual official prohibition of free research into Japan's past had been removed by the defeat of 1945.

Obviously it is necessary for all of us, no matter what our academic tradition, to make a conscious effort to free ourselves from these same chronological limitations and their implications, since we now know them to be just as harmful to free inquiry as they have always been rooted in false assumptions and erroneous aims. Unless we are able to do this, it will be quite impossible to take proper cognizance of any of the important data that we now have at hand, both concerning the chronology

[105]

that may be established for the habitation of the Japanese archipelago by *Homo sapiens* and concerning the origins of the Japanese language. From this point on in the discussion we could, if we wished, discard the technical designation *Homo sapiens* and simply call the creature involved in all this "man," for that is what the creature, by this time at least, was and is; but we shall continue to employ the technical designation in the hope, vain perhaps, that it will help to focus attention on the fairly narrow epistemological window through which all data of this variety must necessarily be filtered.

One always wishes to begin at the beginning; but in this variety of discourse, it is generally necessary to settle for second best, and to begin as far back as one is able to go, meanwhile realizing that beyond this earliest stage for which evidence is presently available, other, still earlier stages may very well remain unstudied. In the present case, the earliest evidence we have is, as a matter of fact, quite early indeed, by any standards of chronology.

Archaeology has in recent years managed to document, in more and more detail, the initial settlement of the Japanese archipelago by Paleolithic man, who seems to have come across to the islands from the Asiatic mainland for the first time some 25,000 or more years ago. This is, at the present stage of these studies, the earliest datum that may be established for *Homo sapiens*—or for someone close to *Homo sapiens*—in Japan.

Documentation for the presence, as well as for the activities, of Paleolithic man in Japan comes from hundreds of archaeological sites. Among these the most important, and most revealing, is one on the shores of Lake Nojiri, in Nagano Prefecture, where excavations have been in progress on a more-or-less regular basis each summer since 1962, under the direction of Professor Gohara Yasumasa. Each year's work on this site turns up more striking evidence relating to the extremely remote period that can, without any significant exaggeration, be termed the dawn of Japanese civilization.

The Lake Nojiri site is now understood to mark the remains of an important Paleolithic hunting ground. Evidence for human (or hominid) activities turned up in the excavations to date includes a spearhead and a carved figure that closely resembles the cult figures or talismans well known from other parts of the Paleolithic world—objects that archaeologists customarily identify as Old Stone Age Venus figures. Their use and significance are of course obscure to us today, but it does seem a reasonable assumption that these Venus figures were cult, magic, or religious objects of some variety; and it has been suggested, again with considerable plausibility, that they served as talismans for the hunt, or perhaps also for childbirth. The Lake Nojiri specimen was discovered in what archaeologists working on the site now regard as its "middle layer," a stratum of the dig that they presently assign to a period roughly 25,000 years ago. Further remains located here include specimens of the animal known to science as Nauman's elephant, a distinctive local variety related to the woolly, or northern, mammoth that was commonly hunted by Paleolithic men all over Asia.

Such evidence for the Paleolithic in Japan is extremely valuable for several reasons. Among these, first place should probably still be given to the fact that such evidence offers conclusive proof for the utter impossibility of restricting the development of Japanese civilization within the narrow chronological "window" set by the pre-1945 orthodoxy. Second in order of importance is probably the evidence that this archaeological data offer for documenting Japan's early participation in the civilization and culture of the rest of Asia—whatever that civilization and culture may have been. Indeed, we should here probably refer not solely and specifically to Asia alone, but rather to Eurasia, since the evidence for Paleolithic activities of humans (or hominids) in Japan is completely congruent with evidence for the Paleolithic in other parts of Asia, and in Europe as well.

Given the dates suggested above for the so-called middle layer of the Lake Nojiri hunting-ground site, something on the order of 25,000 years ago, we are in turn able to place the Japanese Paleolithic and the Paleolithic in Europe in chronological relationship: the Paleolithic activities for which evidence is now forthcoming from Japan are, in European terms, events to be dated in the late Paleolithic. Apart from this, and particularly in the substance of the finds, there are few important differences. The Paleolithic hunters who came to Japan from the Asiatic mainland did not leave behind them, in Japan, any remains that indicate to us that they were substantially or significantly different from the inhabitants of the other Paleolithic communities in Europe and Asia. When they got to Japan, they continued the same activities, hunted the same animals, and apparently went about their lives much as they had done before their move, and also much as the other Paleolithic populations who remained behind had themselves continued to do.

Paleolithic Japan was culturally a part of greater Eurasia; its civilization was not unique, or special, or distinctively different from Paleolithic civilization elsewhere in the world. If we must find some difference here, it will be solely one of chronology. The Paleolithic may have been a little later in Japan than elsewhere, simply because of the geographical location of the islands, and because it took some time, then as now, for developments and advances from other parts of the globe to reach the archipelago.

But with these two important points understood, we had better detach our attention from further consideration of the Paleolithic in Japan, since here we are discussing origins of the Japanese language, and the simple, unfortunate fact is that we have absolutely no evidence about the language of man, or his near relatives, for the Paleolithic, even when we exploit the resources of the comparative method to the maximum extent possible. If the Paleolithic hunters who tracked down Nauman's elephant on the shores of Lake Nojiri some 25,000 years ago were indeed of the species *Homo sapiens,* then (by definition) we assume that they used language. But unfortunately we have no methodology or materials that will tell us what that language was.

The consensus of historical linguists, familiar with the comparative method, is that the techniques of that method in general take us back at the earliest to the late Neolithic, and that the reconstructions performed in terms of the assumptions of the comparative method provide us with data concerning the existence, and substance, of linguistic communities of roughly that date—but most likely of no earlier periods. The same late Neolithic datum is true both of the Indo-European and of the Altaic linguistic communities, two of the most important of the earlier linguistic entities that have already been reconstructed, in larger or lesser part, by the application of the comparative method of historical linguistics.

This means that we may trace the origins of any of the attested Indo-European languages, such as English, French, or Hindi, back to the late Neolithic, but no further. So also for the Altaic languages, where, as we have seen, the linguistic unity that we call Altaic—something that is attested only through the reconstructions that are rendered feasible by the assumptions and methodology of the comparative method—is believed to have been a late Neolithic community. In these terms, then, we may also expect to be able to pursue the history of the individual, historically attested languages, such as Turkish, Mongolian, Manchu, or Japanese, back as far as that late Neolithic community, but again, no further. Historical linguistics—at least historical linguistics as we generally understand the term, and based on the assumptions and reconstruction techniques of the comparative method—is unable to bridge the gap between the old and the new Stone Age civilizations; apparently it can tell us nothing about the language of the former, only something about the latter.

Disappointing as this is, it is not wholly unexpected. What can be recovered of the characteristics of the human or human-like figures commonly associated with the Paleolithic—such as the Heidelberg, Peking, Neanderthal, and Cro-Magnon "men"—and what we know of the culture that these figures had developed contrast sharply with what we know of the inhabitants of the later Neolithic periods, and also with their subsequent culture. The differences between these two great epochs in the history of mankind are monumental; something happened between the two, at different times in different parts of the world perhaps, but nevertheless something enormously important happened. We cannot even speculate about what the linguistic implications of that "something" may have been, apart from the fact that these linguistic implications also must surely have been far-reaching.

Whether Paleolithic populations evolved into Neolithic or whether they were replaced by them—or whether, as would seem quite possible, the two processes, evolution and replacement, took place over and over, back and forth, in a very complex pattern of development—we find, in turn, even more and better documented evidence from Japanese archaeology for the permeation of Neolithic culture throughout the archipelago; and it is to that Neolithic culture, and particularly to its linguistic implications, insofar as they may be established, that we now turn.

Every possible topic in every imaginable area of Japanese studies is plagued with terminological problems; we have noted a few of them already in connection with such words as *kigen* "origin," *keitō* "genetic relationship (of languages)," and the like; and as we might guess, the study of Japanese archaeology and pre-history is particularly rife with such vexatious problems concerning what words are used to identify certain things, and what certain words actually mean when they are so used.

When Japanese scholars write or speak of the *shinsekki jidai,* they are employing a term that is a neologism or newly coined word in Japanese; it translates "Neolithic period" very literally *(shin* "new," *sekki* "stone implement," *jidai* "period, age"). But simply because this is what the constituent elements of this scholarly term mean individually, it does not necessarily follow that when Japanese scholars use this term they mean precisely what we would mean by Neolithic in English, or that they use *shinsekki* or *shinsekki jidai* on any or all occasions when we would refer to the Neolithic. Usually, Japanese scholars employ the term *shinsekki* "Neolithic" consistently with the employment of the term Neolithic throughout the archaeology and pre-history of northeast Asia, which is simply to indicate the exis-tence of ground stone tools and pottery but not—as the general reader might expect—to imply the use of stone tools for producing food.

Sites to which Japanese scholars apply their term *shinsekki* "Neolithic" would in many instances be more likely to be labeled Mesolithic if they were being studied, and named, by Western scholars employing these terms in their more generally understood senses. This means that, for example, Neolithic in an Indo-Euro-pean archaeological context can have a rather different implica-tion than literal translation of *shinsekki* will produce for a Japa-nese context. But the term is so universally employed in the Japanese literature, and so generally rendered literally when

Japanese technical publications on these subjects are translated, that in what follows it has seemed the better part of academic caution to translate *shinsekki* literally as Neolithic, even in Japanese contexts where the implications of such rather mechanical rendering must be evaluated in the light of Japanese academic usage, and also to follow Japanese usage in this connection and refer, in English, to what the Japanese would call *shinsekki* or *shinsekki jidai* in what follows below simply as Neolithic, without further qualification.

Understood in this fashion, the Japanese Neolithic runs in close parallel with the same period on the Korean peninsula. The same, or largely the same, features tend to appear in Japan somewhat later than on the peninsula, again no doubt as a result of the time necessary for travel. (From Korea, too, we now have increasingly rich documentation for the Paleolithic period and its culture; but once again, the differences between these earliest remains and those of the Neolithic that follows are so enormous as to necessitate the assumption of some sort of a decisive break or interruption between the two.)

In the Korean peninsula, the Neolithic culture is distinguished by the presence of four major types of pottery remains. One is a rather coarse, undecorated pottery, featuring vessels with flat bases. This variety is most often discovered in Neolithic sites fairly well inland on the peninsula, and the finds are often accompanied by the remains of Neolithic agricultural implements, together with, in some cases, traces of the early metal weapons and ornaments that the populations associated with this particular variety of pottery already appear to have been employing. A second variety is pottery of a much more sophisticated and highly developed type, generally red in color, burnished, and thin-walled. This second variety of Korean Neolithic pottery is usually regarded by scholars as deriving quite closely from prototypes of models outside of Korea itself, either to the north, in the Tungusic-Manchu area, or—perhaps coming into Korea through that northern region—eventually from China.

The third variety of Korean Neolithic pottery may only be a subvariety of the third. Like the third, it is a well-finished, fairly sophisticated product, hard and durable, which appears to have entered Korea from the outside—again, most likely from the Chinese cultural area via the northern, or Tungusic-Manchu route. Particularly associated, in the sites in which it is found, with the employment of iron implements, this variety of pottery is especially important for Korean cultural history because it appears to be the ancestor of several famous ceramic wares with which we are familiar from Korea in the historical period, notably the pottery of the Silla kingdom. It is also most likely the immediate ancestor of the distinctive, hard-finished ceramic objects used for funerary and other ritual purposes in the Tumulus* period in Japan, where they are known as Sue ware. In certain regions of Japan, this Sue ware—a characteristic culture item of Japan's Iron Age, and not an indicator of the Japanese Neolithic in any sense of that difficult term—continued to be produced in considerable quantities down into historical times.

As interesting and valuable for the scholar as each of these three types of Korean Neolithic ware may be, it is the fourth variety that is especially significant for us in any consideration of the origins of the Japanese language, particularly now that we have advanced our discussion to the consideration of the early dispersal of the various Altaic subgroups from their second, Central Asian homeland. This fourth variety, which is actually believed to be chronologically the earliest of the four, is generally called comb-pattern pottery, because most of it carries a striking and characteristic impressed or incised decorative device that

* The term "Tumulus period" is commonly used to render the Japanese historical and archaeological term *kofun jidai,* and refers to a brief but extremely important early Japanese culture to be dated roughly from the fourth to the first part of the seventh century; the culture was characterized by the construction of enormous and extremely costly burial mounds, usually surrounded by moats, and often of a distinctive keyhole shape. The Tumulus period saw the extensive use of iron and bronze for weapons and ceremonial objects, and evidently prized the horse highly, though what use it made of the animal, apart from the evidence provided by ceremonial burials of horse gear in the mounds, is less clear. Sue ware is a distinctive thin-walled pottery thrown on a wheel and fired in enclosed kilns at extremely high temperatures, its manufacture thus reflecting significant borrowings of continental ceramic technology. Sue ware, generally dated from the fifth to the eighth century, is particularly rich in Korean analogs in form and design as well as in craftsmanship, and is common in burial mounds from the end of the Tumulus period.

looks as if it might have been made by pressing the teeth of a comb up against the unbaked clay biscuit of the ware. Whether or not the designs that characterize this ware were actually made by using combs in this fashion is of course inconsequential; at any rate, they must have been made by some sort of comblike tool, perhaps even a specialized device developed for this particular purpose.

The Korean examples of this important comb-pattern pottery of the Neolithic period generally have circular bases decorated with parallel lines and dots. The ware itself is found in Korean Neolithic contexts, particularly along rivers and in close proximity to the seacoast, and it is found most often together with bone and stone implements. The fact that these implements are found in context with the ware clearly indicates that it was made and used by a Neolithic population who primarily obtained their food supply by fishing. Most important, Korean archaeologists have for some time been aware of striking stylistic parallels between this comb-pattern pottery, as found in the sites and in the archaeological contexts just described, and certain Neolithic wares from the Eurasian steppe regions, which are also known as comb-pattern because they carry the same kind of carefully impressed or incised decorations.

Significant linguistic evidence may be cited that testifies to the great importance of fishing as a socioeconomic occupation par excellence among those Altaic speakers who had managed to reach the general area of the Korean peninsula, as well as among those who later completed the great trek to the Japanese islands. Cognate with the Japanese verb *izar-* "to catch fish at sea" are words in both Turkic, at one extreme of the Altaic linguistic community, and Korean, at the other, which in those languages mean simply "work, business": Uig. *yš̌*, *iš̌*, Tkm. *īš̌*, and Korean *īl*. These words, together with the Japanese verb just cited, all reflect an original Altaic noun *$\bar{i}l_2$, meaning "work, occupation." (It is important to note that even the vowel length in the Turkic and Korean forms, though in languages far removed from each other geographically, agrees exactly: both languages show a long vowel in the word in question. The Japanese verb is a denominal formation, and was originally *isa-r-;* in this original form, the *-s-*, which is the expected Japanese correspondence of Altaic *l_2*, as, for example, in the word for "stone," was later regularly changed to -*z*- under the influence of the suffixed Japanese -*r*-, which is from an original Altaic *-*l*- suffix meaning "to do or perform the act or action of the underlying noun," as already described above.) The work of gathering the community's principal food supply from the ocean was so important to the early Japanese that they referred to it with a word that simply meant "to do work," that is, to carry out *the* work, the most important business or occupation of the social group.

Taking into account all this evidence, specialists in Korean archaeology have evolved the theory that this comb-pattern pottery, the fourth major variety of Korean Neolithic ware, was introduced into the life of the Korean peninsula sometime between 3000 and 100 B.C., at the hands of a new Neolithic population that came down into the region from the north, bringing with them not only their earlier socioeconomic pattern that focused on hunting and fishing along rivers and sea coasts but also the technique of manufacturing and decorating this distinctive comb-pattern pottery that today serves as the principal archaeological evidence for their existence.

It is surely not difficult to understand how well this assumption on the part of archaeologists, working solely to provide a unified and logical explanation for the concrete evidence of their excavations, and for the cultural contexts in which the objects concerned are characteristically uncovered, dovetails into the scheme that we have already sketched, entirely on the basis of linguistic evidence and following up the assumptions and implications of the comparative method, for the early dispersals and migrations of the Altaic subgroups. It is also quite congruent with the assumption noted above concerning the extremely early breaking off of the ancestors of the speakers of the later Tungusic subgroup of Altaic languages, and their long overland journey away from Central Asia, through the northeastern reaches of Eurasia, and eventually all the way to the Pacific coastal regions. This is the same trek, of formidable scale both geographically and chronologically, that we have characterized as irreversible, because the conditions under which it was undertaken determined that the Tungusic speakers would ever after be separated from the rest of the Altaic subgroups in a rather different way than, for example, was to be true of the Mongolian or Turkic linguistic ancestors.

By the time the ancestors of the later Tungusic speakers had reached the northeasternmost limits of their travels, and particularly by the time they had learned to live in the demanding ecological circumstances of the Pacific maritime regions, their daily lives, their socioeconomy, their habits of livelihood, and their language had all undergone tremendous changes. Most of these changes were imposed by the physical circumstances of their new environments. Along with their newly evolved nomadic herding of reindeer, these peoples had soon adapted themselves to the rich resources of the rivers, streams, lakes, and particularly to the ocean with which they now came into contact. The physical geography and climate of northeast Eurasia placed heavy demands on them for survival, but they also provided resources that could help to support life, once the necessary manipulative techniques had been mastered.

Like their reindeer, the people learned to exploit the nutritive resources of the many varieties of moss and lichen that constitute the only ground cover in much of the area. The linguistic evidence for words signifying edible moss and lichens is not substantial enough to permit us to recover a single original Altaic word, but many of the later languages do share a few common forms in this meaning—forms that are most likely related in some way, even though the precise details of that relationship escape us at the present time. For example, Middle Korean had the term *is* for "moss, lichen," and this happens to be one of the relatively small number of Middle Korean forms for which we may with confidence point to an Old Korean original, since by a lucky philological accident the word is also attested in the language of the Old Silla kingdom as *isi*. But both these early Korean forms for "moss, lichen," are from a still earlier *nisi, and this in turn was directly cognate with Manchu *nisi.kte* "moss, lichen," where the final *.kte* was a Tungusic collective suffix used to mark nouns having reference to items or things of no considerable size, naturally belonging together, and having little importance as separate pieces—surely a fitting suffix for a word meaning "moss, lichen."

The etymological relationship of these words from Korean

and Tungusic to Old Japanese *nŏri,* and modern Japanese *nori,* both meaning "edible seaweed," is far from clear; nevertheless these Japanese words also tell us something of the history of early migration and food adaptation in northern Asia, particularly when we realize that the formal, etymological equivalent of standard Japanese *nori* in the Ryukyu language is *nuuri,* but in the Ryukyu language *nuuri* does not mean "edible seaweed," but "moss." Even though there are several missing links in this etymological picture, and we are at present unable directly to connect the Korean and Tungusic forms with the Japanese ones, on the semantic level at least Ryukyu *nuuri* "moss" and Japanese *nori* "edible seaweed" do seem to indicate a full round on a circle of historical change in the forms and meanings of language, reflecting the various circumstances of ecology encountered by a single people throughout a long history of migration.

Most important, of course, the same people also soon learned to become skilled harvesters of the bounty of stream and ocean, mastering fishing techniques that they could hardly have brought with them from their Altaic homelands in Central and Inner Asia. When this particular branch of the survivors of the long Tungusic migratory trek continued their wanderings even farther, this time altering their general course of advance in the direction of the south, they brought with them their by-now totally acclimatized skills for harvesting a plentiful food supply from streams, lakes, and oceans, employing them with renewed vigor in the relatively salubrious climate of the Korean peninsula.

That they should now turn the direction of their advance to the south was also quite simply determined by the physical geography of the area in which they found themselves. They also most probably, at the same time or perhaps a little later, took off across the narrow tongue of sea that separates northeast Asia from the Japanese archipelago, to bring their pottery culture, their techniques for the exploitation of the ecology by hunting and particularly by fishing, and above all else, their language, to these islands. In their never-ending search for new terrain fit to sustain human life, these early Tungusic-speaking splinter groups from the second Altaic homeland had nowhere else to go but the two directions which they took, probably sometime between 3000 and 2000 B.C.—south into the Korean peninsula, and across the narrow stretch of sea into Japan.

But to stress that these early Tungusic-speaking splinter groups from the second Altaic homeland moved down into the Korean peninsula, and came across to the Japanese islands, because they had nowhere else to go is to oversimplify their motivations. There was, to be sure, that aspect to it; in a sense, they were now cornered by the physical geography of Asia, and if they were to go anywhere, it was to Korea and to Japan. But viewed in a more positive fashion, these movements were those of a people also consciously expanding their activities within a single new, and awaiting, ecological zone—Korea and Japan.

Finally, at this point, two disparate strands that have characterized our pursuit after the origins of the Japanese language— the knowledge concerning early Altaic movements that has been accumulated, largely by applying the comparative method to the data available from the attested Altaic languages, and the quite separate findings of archaeological evidence and its analysis— begin to converge. The comb-pattern pottery that we have identified from Korean Neolithic sites, where it clearly represents a sudden interruption or innovation resulting from the advent of a newly arrived population in the Korean cultural setting, also quite suddenly begins to be found in Neolithic Japan, where in parallel fashion it is once again an interruption, a sudden and a striking innovation in the established cultural picture.

In Japan, the established cultural pattern before this comb-pattern pottery interrupted it was that of a cord-decorated pottery culture well known under the archaeological term "Jōmon ware." The word *jōmon* is simply a modern Japanese archaeological term meaning "cord impression," descriptive of the principal technique used for decorating the relatively thick-walled, heavy-bodied, low-fired earthenware that persisted throughout many centuries of the Japanese Neolithic until, almost in historical times, it was replaced by thin-walled, smooth-finished, highly fired ware obviously deriving directly from the Korean prototypes noted above. Of course, we do not know what name the Japanese Neolithic populations that we call Jōmon used for themselves, or even if they had any ethnic specific term or designation of their own.

[117]

The Japanese Neolithic culture that we call the Jōmon existed from much earlier than 5000 B.C. until, at least in certain regions of the country, around 400 B.C. For a long time Japanese archaeology and prehistory displayed a pronounced tendency to constrict the chronology of this enormously long Jōmon culture period to far too narrow a chronological horizon. This was largely a result of the inhibiting influences of the pre-1945 official policy and orthodoxy concerning the history of early Japan. Another important reason for the stubborn persistence in an unrealistically short Jōmon chronology is probably the tendency on the part of much Japanese scholarship to discriminate against nonagricultural and preliterate societies.

It was difficult for scholars who shared this prejudice to accept the identification of the earliest periods of Japanese civilization with peoples who engaged in hunting and gathering, and were preliterate. They preferred to make their identifications from evidence available for much later periods, even wishing to push the entire scheme of chronology down into the quite recent past, where it would become involved with Buddhism and literacy, as well as with settled, highly developed agrarianism. The Yayoi period met these qualifications, but they were out of the question for Jōmon. Hence if Jōmon were to be accommodated at all, it would have to be very much constricted in time.

But everything that has been learned since Japanese scholars began to investigate the early history of their own country under circumstances of unrestricted inquiry and academic freedom suggests a very early beginning for the Jōmon culture. Shortly after 1945, it was still customary in Japanese academic circles to consider about 3000 B.C. as the upper limit for Jōmon. Soon this was adjusted to around 5000 B.C. But now we can see that to set even this chronological limit is only a little less restricting than was the fascist-nationalist orthodoxy of constricting everything in the development of Japanese civilization into the period subsequent to 660 B.C.

Considerations of relative stratigraphy in Japanese Neolithic sites—that is, the levels and layers in which different objects are discovered in relation to one another, and the evidence derived from this and similar data for the chronological interrelationship of those objects and the sites in which they are found—have for some time made it possible to assign relative datings to Jōmon remains, and to identify certain sites as early, middle, or late with respect to the total Jōmon culture.

As Jōmon finds grew in number and as archaeologists grew more familiar with the different kinds of objects found in such sites, and more aware of the relative placement with respect to physical levels in the sites at which objects with this or that kind of technique or decoration most often were located, it became possible for them to carry out a more refined classification of these three major chronological categories. Japanese archaeologists have evolved a truly elaborate system of terminology for this purpose, employing terms that may be translated as Incipient, Earliest or Initial, Early, Middle, Late, and Latest or Final; furthermore, each of these six chronological categories is often subdivided into an earlier half and a later half, the entire system thus providing for a sometimes rather bewildering series of interrelated gradations for relative dating. In its terms, one can and often does find references to a given object or site as belonging, for example, to the early half of the Early Jōmon, or to the later half of the Incipient Jōmon, and so forth.

But the relation of each segment in such a system of stratigraphic chronology to every other segment remains entirely relative, no matter how elaborate the distinctions of such a system, or the principles of categorization behind it. We know that something is earlier than something else, or that something else is later than some other object; but we do not really know, on this basis alone, when any of these objects were produced. What we can learn in this way is very important; but in and of itself it is insufficient for relating the entire scheme to any absolute dating outside of the scheme itself—insufficient, in a word, to give us an idea of when anything happened.

Fortunately, this situation was altered when it finally became possible to obtain absolute datings for selected Jōmon materials from Japan through the technique of carbon-14 dating. This is a system of projecting absolute dates for archaeological objects, based on the assumption of a regular rate of decay and half-life for certain radiocarbon isotopes. The technique permits early archaeological evidence from parts of the world where

[119]

no absolute historical dating is possible on the basis of written records to be brought into congruence with objects from other parts of the world, notably from the ancient Near and Middle East, where such items have survived from very early periods within a well-documented historical context. It must, however, be emphasized that all carbon-14 dating is a relative, or statistical, matter, not one of absolute chronology, such as looking up a date in past history by consulting tables of earlier years and days of the month. In the case of any given carbon-14 date, there is one chance in three that the date established by this technique does not fall within the plus-minus factor that each carbon-14 date carries. It is also known now that by 3000 B.C., carbon-14 dates and so-called calendar years (obtained from the study of tree rings) diverge by 700 years, the carbon-14 dates being too young. As is equally true of any scientific technique that incorporates a large number of methodological assumptions and premises, it is important to understand the limitations of the data generated by the carbon-14 dating procedures if we are not to overstress their value for the study of prehistory.

Applications of this carbon-14 dating technique to Jōmon remains immediately demonstrated that the upper chronological limits for the Japanese Neolithic had to be extended quite far back, certainly well beyond the 3000 B.C. figure often mentioned in the early post-1945 Japanese literature. Items recovered from a typical Middle Jōmon site—identified as Middle in the stratigraphic terms already explained—have been shown, by carbon-14 dating, to go back to around 2540 B.C.; other objects from an early Middle Jōmon site are actually to be dated around 3120 B.C. The conclusions to be drawn from this are obvious. By the general date of 3000 B.C. the Jōmon culture had already undergone a long period of growth and development, and any absolute chronology for the Japanese Neolithic as a whole must provide for this fact.

If we place, as here, an upper limit of well beyond 5000 B.C. on the Japanese Neolithic, we are barely providing a time span long enough to accommodate the extensive history of developments that must be assumed to have preceded the Middle Jōmon culture for which carbon-14 datings are now available. In terms of this absolute chronology, then, that sudden interruption into the Japanese Neolithic represented by the advent of the comb-pattern pottery makers from the continent, whom we are here identifying with the Tungusic subgroup of the Altaic linguistic unity, comes well into the middle, or in different places in Japan most likely somewhat after the middle, of the Jōmon—sometime in the earlier part of the millennium between 3000 and 2000 B.C.

In geographical terms, we are even able to point to two principal locations as typical of the evidence that has been discovered in Japan for this interruption of the long-established Neolithic culture of the Jōmon pottery-making people by this sudden intrusion of the comb-pattern pottery makers, together with their characteristic new culture and also, we are here assuming (though of course no direct, concrete evidence for this last is forthcoming), with their language.

The first of these two locations is the older. The Sobata shell mound in modern Kumamoto Prefecture, on the island of Kyushu, has yielded impressive specimens of comb-pattern pottery showing strong links with the comb-pattern pottery of the Asiatic mainland, and specifically with that of the Korean peninsula, which is, after all, only a short distance across the water from Kyushu. The stratigraphical contexts in which this pottery has been found at the Sobata site suggest that, in relative terms, it is to be dated near the end of the Early third of the Jōmon Neolithic. Particularly in view of the results of carbon-14 dating for Middle Jōmon noted above, such a relative dating for these comb-pottery finds at the Sobata shell mound would, if mechanically transferred to what appears now to be a more realistic absolute chronology of the Jōmon period, place them at somewhere between 4000 and 3000 B.C., if not as much as a millennium earlier. In fact, Professor J. Edward Kidder, who has been able to work at firsthand with Jōmon sites and remains for over two decades, and to whom we owe most of the attention that has been devoted to obtaining the necessary specimens from Jōmon sites and submitting them to the process of carbon-14 dating, is himself now of the opinion that a date around 5000 B.C. would be closer to the facts for the intrusive comb-pattern pottery finds at the Sobata shell mound. Here we have, it is clear, several still unsolved problems, as well as yet another graphic illustration of the principle alluded to earlier, that the more we find out about the Neolithic in Japan—or indeed about any portion of the chronology of prehistoric Japan—the greater the necessity to push our absolute dates further and further back into the past.

The unsolved problems have to do with the anomaly, which will already have been noted by the reader, that the Sobata comb-pattern pottery appears to antedate by a considerable period the appearance of the same ware in Korea—perhaps by a millennium or more. This is, to be sure, no small chronological factor, even when we are maneuvering within the admittedly generous boundaries of the prehistoric past. But this discrepancy in absolute dates is almost surely more apparent than real. We must remember that the discrepancy here is between dates from Japan, where we are constantly in the process of adjusting the entire Neolithic chronology as carbon-14 dating combines with other information to show us that more time is required if our scheme is to accommodate the established data, and dates from Korea, where in large measure we still unfortunately lack the kind of solid information concerning absolute chronology that is provided by the carbon-14 datings now available from Japan.

In other words, every possibility exists that the dates established for the Japanese materials represent the more accurate system of the two, and that in the future, as more information becomes available from Korean sources, it will be necessary to adjust most of the presently accepted Korean chronology for the Neolithic back into the past, more or less in parallel with the process that we have already noted in Japan. We must remember that Korean scholars too still suffer from much the same inhibiting inheritance with respect to systems of prehistoric chronology as Japanese scholars do. Korea was a Japanese colony until 1945, and after liberation from Japanese colonial rule, Korean scholars also had to begin their study of the Korean past almost from scratch, particularly for the earliest periods. As long as Korea was part of the Japanese state, it was quite as impossible to provide official recognition for Korean evidence that did not fit the confines of the official orthodoxy as it was when such evidence turned up in the Japanese home islands themselves. Like their Japanese colleagues, Korean archaeologists have made impressive advances in the three short decades since they achieved academic freedom; but also like the situation in Japan, inherited patterns of conceptualization and approach are difficult to overcome, particularly for the older generation of scholars that, in both countries, still in large measure sets the overall tone for these and related studies.

Another serious problem that continues to delay progress in clarifying the formative phases of Korean prehistory is connected with the modern political situation on the peninsula, and in particular with the partition of the country into north and south. Many important archaeological sites, from which there is every reason to expect finds that would do much to improve our understanding of the dating of early developments in Korean culture and civilization, are located in the north. This means that such sites are totally inaccessible to scholars from the south, as well as to scholars from Japan and the West. A relaxation of political tensions that would permit free passage back and forth by scholars, and the unhampered publication and exchange of data and findings between the north and the south, as well as between all parts of the Korean peninsula and the rest of the world, would surely work to the best interests of scholarship. It could also be expected to facilitate rapid advances in our understanding of the absolute chronology for these developments in the Korean Neolithic—developments that hold the greatest importance not only for Korean studies but also for the study of early Japanese civilization.

At present, however, there is little indication that this necessary political relaxation will take place in the near future. We can only note the apparent—but probably not real—discrepancy between the Japanese dating for the intrusion of the comb-pattern pottery makers and the Korean dating, as we now have it, for the same Neolithic interruption, at the same time suggesting that the facts probably lie closer to the Japanese evidence, if only because it is based to an important extent on evidence from carbon-14 dating.

The earliest known site for this sudden interruption of comb-pattern pottery makers into Japanese Neolithic culture is the Sobata shell mound on the island of Kyushu (see figure 2). But once the peoples who brought this culture to Japan from the Asiatic mainland had established themselves here—if

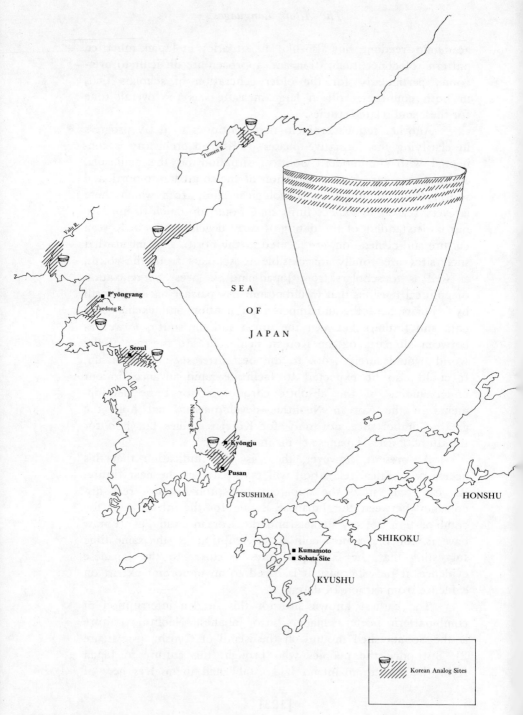

SEA

OF

JAPAN

Tumen R.

Yalu R.

P'yŏngyang

Taedong R.

Seoul

Nakdong R.

Kyŏngju

Pusan

TSUSHIMA

HONSHU

SHIKOKU

Kumamoto
Sobata Site

KYUSHU

Korean Analog Sites

Fig. 2. The Sobata site (Kyushu). Locations of sites with Korean analogs, and specimen of comb-pattern potter

this was actually their first and sole point of intrusion into Japan, an important question about which we ought to know more than we do—it is clear that they did not limit their influence to this single site, or to the island of Kyushu, or, for that matter, to the extremely early period at which they made what appears to be their initial impact.

Archaeologists and others studying early Japan use the term Yayoi as a convenient designation for a cultural period that is transitional between the end of the Jōmon and the inception of the historical period. (The term Yayoi itself, unlike the term Jōmon, is neither descriptive nor meaningful; it originates in a late Old Japanese word *yayoFi* meaning "spring" or "early part of the year," but it was selected for the period only because Yayoi was the name of a Tokyo neighborhood where excavators first discovered some of the pottery that became an archaeological bench mark of the distinctive ceramic ware of this period.) Culturally, the Japanese Yayoi period is distinguished by its intimate connections with the Asiatic continent, particularly the Korean peninsula. The cultivation of wet rice, the import and use—and later the indigenous manufacture—of iron and bronze implements, and the weaving of textiles, are all characteristics of the Yayoi culture that provide vivid testimony for the closeness of the intercourse between Japan and its advanced neighbors to the west during this period.

According to the chronology usually accepted in Japanese archaeological circles, the relative period of Middle Yayoi would fall somewhere between 100 B.C. and A.D. 100. Again, there is much reason to suppose that this dating should be made somewhat earlier, even though as we approach the beginning of historical times, Japanese developments are more closely linked to parallel developments on the Asiatic mainland, hence not only easier to control but also less subject to backward revision.

At any rate—and whatever the more correct absolute dating for Middle Yayoi may eventually turn out to be—it is in the Middle Yayoi that we find an interruption of this same comb-pattern pottery into what was until then the quite uniform and consistent development of Yayoi culture in the portion of Japan known as the Kinai. This is a traditional geographical designation referring to the region that in modern terms we may identify

[125]

somewhat more usefully, for most Westerners at least, as the Kyoto-Nara region. The Kinai is, in other words, the area in which the oldest stages of Japanese culture were centered in early historical times, as well as in those slightly earlier periods that witnessed the transition from the prehistoric Yayoi to the periods for which we have the more or less secure, and datable, evidence of written records. The Kinai is, in a word, the historical heartland of Japanese civilization.

In fact, so closely linked with the development of Japanese culture throughout all the early historical periods is this Kinai region that there has long been a considerable body of opinion in Japanese academic circles that the ultimate origin of all Japanese civilization is to be placed in this region, and that the developments of Japanese life and culture throughout the other portions of the archipelago are to be identified as nothing more than subsequent, regional offshoots of an original center in the Kyoto-Nara area. Sharply opposed to this view, however, has been another body of opinion that would find the original center for Japanese civilization somewhere in the southern part of the island of Kyushu, and which would make all other parts of Japan, including the Kyoto-Nara region, secondary developments out of this southern Kyushu location.

Fortunately, for our present purposes we need take little notice of these conflicting views concerning the geographical identification of the oldest Japanese cultural center in Japan, mainly because all these theories were developed, and continue to be argued, entirely apart from any consideration of questions of historical linguistics, or of the problems of the history and origins of the Japanese language. In the main, the arguments either for the Kyoto-Nara area or for southern Kyushu as the more likely original center of Japanese civilization have not been based on any linguistic evidence at all, and not even on any major amount of critical archaeological data, but rather on the extremely difficult and tenuous testimony of a few passages in some of the Chinese dynastic histories—passages that apparently provide descriptions of the geography, natural features, and population of some part of the main islands of the Japanese archipelago during the third century of our era. (Thus, if the chronology is correct, these early Chinese documentary sources probably describe Japan at the very end of its Neolithic period or perhaps already started on the way toward the transition to its largely borrowed Bronze Age culture of the early Yayoi.) Unfortunately, these arguments either for the Kyoto-Nara area or for the southern Kyushu region as the original center of Japanese culture soon became extensively entangled with the official orthodoxy of the fascist-nationalistic period, and particularly with the almost entirely spurious case that this orthodoxy made for the original, continuing, and unchanging authority of the Japanese imperial house.

The fascist-nationalist ideologists erected an elaborate and extremely mischievous myth, one that attempted to project the power, authority, and quasi-divine role of the late- and post-Meiji imperial figure back into the remote past, in a thoroughly unhistoric and indeed quite anachronistic manner. In defending this indefensible myth against the plain evidence of history, the location as well as the identification of Japan's earliest center of culture became a matter of great ideological urgency for them. As a result, even the study of this aspect of early Japan was sharply regulated, and these questions could not be studied in anything resembling the spirit of free inquiry without the danger of repressive measures of the most severe sort.

For us today, this controversy about whether Kyushu or the Kyoto-Nara area was the original center of Japanese civilization seems almost a trivial question. We are not concerned about the early authority or role of the imperial line and its representative figure, though we have plenty of evidence that both were anciently quite different from what they became following the so-called Meiji Restoration of 1867. We certainly find it difficult to believe that Japanese culture did not have important, and extremely early, centers in southern Kyushu, given the archaeological evidence from that area, and particularly in view of this region's proximity to the mainland of Asia, not to mention its easy access to Korea. But to say that this is so does not rule out the simultaneous presence of very early—perhaps equally early—centers in the Kyoto-Nara region. We need not select one of these possibilities by putting the other totally out of consideration. Most fortunately of all, we need not give serious concern to the tedious questions of interpreting the early Chinese notices, since they contain almost no useful linguistic data, and the materials that they do preserve relate hardly at all to our present topic of inquiry, the origins of the Japanese language.

The importance of simultaneously considering both the early Kyushu centers for Japanese civilization and the evidence for early activities in the Kyoto-Nara region is particularly well illustrated by the materials available concerning the spread throughout Japan of the comb-pattern pottery population and its culture. We are particularly concerned with evidence for the spread of this population for the reasons already explained; these reasons center on its identification with some of the very earliest, if not the earliest, intrusions of Altaic speakers as a large and unified group, first into the Korean peninsula, and subsequently into the Japanese archipelago, bringing with them an Altaic language that had close links with the later Tungusic subgroup of the Altaic family.

At least as far as this comb-pattern pottery population is concerned, the filiation of the Kyushu centers with those in the Kyoto-Nara region of Japan appears to be quite clear. The comb-pattern pottery suddenly intrudes into the middle strata of Neolithic sites in Kyushu, and from these sites is slowly carried, over a considerable period of time, to other parts of Japan. It does not reach the Kyoto-Nara region until much later, perhaps as late as the two-century period from 100 B.C. to A.D. 100—in the usual Japanese chronology and terminology, Middle Yayoi—though this dating may also need to be pushed further back into the past.

At any rate, the Yayoi culture was, by the approximate time of the beginning of our era, well established throughout the Kyoto-Nara region of Japan. The archæological evidence for the Middle Yayoi in this area shows a considerable amount of cultural uniformity throughout the region, with only a few traces of special local developments here and there. Not only is the cultural horizon quite uniform throughout the Kyoto-Nara area at the time, but further consideration of a wider chronological range of evidence shows that this uniformity had been the rule from a considerably earlier time, and in most places even from those earliest times at which the transition from Jōmon to Yayoi can be traced. This was the situation that was radically

[128]

altered by the sudden intrusion of the comb-pattern pottery makers into the Kyoto-Nara area in the middle of the Yayoi culture period.

This new pottery, with which we are already familiar both from Korea and from other parts of Eurasia, as well as from the Sobata site in Kyushu, first begins to appear on a large scale within the confines of a fairly restricted geographical area— the drainage basin of the Yamato River. This river, which flows out of the Yamato basin through the Kawachi Plain and eventually into Osaka Bay, is one of the two great streams of the area (the other is the Yodo River). Familiar as we now are with the affinity of the comb-pattern pottery making population for the socio-economy of riverbank and coastal areas, we are able to find particular significance in this river-related location of the intrusion—late though it is—of their distinctive culture into the until then mostly uniform cultural pattern of the Middle Yayoi in the Kyoto-Nara area. There is other evidence for substantial changes in the culture and life of this region that came about with the intrusion of the makers of the comb-pattern pottery— evidence of particular importance for our pursuit of the origins of the Japanese language. One Japanese archaeologist has described the sudden increase in the numbers of stone implements found in sites related to the intrusion of the comb-pattern pottery in the Kyoto-Nara area as a veritable "explosion in production." This "explosive" increase in lithic activities was clearly limited to the geographical area most closely associated with the Yamato River and its drainage basin. Again, one must remark on the significance of the intimate connection of this comb-pattern pottery population with the economic, and life-supporting, possibilities provided by the riparian ecology with which they characteristically associated themselves.

We also know that from this new stronghold in the Kyoto-Nara region, the culture and civilization of these comb-pattern pottery makers spread, in turn, to other parts of Japan. This permeation of the new, intrusive culture took place almost literally in all directions. It is also clear that it was soon transmitted back in the general direction from which it most likely came in the first place—that is, back into Kyushu, where particularly in the northern part of the island, a number of coastal areas now came under the influence of a distinctively Kinai variety of the comb-pattern pottery, in a series of apparently rapid cultural developments that are to be dated in the latter half of the Middle Yayoi.

So quickly did this reintroduction of the comb-pattern culture in the Kyushu area from its new, clearly secondary, focus in the Kyoto-Nara area take place, that archaeologists have speculated whether its transmittal in this case might not have been associated with some sort of organized advance or even by military invasion of Kinai forces into the Kyushu region. If so, then these Kinai forces, or even Kinai authorities, as they have been referred to in the literature, were themselves the direct cultural heirs of the same Tungusic comb-pattern pottery populations with which we have been particularly concerned. This also implies that their advance into a dominant position in Kyushu, and their extension of Kyoto-Nara authority into other areas of Japan, is of paramount importance for the understanding of all subsequent developments in the formation of the Japanese nation and state.

To sum up this presentation concerning what now appears to Western scholarship to be the most likely dating and circumstances for the earliest major introduction of Altaic speakers into the Japanese archipelago, it is necessary to mention, if only briefly, a number of related topics and issues; all are important, and all deserve more detailed treatment than they can be given here.

First, there is the problem of what may be called the "continuity" of prehistoric Japanese culture. By this we mean that, both in the Jōmon culture sites and later, down into the Yayoi, and so almost into historical times, we generally find a series of easy, overlapping gradations from one period of historical development to another, rather than evidence for a number of abrupt changes in direction of growth and innovation. The intrusion of the comb-pattern pottery into the Jōmon and Yayoi contexts is an exception to this general statement. This is one of the reasons why we must attach considerable importance to the evidence that the materials relating to this intrusion preserve for their own fairly recent and direct continental filiations, as well as other data now available that point in this same direction. Otherwise, the more usual situation is to find one level of historical development blending into the next with considerable smoothness, making it difficult to set hard-and-fast lines of chronological demarcation on stratigraphic grounds, and at the same time inclining us to interpret the bulk of the evidence as somehow pointing to uninterrupted periods of long, slow, continuous inhabitation, together with the kind of continuous growth and development of cultural patterns that go with this sort of habitation.

At the same time, this pattern of continuity is balanced by almost its precise opposite, in the sense that, particularly for the earlier stages of the Jōmon culture (but also persisting with more or less clear-cut results throughout the entire time span of prehistoric Japan), we must reckon with a large number of localized sites, each with its own characteristic culture. Especially striking is the lack of evidence for overall, regional trends, trends that if they had been somewhat more pervasive might eventually have swept before them many of the localized variations. But that did not happen. Instead, the early chronological strata of the Jōmon culture in particular preserve evidence for a profusion of local types and localized cultures, in a pattern that would support a hypothesis for the existence of a large number of separate and distinct local linguistic communities. Of course, this must always remain on the level of hypothesis, since for reasons already explained, we lack linguistic materials for the periods in question. Nor do the techniques of the comparative method make it possible for us to advance our reconstructions this far back into prehistory.

When we try to account for a cultural (as well as a linguistic) distribution pattern of this sort, the most satisfactory hypothesis, because it accounts for the data in the most economical fashion, is one that postulates a large number of very early, and separate, crossings over from the continent to Japan, long before the major intrusions by the comb-pattern pottery makers that we have here associated with the earliest phases of the dispersal of the Tungusic subgroup of the Altaic linguistic unity.

It would perhaps be equally feasible to postulate continuous local development from the Japanese Paleolithic through

[131]

the so-called Incipient Jōmon and on into the Jōmon itself; but in order best to account for the distribution, and particularly for the strongly evident local-culture orientation of the bulk of the Jōmon evidence, we prefer to postulate a large number of earlier, separate arrivals in Japan. Not only does such a thesis fit in with the archaeological data, but it also correlates best with what we know of the linguistic evidence—not only the linguistic evidence from Japan, but also the linguistic evidence from the continent. For these reasons, we prefer to work in terms of a succession of fairly frequent, earlier, separate arrivals in Japan. The people involved in these arrivals must also have come from somewhere; and if they were *Homo sapiens,* which seems equally certain, they spoke some language or languages.

It is quite possible, and indeed even probable, that many of these extremely early intruders into the Japanese islands spoke some early variety of the original Altaic language, closely related as a consequence to the language of the original Altaic homeland. Again, we can learn very little about languages and their movements at this extremely remote period in the history of our species, because of course there are no directly surviving linguistic data that may be brought into evidence, and also because here the techniques of the comparative method will not serve us effectively. But there can be little question that Paleolithic man, like all his subsequent descendants, was a great traveler. Indeed, there is reason to believe that Paleolithic man probably traveled more extensively than his Neolithic descendants; he probably indulged himself less in building permanent camping sites, and he probably followed game over larger territories than was common in later periods. If he did not travel very quickly, it seems certain that he made up for this in the length of time and amount of energy he was willing to devote to his journeys, treks, and migrations.

In Polynesia, where what was in many respects a Neolithic culture survived with very little technological advancement over Stone Age levels until well into the period of European exploration and colonization, we know of tremendous voyages undertaken by the early Tahitians, for example, in the course of invading and settling remote islands such as those of the Hawaiian chain. Compared with the tremendous feats of travel successfully undertaken by these Stone Age voyagers of Polynesia—feats that we can, in a sense, verify firsthand because some of them were undertaken well into the historical period—the difficulty of movement back and forth across Eurasia by continental Paleolithic man hardly deserves mention in the same context. Of course, we must also not forget that human adaptation to the challenges provided by environment involves more than levels of technological development. Innovations in social organization, ways of evolving effective group size for cooperative activities, and above all techniques for developing generally accepted systems for group decision making certainly play vital roles in determining the ease with which an early people will be able to move around the globe. The physical evidence of technological developments is all that remains, in most cases, for the archaeologist to uncover and study, and this in turn can lead to an unconscious tendency to denigrate the importance of other, equally vital innovations in social life that have unfortunately left no "hard evidence" for the spade to discover.

When we stress the importance of the comb-pattern pottery makers and the significance of the sudden intrusion of their culture into Japanese civilization, whether we find this taking place in Middle Jōmon or Middle Yayoi, or on Kyushu or Honshu, we do so because this intrusion may be linked, as we have explained, directly to major developments on the Asiatic mainland, particularly in Korea, and may also be associated directly with the earliest stages in the major dispersal of the Altaic speakers from their second, Central Asian homeland, particularly with the separation of the Tungusic languages from the original linguistic unity. But these Altaic speakers, when they did arrive in Japan, found *Homo sapiens* already in place; and although we cannot prove it, certainly there is an excellent chance that at least some of these still earlier arrivals were Altaic speakers.

With this, we have established a pattern for the course of the development of the earliest stages of Japanese civilization, especially when those stages are viewed in the full context of Japan's early contacts with the rest of the world, particularly with the rest of Asia. This is a pattern that may be described as the vertical accumulation of successive layers of migration and influence from abroad, or more simply, as the piling up of one successive historic layer of Altaic migration into the islands upon another. And it was this pattern that in one variation or another was to continue to characterize Japanese civilization and its development for millennia.

LINGUISTIC EVIDENCE FOR CONTINENTAL INCURSIONS

Wave after wave of intruders from the continent must be reckoned with in any comprehensive account of Japanese origins. It is particularly in the language, and especially when we analyze its vocabulary and morphology on the comparative level, that we find the most impressive evidence for these successive waves of intruders from abroad. No other thesis can so efficiently account for many of the phenomena that we observe in the language—phenomena that remain without any explanation if we refuse to compare their evidence with parallel evidence from the languages of the continent, and phenomena that are also impossible to reconcile with any unique arrival into, or invasion of, the islands at a single point in the past.

The linguistic evidence that bears on this point is of an extremely complex nature, and not a simple matter to summarize; but even the citation of a small number of the relevant forms will probably serve a useful purpose, and help to illustrate the nature of the evidence that historical linguistics is able to bring to bear on this issue.

At the outset, it is important to explain what we are looking for, so that we will be able to recognize it when we see it. What we are looking for is linguistic evidence—by which we mean, quite simply, evidence in the form of words in the language—from within Japanese, that will point to how the Japanese language has inherited two or more different historical stages or different kinds of historical developments from a single linguistic feature or item in original Altaic. The assumption that follows from the identification of such data is that each of these different stages or developments may today be identified in the language because it was brought to the islands, and entered the language, in the course of a different wave of invasion from the continent. The internal evidence from within Japanese for this would be most likely to take the form of what are called doublets,

or pairs of words in a single language—in this case, in Japanese—
that are closely related to each other in forms and meanings,
but which are nevertheless different in both.

We know from the study of the comparative historical
phonology of the Altaic languages that when the consonant
*d of the original language appeared in that language between two
vowels, it subsequently underwent different historical changes
in different parts of the original linguistic unity. In many instances, and in some of the later languages, this consonant between vowels changes relatively little, sometimes remaining
as *-d-*, or unvoicing to *-t-*, or becoming a voiced affricate *-ǰ-*.
(like the "j" in English "just" or "jeep"); examples include such
words as Proto-Altaic **pādī-* "distinguishing, separating one's self
from others," reflected in Mo. *aǰira-* "mind, pay attention to,"
Goldi *pāǰila-* "separate, distinguish," and Japanese *haji* "shame,"
from Old Japanese *Fadi-r-* "feel one's self inferior to others";
Proto-Altaic **gède, gèdi* "back, rear (esp. part of the body)," Mo.
gede "back, nape of the neck," Ev. *gedimuk* "id.," Japanese *kita*
"north" (the direction that is "behind, rear" in a system of southern orientation), also Japanese *ketsu* "buttocks, rear end." The
difference between Japanese *-d-* and *-t-* in these words does not
reflect an original Altaic distinction but rather a later set of
changes wholly within Japanese; at first all these cases of **-d-*
yielded Japanese *-d-*, which remained as such when the initial of
the word in question was unvoiced, as in the word for "shame,"
but changed to the unvoiced *-t-* when the original initial of the
word in Altaic was voiced, as in the words for "north" and
"buttocks." The precision of detail with which such changes even
within later stages of Japanese may be stated increases our confidence that we are dealing here with examples of regular genetic
relationship.

But in other portions of the Altaic linguistic unity, and
particularly in the Turkic subgroup, this original **-d-* when found
between vowels underwent a series of other, more far-reaching
phonological changes. These are well known and often studied
for the light they throw on the historical relationships between
the various Turkic languages; what is less well understood is how
these more involved developments also left their mark in certain
of the later languages outside Turkic as well, where they provide

valuable clues for tracing a number of the relationships that may be recovered when we reconstruct the details of the Altaic linguistic unity.

In certain of the Turkic languages, original Altaic *-d- when occurring between two vowels was, as summarized above, preserved unchanged or virtually unchanged; but in many others it was instead later pronounced as a voiced spirant -δ- (more or less like the "th" in English "this" or "then"). In still other Turkic languages, *-d- changed into -y-, and in yet others, into -r-. It certainly is not difficult to understand, given this wide diversity of phonological developments for this single original consonant, why tracing the changes of this original *-d- in the later languages provides excellent grounds for the historical identification and classification of those languages into a number of large categories; thus, one may speak of "-y-languages," or "-δ-languages," or "-r-languages," all within Turkic, depending on how they treated this original *-d-. But even more important, for our present purposes, is the way in which the varied developments of this original *-d- also attest to the inheritance of the original Altaic language in Japan in the course of several different waves of introduction from the continent—in other words, successive invasions.

This is because, within Japanese itself, we find not only the regular, relatively unchanged representation of original Altaic *-d- by Old Japanese -d- or -t- illustrated by the words meaning "shame" and "north; buttocks" cited above, but we also find doublets that preserve evidence for two other developments for this *-d- within Japanese: these are two out of the three characteristically Turkic developments of Altaic *-d-, that is, sometimes as Japanese -y-, sometimes as Japanese -r-. Such evidence can only point to separate, different introductions of Altaic linguistic forms to Japan at different times in history, by people whose language at the time they reached Japan already reflected different secondary stages within the total development of the Altaic linguistic unity—secondary stages that are particularly well attested from within the Turkic subgroup but which are, as the Japanese evidence in turn shows, by no means purely Turkic innovations.

The evidence is best illustrated by a number of Japanese

words that within Japanese continue the lexical inheritance of
Proto-Altaic *padák* "extremity; foot," a word that in the
original language was both a designation for a part of the human
or animal body and a geographical term, particularly with reference to the lower reaches of rivers. (Again, it is important to
keep in mind that when we gloss or translate this Altaic form
as "foot" or "extremity" we are not giving its "meaning," we are
only giving a few minimal translation-identifications that will
help us to understand the very general outlines of what its "meaning" was. Amateurs of linguistic comparison who have not understood this simple principle have sometimes not been able to understand how a word they believe means "foot" in one language
can be related historically to a word that means something like
"mouth of a river" in another. These problems only arise when
one confuses "meaning" with "translation.")

Following a considerable number of sound changes that
can be stated in regular fashion, this original Altaic word may
be traced in such later and often much changed forms as Mo.
adaγ "end; estuary; lower part of a river," Korean *patak* "bottom,
sole (of foot); river bed," and Old Tk. *adaq* "foot." These words
all show the original *-d-* between vowels, either more or less
unchanged, as in the Mongolian and Old Turkish examples, or
simply unvoiced to become *-t-*, as regularly expected in Korean.
But in one important Turkic language, Chuvash, an original
-d- in the circumstances in which it is found in this word changed
radically, to become *-r-;* and this change, together with other
regular changes, resulted in the cognate form for Altaic *padák*
becoming Chuvash *ura* "foot" (the other changes in the word,
including the loss of the initial *p-* and the development of the
-a- to *u-*, are also regular and expected in Chuvash). It is not
difficult to connect this Chuvash word with Japanese *ura* "bottom, inside; sole (of foot)," a form that is attested in these meanings since the Old Japanese period, and one that shows the same
development of *-d-* to *-r-* that is seen in Chuvash, together with
other quite Turkic-like developments that are equally striking.
The Japanese word, of course, does not come from Chuvash
or any other Turkic language; the point is rather that the Japanese
form tells us that phonological changes of the same type that
happened in the pre-Chuvash sector of the Turkic subgroup

of Altaic were also brought to Japan by Altaic speakers from the continent at an extremely early period.

But at the same time, Japanese *ura* "bottom, sole" is by no means the only form in the language that may be identified as having resulted from the Japanese inheritance of Altaic **padák*. Another early Altaic development, parallel to the Turkic changes in which **-d-* shifted to *-y-*, is also attested in the Japanese verb *ayum-* "walk (a step at a time)." Furthermore, within Japanese and alongside this verb, we also have a doublet in *-r-*, Japanese *aruk-* "walk (in general)," and Japanese *arik-* "id." (In the modern language the verb *arik-* has become obsolete, and only *aruk-* is used; in the Heian period, *aruk-* was generally a formal word most often employed by men, while *arik-* was part of women's language. Apart from these sociolinguistic differences, *aruk-* and *arik-* both apparently covered nearly identical semantic areas.)

Japanese *ayum-*, *aruk-*, and *arik-* are all verbs formed from underlying nouns (denominal verbs) through the addition, to nouns, of inherited Altaic verb-stem formant suffixes *-m-* and *-k-*. These two suffixes, each of which made verbs from nouns, had slightly different semantic roles in the original language, which may be traced in the later languages, even in one of the later languages as far removed from the original Altaic language as is Japanese. The *-k-* suffix was especially common in this function, and has already been discussed, with examples; it formed verbs that meant "do something with or with direct reference to the underlying noun" involved in the formation. The *-m-* suffix was somewhat less common, and at least in its Japanese version is fairly well specialized for forming deverbal nouns that refer to the functioning or operation of parts of the body, sometimes literally, sometimes by semantic extension into areas of the abstract or emotional (e.g., with the noun *kokoro* "heart, mind," the verb *kokorom-* "ponder; explore mentally").

Subtracting the suffixes *-k-* and *-m-* from the three denominal verbs being discussed, we arrive at the underlying nouns **ayu-*, **aru-*, and **ari-*. None of these three different nouns has survived as a free or independently occurring form in the language; but from the semantic function of these two suffixes, and also from the class meaning of the three resulting verbs, "walk," we

[138]

may postulate that *ayu-*, *aru-*, and *ari-* were all nouns that had semantic reference to "foot" or "bottom (of the foot)," which after all is the part of the body essentially involved in the act of walking. Japanese *arik-* and *aruk-* are, in other words, actually *ari+k-* and *aru+k-*, the results of suffixing *-k-* to original underlying nouns meaning "foot," just as *kabu* "head" with the same suffix *-k-* produced the denominal verb *kabuk-* "incline the head," and the other examples with this *-k-* suffix discussed above. In the same way, the verb *ayum-* goes back to *ayu+m-*.

Thus, *ayu-*, *aru-*, and *ari-* were all nouns meaning "foot," but each of these three forms represents a different historical stage in the development of original Altaic **padák* "foot." The first of these underlying nouns shows a development as *-y-* for **-d-*, the last two show a development as *-r-* for the same phoneme. And each of these developments has a precise parallel, to be illustrated with the same lexical item, in the Turkic subgroup of Altaic.

In other words, we must conclude that these forms were brought to the Japanese islands, and entered the Japanese language, as the result of different waves of Altaic speakers entering upon the Japanese linguistic scene at various times. It is the linguistic evidence of doublets of this sort that points to multiple waves of intrusion, invasions bringing to Japanese multiple forms that relate directly to separate, and originally localized, developments within the original Altaic linguistic unity. Most important, we should also note that it is only comparison with the other, related languages that makes it possible to explain the interrelations within Japanese itself that are observed in such sets of forms as *ura*, *ayum-*, *aruk-*, and *arik-*. As long as we restrict ourselves solely to Japanese linguistic materials, no explanation for such sets of forms is forthcoming. Only comparative evidence can throw light on how they arose.

Similarly valuable linguistic evidence for successive waves of introduction of Altaic to the islands is provided by such doublets as Old Japanese *tadu* and *turu,* both words meaning "crane," the former specialized as a term in Old Japanese poetic diction, the other apparently the usual word in spoken Old Japanese, and the form that underlies modern Japanese *tsuru* "crane." Both words are somehow related to Proto-Turkic *tur(u)ńa* "crane." The existence of the doublet in Old Japanese is to be explained by successive introductions of forms that go back to different localized stages in the linguistic development of Altaic.

Another important example that may be cited has to do with a word that is particularly significant because of its role in the early Japanese food economy. Japanese *kuri* "chestnut" goes etymologically, as we have seen above, with Proto-Altaic *$k\ddot{u}r_2$- "dark brown"; and in a form of this phonological shape, Japanese *-r-* is the regular development of the original Altaic phoneme that we reconstruct and write as *r_2*. But Altaic *r_2* regularly changed into *-z-* in the Turkic languages (except in Chuvash, where it became *-r-*), so it does not surprise us when we discover an anomalous and aberrant Old Japanese form *kuzi* "chestnut" recorded phonetically as a local variant form in at least one Old Japanese source. The linguistic form Old Japanese *kuzi* "chestnut" must have come to the islands at a different time than the form *kuri* did, and it also must represent a different, though related, inheritance from a different part of the original Altaic linguistic unity.

We cannot even guess when the earliest of these waves of intrusion took place; but we have already discussed the extremely remote period during which Paleolithic man, whatever type he may have represented, and however close it may have been to our own, is known to have lived in Japan, making his Venus figures and hunting Nauman's elephant on the shores of Lake Nojiri. With the dawn of the Neolithic, we are surely dealing with our own species of *Homo sapiens,* who just as surely came to these islands time and time again, always finding that someone had got there before him, but then himself settling in to receive, in his own turn, the same treatment from still other, subsequent invaders. This pattern, established so very long ago, continued to distinguish Japanese life until well into the early historical period.

Two points deserve special mention in this connection. One is that there is every possibility that non-Altaic speakers, and hence non-Altaic languages, also from time to time entered into this picture of multiple arrivals and frequent invasions of Japan from the Asiatic mainland, throughout both pre- and early recorded history. These non-Altaic speakers can never have been very numerous; but neither, for that matter, were the Altaic speakers, at any given time, with the possible exception of the initial wave of the comb-pattern pottery makers. Unless all these non-Altaic speakers were systematically exterminated immediately upon arrival by the earlier Altaic invaders, they, their genes, and in some fashion or other their languages, too, must be assumed to have survived in Japan.

Total or mass extermination even of small human populations is an unlikely hypothesis for early periods in the history of our species. The technology that makes such slaughter possible largely had to wait for later stages in human development, as we all know only too well from the terrible events of the 1940s in Europe. The reasonable expectation is that significant segments of any non-Altaic speakers, however many may have come to early Japan, did survive their early confrontations with the Altaic speakers whom they confronted in the islands; it also follows that in some way or other they also made a contribution to the development of the Japanese language, just as they surely contributed to the Japanese gene pool.

But it is also clear that, no matter how many different waves of invasions there were, it was the language of the Altaic speakers that proved to be the dominant element in the formation of the Japanese language. What happened in this connection in early Japan must have been quite close to what happened in other, parallel sociolinguistic confrontations elsewhere in the world, where we are able to document the events in question rather more fully because they happened in the historical period.

History is full of well-documented examples of the imposition of an invader's language on an indigenous population. If the invader stays long enough, and especially if his culture is of a significantly lower order than that of the indigenous population, he may find his own language replaced by the language of those whom he has conquered. The virtual extinction of the Manchu language during the period of Manchu rule in China, and its replacement by Chinese, even in the daily life of the noble Manchu families, is a good example. But usually it is the conqueror's language that is dominant, for the simple reason that he himself is dominant.

In this way, the Latin language of the Roman soldiers and

colonists replaced the original Gaulish language of the region that later became France. Even earlier, Latin itself, originally the language of an unimportant village on the Tiber, had spread throughout the Italian peninsula, replacing other languages, such as Etruscan, that were in place long before its coming. Particularly clear and well-documented examples of the same phenomenon are close at hand in Mexico and other parts of Central and South America, where the Spanish of the conquering explorers and colonists—itself a later, changed form of Latin—was soon adopted by most of the indigenous population. Sometimes their survivors have continued to employ their own, preconquest languages, but more often they have exchanged these languages for the Spanish of their conquerers, which of course itself has gone on to change and develop in the New World in ways different from the ways in which it has changed and developed in the homeland of Spain.

In other words, when we are in full, or practically full, control of the historical facts, we experience no difficulty in identifying the genetic mainstream of languages, even when they have been imposed on indigenous populations through invasion and conquest. The Spanish of Mexico is different from the Spanish of Spain; the Portuguese of Brazil is different from European Portuguese. The Latin spoken in the Roman province of Gaul was surely quite different from the Latin of the city of Rome, and modern French is no longer mutually intelligible with modern Italian, or modern Spanish, even though these languages are all later, changed forms of Latin. But in none of these cases do we have any difficulty in identifying the genetic relationship of the languages involved, despite the many changes they have undergone.

What we must do, therefore, is capitalize on the facts that may be established almost without question from these well-documented cases of language replacement, and of eventual dominance by the imported language of conquering forces, and extend them by logical analogy to those circumstances where equally detailed documentation is not available, such as the problem of the origins of Japanese. Working in this fashion, we will be able to build on what is known about how other languages have grown and developed, and to extend that knowledge to our hypothesis of how Japanese most likely also grew and developed. Of course, in order to do this, we must begin with the assumption that Japanese is in its essence nothing more or less than another language, hence much like all other human languages, not something unique or set apart from the other linguistic structures of mankind. This is an assumption many of our Japanese colleagues might be unwilling to join us in making. But for linguists in the West, at least, such an assumption seems to be as obvious as it is necessary.

Once we make the assumption that Japanese is a language that may reasonably be expected to have grown and developed like other languages—in other words, the assumption that like causes produce like results, other circumstances and conditions being equal—we will be in a position to draw on our knowledge of the history of English, where again the historical documentation is often remarkably complete, in order to help us understand many of the events that must have taken place in the history of Japanese, even though in the case of Japanese we will not always be able to document these events with equal precision. In fact, the linguistic history of English—which is, after all, like Japanese, now an important language but originally one spoken only by a small population living on a few tiny islands just off a major land mass—can teach us about many trends and directions that surely have enormous relevance for our approach to the overall question of Japanese linguistic origins.

In the case of English, for example, we entertain no doubts concerning its genetic relationship: it is a Germanic language, and also a member, along with all the Germanic languages, of the Indo-European family. But we also know that English incorporates many layers of different, disparate elements in its vocabulary—especially borrowings from Latin, from Norman French, and from early forms in the Scandinavian languages. These borrowings reflect the involved course of the early stages of English history, and often overlap and intertwine with one another in a most complicated fashion. Fortunately, in the case of English, most of the linguistic developments that produced these many different layers of lexical materials originating in various languages took place during the historical period, with the result that for a considerable number of these words we have quite detailed

[143]

information about how and when the linguistic contacts that produced them took place. Sometimes these linguistic contacts were simply the result of cultural contacts. Words were often borrowed from other languages into English in the course of the ordinary civilized exchange between nations that characterized much of European history, particularly after the spread of Christianity and during the period in which the Roman Church served as a focal point for Western culture. To contacts of this variety are to be assigned most of the borrowings into English from Latin, as well as from other languages, notably French, that were themselves later, changed forms of the earlier Latin of the Roman Empire—a language related to but of course different from the Latin that continued, until our own time, to be used throughout those portions of Christian Europe that were in communion with the Roman Church.

But such peaceful and edifying contacts were not the only way by which new words were borrowed during the long history of the English language. We also know that early invasions by Scandinavian ethnic groups from northern Europe also brought new words into the English language that sometimes were closely related to, but still different from, words that already existed in English—words that continued thereafter to coexist alongside the new words. An example is provided by modern English "shirt" and "skirt." We know that "shirt" is a later, changed form of Old English "scyrte"; but we also know that the word "skirt" is related to "shirt" in a very complex fashion. Modern English "skirt" is a later, changed form of Old Norse "skyrta," a word that was brought into the English islands by the Scandinavian invaders probably a millennium ago. Originally, both Old English "scyrte" and Old Norse "skyrta" were themselves later, changed forms of a still earlier word—a word that belonged to one of the subsections of the original Germanic linguistic unity, which was in turn a subgroup of the much larger, and older, Indo-European linguistic community. The original Germanic form that changed in different ways in different parts of Europe, in some places becoming Old English "scyrte," in other places becoming Old Norse "skyrta," thus serves as the ultimate origin for both modern English "shirt" and modern English "skirt"; but the history of the word "skirt" is further complicated by the fact that

[144]

although it is historically related to "shirt," it is also a borrowing into English, at a relatively late period in linguistic history, of yet another development of the original Germanic, and Indo-European, word that underlies all these later, changed forms.

The most important thing about the example above, which is representative of many others that could be cited from the history of English, is that all the languages concerned with the illustration, that is, Old English, Modern English, Old Norse, and so on, are genetically related to one another. All are Indo-European languages, and all are members of the Germanic subgroup of Indo-European. Thus, even when all the languages concerned can be demonstrated, with considerable power of conviction, to be genetically related, we know that historical contacts—both peaceful, as in the cultural borrowings back and forth in Christian Europe, or warlike, as in the Scandinavian invasions of early England—can greatly complicate the picture, producing many different layers of borrowings that the historical linguist must be prepared to distinguish not only from one another but also from the nonborrowed body of inherited linguistic resources.

It is this nonborrowed body of inherited materials and this body alone that is relevant to questions of genetic relationship, and that may be cited in questions of linguistic origins. It is also this inherited body of linguistic materials that we refer to when we say that English is a Germanic language, or that French, for example, is a Romance language. In the same way, it is this body of inherited, nonborrowed materials that we refer to when we say that Japanese is an Altaic language, even though we know that the history of Japanese, like the history of English, is rendered extremely complicated by a large number of borrowings from other languages that took place under different circumstances at various times in its history.

Of almost equal importance is the fact that in the case of the history of English, almost all the developments that have been sketched above took place well within the historical period. As a result, the circumstances of these changes can often be documented from historical records, and the linguistic changes themselves may often be verified from written records of the various languages concerned. Here the suggested parallel with

[145]

Japan, and otherwise informative parallels with the history of the Japanese language, begin to break down. Nevertheless, consideration of the two areas—Japan and England—together still provides us with many useful ideas that help explain the probable course of events in the history of Japanese.

The suggested parallels begin to break down for two reasons. One is that the events resulting in the borrowing of many different types of linguistic resources into Japanese from other languages—some of them Altaic, but others belonging to totally unrelated linguistic stocks—generally took place far earlier in the history of Japanese than did parallel events in the history of English. The other, a direct consequence of the first, is that for Japanese we generally lack historical documentation of the sort available for parallel developments in English.

JAPANESE AND KOREAN

For Japanese, this is particularly true—and particularly unfortunate—with respect to most of the early linguistic contacts between very early forms of the Japanese language and equally early forms of the various languages of Old Korea. We have reason to believe that Korean is itself an Altaic language, and hence genetically of the same stock as Japanese (in much the same way that Old English and Old Norse were both Indo-European languages), and also that both Korean and Japanese probably stood in a particularly close historical relationship not only to each other but also to the Tungusic subgroup of Altaic (again, in much the same way that both Old English and Old Norse were not only Indo-European but also Germanic languages). We also know that there were extensive cultural relations between the Old Korean kingdoms and Old Japan, particularly because the introduction of Mahāyāna Buddhism into Japan took place largely through Korean intermediaries (see figure 3).

Buddhism played much the same role in the formation of Japanese civilization and culture that Christianity did in the development of English civilization and culture. Each of these world religions provided an impetus for the ever-closer association of life on the islands concerned with life on the land mass

Fig. 3. The Old Korean kingdoms and Japan

adjacent to them. Latin was the language of Western Christianity and of the Roman Church; both as the language of the church and as the later, changed languages of some of the successor states of the Roman Empire in Western Europe, as for example Norman France, the Latin language left lasting marks on the English language. (Britain had, of course, even before its conversion to Christianity been occupied by Latin-speaking Roman armies, but their linguistic impact was trivial compared with the massive borrowings that resulted from the linguistic contacts of later Christian periods.)

There can be no question that one variety or another of the Old Korean language played much the same role in early Buddhist Japan as Latin did in Christian England. Most likely the language through which Mahāyāna Buddhism was first transmitted to Japan was the particular variety of Old Korean spoken in the Paekche kingdom, one of the three quite separate states into which ancient Korea was divided. We know that it was the Paekche kingdom that was most influential in introducing Buddhism to Japan, and we know enough about the circumstances of that introduction to make it clear that the Paekche language must have been the linguistic vehicle by means of which this world religion was first introduced to the Japanese. We also know that the Japanese continued their relations with Paekche until well into the historical period. They even sent an invasion force to Korea to attempt to assist the Paekche rulers when, in the seventh century, they were attacked by an alliance of T'ang China and the other Korean kingdoms. The Japanese expeditionary force failed in its mission, badly defeated by the Chinese and Korean allies at the battle of Paekch'ŏn'gang in A.D. 663. But cultural and political ties between Japan and Paekche were even then so strong that the retreating Japanese forces brought back with them to Japan thousands of Paekche refugees, who apparently preferred the risk involved in fleeing to a new and unknown land, together with their now defeated Japanese allies, to remaining in their homes and facing almost certain death at the hands of their victorious enemies.

We also know that population remnants surviving from this massive evacuation of Paekche refugees continued to maintain their ethnic identity in Japan for several generations to follow. All this can be established from historical records; and it leads us to believe that linguistic contacts between Japan and early Korea, particularly linguistic contacts with the Paekche kingdom, played an important role in the development of the Japanese language, most likely a role equally important to that played by Latin and the later Romance languages in the development of English. What we do not know—and what we lack to fill out most of the details in the case of Japan—is very much about the Old Paekche language itself.

Like the Paekche kingdom, the Old Paekche language—together with the two other important Old Korean languages, Old Silla and Old Koguryŏ—has almost completely disappeared from history without leaving behind any substantial evidence. This makes the study of the problem here under consideration very difficult, and means that the otherwise promising parallel with the linguistic situation in early England tends to break down at this point, to our disadvantage. We of course know a great deal about all the forms of Latin that played a role in the development of the English language. We have the classical Latin of the literary texts from Roman antiquity, together with copious records of the later forms of the language as used by both church and state in all parts of Europe, not to mention the equally important evidence of the Romance languages themselves (Italian, French, Spanish, and many others). Applying the comparative method to these living Romance languages makes it possible to reconstruct linguistic data directly relating to the one important form of Latin for which we do not have evidence from written records, namely the spoken Latin of the Roman armies and their empire—the form in which the Latin language was carried to all parts of Western Europe and Africa by Roman military forces and colonists, including those who reached England. This is a particularly rich fund of information, which generally makes it possible for the historical linguist to determine the precise nature of linguistic contacts between early forms of English and Latin with considerable confidence.

We have every reason to suppose that the Old Korean languages, particularly the Old Paekche language, played much the same role in the development of early forms of Japanese that Latin did in the development of English. The significant difference between the two is that we know a great deal about the various forms of Latin that were so important for the history of English, while we know almost nothing about the early forms of Korean that we believe to have been equally important for the history of Japanese.

The Old Paekche language is a good case in point. The role of the Paekche kingdom in introducing Buddhism to early Japan is well established from the historical record. So also is the continuing importance of several later generations of Paekche refugee and other immigrant families domiciled in Japan. It is most likely that Old Paekche, like the other Old Korean languages, was itself an Altaic language and, as such, genetically related to Old Japanese. But at the same time, it seems certain that owing to the intimate nature of the cultural and particularly the religious associations between these two early states, Japan and the Paekche kingdom of Korea, the Old Paekche language was also the source of a great number of borrowings, or linguistic imitations, by means of which Paekche words entered the vocabulary of Japanese in the course of cultural contacts between the two countries. Since the two languages were genetically related, the Paekche words that were, by this process, borrowed into Old Japanese would sometimes be cognate with already existing Old Japanese words; but at the same time, these new words would also be different, probably different in both their forms and their meanings. (A close parallel would be such words as English "skirt" and "shirt" noted above, in which a word coming from another but genetically related language—a form of Old Scandinavian—was borrowed into Old English, where it continued to exist alongside an older and originally English word, close to it in both sound and meaning, to which it was also genetically related.)

In this way, early linguistic contacts between Japanese and Korean appear to have led to many different levels of borrowings. Until most recent times, these were always borrowings from Korean into Japanese. Borrowings in the other direction become common only in the period of Japanese colonialism, in the modern century.

Since we know very little about the actual Korean-language originals that were the linguistic basis for all the early Korean loanwords into Japanese, it is often difficult to distinguish between these extremely ancient loans and the inherited stock of genetically related forms common to both languages. Of the Old Paekche language, for example, we know today only about ten words. A little more is known about the two other major Old Korean languages, but not significantly more. This lack of Korean data is to be attributed to two causes. One is the troubled political and social developments on the Korean peninsula for most of the historical period; these changes were often so profound that entire early cultures and whole languages disappeared almost without a trace. The other was the early permeation of Chinese literary culture into Korean life and the high degree of Sinicization that early Korean civilization underwent. Particularly in the earliest periods—the periods that would be of most value to us for tracing the process of linguistic contacts and borrowings between Korea and Japan—almost no writing was done in Korean proper; instead, literary Chinese was used for almost all purposes. The earliest substantial texts in Korean that may be utilized for the purposes of historical and comparative linguistic study do not appear until 1445; this means that they are very late indeed, even in terms of the other Altaic languages that, as we have already seen, at best generally lack early written records of any considerable antiquity.

All these factors, when taken together and considered within the context of early Japanese-Korean linguistic contacts, mean that it is often extremely difficult to distinguish between an early borrowing from Korean into Japanese and a word that is the same or much the same in form and meaning in both languages because it is a word that was genetically inherited by both of them separately, and goes back to the common original language to which both Korean and Japanese are in turn related.

We have good reason for assuming that both types, early borrowings and genetically related forms, exist; but too often we still lack the precise information about the early history of Korean that would make it possible to distinguish between these two with the degree of precision we would like. We also have good reason to assume that the borrowings in question belong to many different historical levels, just as the Latin words do that have been borrowed into English; but again, it is sometimes almost as difficult to distinguish with confidence and precision between these different historical layers in the old Korean loanwords in Japanese as it is to distinguish between loans and genetically related forms.

Nevertheless, we are occasionally fortunate enough to be able to estimate fairly confidently whether a given lexical similarity between Korean and Japanese is the result of genetic inheritance or of borrowing, even in the absence of a substantial body of written records that document any very remote stage of the Korean language. Such cases are always of considerable interest, since they can show us the way parallel linguistic developments no doubt took place in the many other cases where we are not so fortunate with respect to our sources and materials. This is particularly true of cases where extralinguistic information, such as our knowledge of the migrations of domesticated plants, can be brought to bear on the question.

For example, a number of interlocking similarities in both forms and meanings exist between the Korean and Japanese words for "hemp" and "morning." For "hemp," modern Korean has *sam,* and modern Japanese *asa;* for "morning," Korean has *achim,* and Japanese *asa.* Since we know that the hemp plant was early domesticated on the Asiatic continent, including the Korean peninsula, and also that it was introduced to Japan from the mainland of Asia at an early period, it seems most likely that its name was also brought to Japan together with the plant itself, and that the Japanese language borrowed the word for hemp, the word that is now Japanese *asa,* from some early form that once existed in a Korean language. What that linguistic form was, and in which Old Korean language it existed, we do not know; all that we do have is the modern Korean word *sam,* which is unlikely to be exactly the same as the ancient Korean word that was borrowed by Japanese, though it is probably a later, changed form of that Korean word.

With this data and its historical analysis thus in hand, we may then with considerable confidence conclude that the similarities in form and meaning between modern Korean *achim* and Japanese *asa,* both of which mean "morning," are either the result of sheer chance, in which case these similarities are without significance for the history of either language, or they are to be accounted for by the genetic inheritance, by each language separately, of a single form that once existed in an earlier common original. This hypothesis of genetic relationship and inheritance would also help to account for the fact that the consonant sound *s* is the same in the words for "hemp" in both languages (the case where we have already, and on the basis of the history of domesticated plants, concluded that the Japanese word is probably borrowed from an earlier Korean form), while the two words for "morning" have different internal consonants in each language (*-ch-* in Korean but *-s-* in Japanese). Since linguistic borrowing is nothing more than a special form of mimicry or imitation, in which speakers of one language attempt to reproduce as exactly as they can a linguistic form that belongs to another language, we often find that a word borrowed from one language into another has identical sounds, or nearly identical sounds, in both of them. But since genetic relationship usually implies that a long period of time has elapsed between the time of each of the languages being compared and the time of the original language to which each is related, we generally find that during this very long period of time much has happened to change either the pronunciation or the meaning, or often both.

If as it then seems safe to conclude, Korean *achim* and Japanese *asa* are genetically related forms, this means that they are both later, changed forms of a lost original word. The difference in internal consonants *(-ch-* in Korean but *-s-* in Japanese) is to be explained by an original consonant in the earlier, but now lost, original word having changed to one thing in the modern Korean form that we now have but to another in the Japanese form. We do not know what the precise pronunciation of that lost original consonant was, but the comparative method of historical linguistics does provide a number of techniques for carefully estimating what it might have been. Similar historical reasoning will also allow us to account for the observed differences in the vowels in the words for "morning" in Japanese and Korean. In this way, we can recover or, as it is sometimes expressed, reconstruct the now lost forms of the original languages that underlie the similarities we observe in forms and meanings in different languages, even, if necessary, in the absence of earlier written records.

Often, however, striking parallels in linguistic forms and their meanings occur between Korean and Japanese that continue to confront us with a number of still largely unsolved problems. As a result we are often quite hard put to distinguish between later loanwords and the earlier inheritance of genetically related (i.e., etymologically identical) forms. All we can be sure of is that both kinds of evidence exist, but to sort them out is often far from easy.

Much of the evidence that is at hand when we compare Korean and Japanese reminds one of the "shirt" and "skirt" doublets from the history of English. The chief difference is that while in the history of English we generally have substantial grounds for deciding which member of such a doublet is the loanword and which is the result of genetic inheritance, we often lack any basis for such categorization in the case of Korean and Japanese.

Thus, modern Korean *mal* "a unit of dry measure" would certainly appear, both in form and meaning, to have some historical connection with two different Japanese forms—one Old Japanese *mari* "a cup-shaped container for liquids," the other modern Japanese *masu* "a box-shaped measure for grain or for liquids." But the direction and nature of the connections between these three linguistic forms are difficult to unravel with confidence.

As far as the phonological shape of the forms is concerned, Old Japanese *mari* would be an excellent candidate for a loanword relationship with some older Korean form, not attested but underlying modern Korean *mal;* but on the semantic level, Japanese *masu* and modern Korean *mal* are closer to each other, and so these forms have been most often associated in the literature to date. But loanwords are imitations of the forms of one language in the sound system of another; and it is difficult to explain why a form of the shape of Korean *mal* would ever have been imitated with an -*s*-, as in Japanese *masu,* when an -*r*- was readily available with which to imitate the Korean *l*. The meanings of all three words are such as tend to make us think in terms of fairly late cultural loans; but the forms and meanings are difficult to sort out into a reasonable scenario of borrowing.

Nor is the problem that we encounter in the comparison

[154]

of Korean and Japanese by any means limited to words that, like *mal, mari,* and *masu,* might be expected to be old cultural loans because of the nature of the real objects to which they refer. The same problem, sometimes on an even more involved level, is found represented in the comparison of Korean and Japanese words from quite ordinary areas of everyday vocabulary—the kind of common, ordinary words that sometimes are misleadingly termed "basic vocabulary."

For example, the modern Korean world *talk* "chicken," which goes back to Middle Korean *tălk,* meaning the same thing, has long been suspected of having some sort of historical connection with Old Japanese *töri,* modern Japanese *tori* "bird." Our suspicion that the two words are somehow related historically is heightened when we recall that in modern Japanese *tori* often means "chicken," and also that the usual Tokyo-dialect word for "chicken" is *niwatori,* literally "garden (or, yard) bird." (Again, we are reminded by this example of the important difference between the true "meaning" of a linguistic form and what can conveniently be expressed by translation glosses, which are simply ad hoc labels that we attach to forms for identification purposes.)

Many students of this question have simply assumed that Japanese *tori* and Korean *talk* are cognates. This would imply that they both go back to a lost, unattested original form, and since the Korean form is more complicated than the Japanese, reconstruction of that lost original form would have to proceed on the working assumption that it was originally closer to the Korean form than to the Japanese, or put another way, that the Japanese form represents a simplification of an earlier, more complex form, a form that had a sequence of consonants something like the sequence of consonants that Korean has preserved in its final -*lk* of the form *talk.*

But there is another Japanese word that is equally relevant to such a discussion, though it has generally been overlooked in the literature. This is Japanese *toki,* which refers to the crested ibis, a beautiful, rare bird that today is threatened with extinction in Japan, even though it proudly bears the resoundingly patriotic scientific name of *Nipponia nippon.* If Japanese *tori* has some historical connection with Korean *talk,* what then about Japanese *toki?*

[155]

A connection between *talk* and *toki* could quite easily be explained in the same fashion, by a simplification of an earlier **-lk*, but with the *-l-* dropping out in Japanese this time, not the *-k*. Both explanations are equally plausible; there are no scientific grounds for selecting one over the other. Yet if one of the Japanese forms is cognate with the Korean form, the other must be a loanword, since it shows a different phonological development. If one is a cognate, then the other is a loan: but the question remains, which is which?

All this is quite reminiscent of English "shirt" and "skirt," but with the added complication that when we compare Korean *talk* with both Japanese *tori* and *toki,* we remain in the dark about the direction as well as the linguistic nature of the connections that we nevertheless feel sure do exist among all these three forms. (Here we have mentioned only the possibilities of borrowings from early forms of Korean into Japanese; it is also possible that borrowings took place in the other direction. In view of the early history of cultural relations between these two countries, borrowings from early Japanese into Korean are generally neither plausible nor very probable, but it must not be forgotten that they *are* possible. In tracing the history of early developmental stages in languages, we can actually rule out nothing as being impossible: an almost infinite variety of change is possible. One of the tasks of the historical linguist is to identify the circumstances and conditions that make one kind of change, or one variety of development, more probable, or more plausible, than another.)

Nor does the problem presented by these Korean and Japanese words stop with the forms cited above. Evidence from several different Turkic languages makes it possible to reconstruct Proto-Turkic **torγa,* which was apparently used to refer to a wide variety of small birds. And not only does this Proto-Turkic form look very much like the modern and Middle Korean words under discussion, but it was borrowed at some early period into Hungarian, where it resulted in *tyúk* "chicken"—showing almost precisely the same kind of simplification that we would assume if we were to try to connect Japanese *toki* with either Korean *talk* or Proto-Turkic **torγa.*

Similarly, Japanese has two verbs that are quite likely

related to one another, *tak-* "burn (something up), set fire to something," and *yak-* "fire (pottery), cook, grill, bake (something)." Most would agree that this Japanese doublet is somehow related to modern Korean *tha-* "burn," which goes back to Middle Korean *thă-* "id." But again the question is how. Middle Korean *thă-* "burn" may very well go back to an earlier **tak-*, since many of the aspirated initials of Korean, such as the *th-* initial of *thă-*, are believed to have resulted from relatively late changes within Korean, in which originally syllable-final consonants shifted both position and pronunciation, so that earlier **tak-* became *thă-*. In that case, Japanese *tak-* might be the inherited form, and cognate with the Korean forms, while Japanese *yak-* might be a very old loan from some early variety of Korean, coming into Japanese through an intermediate form **dak-*, the initial **d-* in such a case regularly changing, after its borrowing into Japanese, to *y-*.

The principal merit of such an explanation is that it not only explains the existence of the *tak-*, *yak-* doublet in Japanese, and the relation of this set to Korean *tha-*, but it also explains the specialized employment of Japanese *yak-* as a technical term for firing ceramic ware, the technology of firing pottery at high temperatures in enclosed kilns quite clearly being an example of early cultural borrowing from Korea into Japan.

CHINESE, MALAYO-POLYNESIAN, AND "MIXED LANGUAGES"

Korean was surely not the only foreign language that, in this complex fashion, contributed to the development of Japanese. What is special about the contribution of Korean is that Korean itself is almost surely genetically related to Japanese, quite apart from early linguistic contacts resulting in loans and borrowings between the two, so that today we often find it difficult to distinguish between the various kinds of relationships that exist between these two languages. It is unlikely that the other languages that had significant early linguistic contacts with Japanese were genetically related to Japanese. This often makes it somewhat easier to identify their contributions to the language as the borrowings that they are.

Most important of these languages, not genetically related

[157]

to Japanese but nevertheless making an important contribution to the historical development of Japanese, were Chinese and many early forms of languages belonging to the Malayo-Polynesian family. There is no serious probability that either Chinese or any of the Malayo-Polynesian languages is genetically related to Japanese; but through early linguistic contacts, each has played a significant role in the development of Japanese.

The contributions of Chinese to the Japanese language are enormous, and relatively easy to document, partly because we know a good deal about the earlier, documented stages of Chinese (almost in the same way that we know a great deal about the early stages of Latin that contributed so strikingly to the history of English) and partly because the process of Chinese loans contributing to the Japanese lexical store still goes on. New words based on Chinese roots are coined almost daily in Japan, particularly in the fields of technology, science, and academic jargon. Observing this process at work today makes it possible to understand a good deal about how it must have worked in the past.

But even apart from such obviously learned borrowings, Chinese loans in Japanese are so common, and used for so many ordinary things, that often we find they have replaced other, older words that Japanese inherited from the original Altaic language. We know, for example, that before the Buddhist prohibition on meat-eating became a part of Japanese life, the Japanese ate the flesh of such animals as boars and deer as part of their regular diet. The Old Japanese word for meat taken as food was *sisi,* a linguistic form that is preserved in written records, and that we can associate historically with other words in the various Altaic languages. But this word soon dropped out of use in Japan, where today it is no longer a living lexical item, but rather has been completely replaced by a Chinese loanword, *niku,* used in this same sense. Many other examples could be given. The most striking, probably, are those provided by the number system. Borrowed Chinese words for the numbers have, in Japanese, almost replaced the set of older number words that Japanese inherited from Altaic. This is particularly true of the higher numbers, where the impact of the Chinese borrowings has been so great that we do not even know for certain—nor can it be established from written records—what the Old Japanese words were for larger numbers such as 43 or 58. With only a few exceptions, for any counting above 10, Chinese borrowings have not only replaced the original Japanese formations but have done this so completely that the inherited Japanese words for the higher combinations of numbers have disappeared from linguistic history.

Early borrowings from the various Malayo-Polynesian languages are also surely of importance in the development of Japanese, but they are much more difficult to document than the Chinese loans. Malayo-Polynesian is, like Altaic and Indo-European, a linguist's term for a now-lost linguistic unity, the later changed forms of which include an enormous number of different languages today spread over the entire Pacific area, from Indonesia and the island of Formosa in one direction all the way to such areas as Tahiti and the Hawaiian Islands in the other. It is obvious, from the present-day distribution of their languages, that the original Malayo-Polynesians were skillful and energetic sailors, and that their voyages took them across enormous distances. One of the last of their major migrations, which carried Malayo-Polynesian speakers from the islands of Tahiti to the Hawaiian chain, took place quite late in history, and hence gives us a fairly concrete idea of how their earlier voyages were accomplished.

It is easy, and dangerous for our purposes, to overstress the navigational and seafaring skills of the early Malayo-Polynesians. Some of them obviously were good sailors, but that does not mean that they all were. There appears to be little hard evidence for successful long-distance voyaging among the Malayo-Polynesian group within East Asia, or even within the insular southeast Asian area. Popular fiction and motion pictures have undoubtedly given us a rather overenthusiastic view of this entire question, and we cannot safely assume, as is sometimes done in contemporary Japanese scholarship, that the early Malayo-Polynesians found it an easy matter to reach the Japanese islands or the Korean peninsula, especially not in the large numbers that would have been necessary if they and their language were to have left any permanent trace. Nevertheless, it is reasonable to assume that more than once in the remote past, and perhaps even down into the early historical period, some small numbers

[159]

of Malayo-Polynesian speakers did come to the Japanese archipelago, bringing with them their language and Neolithic culture, just as they brought them to other islands scattered in remote portions of the Pacific world. But in the case of Japan, their numbers must have been pitifully few, and their arrivals infrequent.

Once such Malayo-Polynesian visitors had reached Japan, they more than likely would have stayed on there, if only because there was no place else for them to go. And surely they could not have survived the rigors of a voyage back to wherever they had come from, at least not without devoting years, even decades, to rebuilding their strength, energies, and numbers. Unless the Malayo-Polynesian visitors were all immediately killed upon arrival by the people they found living in the Japanese islands, they stayed on. And because they stayed on, their language, like their genes, was able to make a contribution to the Japanese scene.

A number of early words that appear to be the result of linguistic contacts between Malayo-Polynesian speakers and Japanese have been identified; as we might expect, most of these terms have to do with the sea or fishing, including many specific terms for various species of fish and other forms of marine life. We will recall that the comb-pattern pottery makers from the continent, whose intrusion into Japanese life apparently represented the first major attested advent of Altaic speakers to the islands, also had a culture that, like the culture of the Malayo-Polynesians, had developed techniques of harvesting seafood to a considerable stage of advancement. The Tungusic comb-pattern pottery makers specialized in the exploitation of streams and coastal areas, while the Malayo-Polynesians were adept at sustaining life during protracted voyages at sea. But apart from these differences, the two cultures tended to converge, with respect at least to their common emphasis on seas and streams and the livelihood to be derived from them. This convergence means that it is not always easy to distinguish between an Altaic, and probably a specifically Tungusic, origin for a given linguistic feature or form that relates to this segment of material culture and one of Malayo-Polynesian origin; the conventional assumption of a Malayo-Polynesian source for all Japanese linguistic

[160]

features relating to maritime economy is surely an oversimplification.

Thus, we have seen above that the Japanese verb *izar-* "to catch fish at sea" is a complex denominal form consisting of two different elements, an inherited noun from Altaic *$\bar{u}l_2$* "work, occupation," to which was added an inherited Altaic denominal verb-stem formant *-l-*. The Japanese verb that resulted from this early process of word-formation is regular throughout in its conformity to all the sound laws that may be established for the Altaic languages, including *-s-* for *l_2*, and the subsequent shift of that *-s-* to later and attested *-z-* under the influence of the suffixed *-l-*, which of course becomes Japanese *-r-*. In other words, everything about *izar-*, an important Old Japanese socioeconomic term, is totally and completely Altaic in its etymology—that is, in its history as a word. It is rather among the various words referring to what was caught that we find an occasional linguistic form in Japanese that seems to have Malayo-Polynesian origins.

An example is Japanese *ika* "squid, cuttlefish." This word can hardly be kept etymologically apart from such forms as Fijian *ᵓika ᵓ*, and Tonga and Futuna *ᶜika ᶜ*, all of which simply mean "fish," and which go back to an original Malayo-Polynesian *ᶜikan* of the same meaning. Of course, we hardly expect that the Altaic speakers would, or could, have brought with them from the mainland of continental Asia a word that meant "squid" or "cuttlefish"; and the Malayo-Polynesian linguistic evidence simply substantiates this hunch. But in other cases, even terms for what might be thought, again along "common sense" lines, to be likely prospects for Malayo-Polynesian etymologies often turn out to be Altaic instead.

A representative as well as a most instructive example of this last point is provided by the words for "crab." It has long been recognized that Japanese *kani* and Korean *kŏi*, both of which mean "crab," are somehow related, the connection between the two probably to be explained by the modern Korean form *kŏi* being a later, changed form from an earlier *kani*, with loss of the intervocalic *-ń-* in pre-Korean and subsequent alteration of the first-syllable *-a-* to attested *-ŏ-* under the influence of the final *-i*. But where did both these words—or to put it more exactly, where did their common, now-lost ancestor form, Proto-Korean-Japanese *kañi* "crab"—come from? One might suspect that Malayo-Polynesian would provide an etymological explanation for this term, but it does not. The word is actually of Altaic origin. It is cognate with Proto-Turkic *känä,* a word that in Turkic referred to various varieties of body parasites, particularly ticks. In Turkic this word appears as Eastern Tk. *känä* "a term for various parasites," modern Tk. *kene* and Kazakh *kenä* "a tick," and Osm. *gene* "a pincer."

From this linguistic evidence it becomes clear that Japanese *kani* and Korean *kŏi* both represent later semantic extensions into marine terminology of an original Altaic word for body lice and related parasites. Encountering the strange new marine animals for the first time when they reached the Pacific littoral, the Proto-Korean-Japanese speakers must have been at a loss for what to call them. Eventually the problem was solved by employing an inherited Altaic word to describe the new, and quite un-Altaic, animals involved—animals whose configurations of claws and pincers called to mind the painful parasitic pests with which these Altaic speakers were already acquainted. Nor is the etymological metaphor involved, and the identification of the crablike body lice with the edible crabs of ocean and land by any means unique to the history of Japanese and Korean. The identification is based on such a strikingly obvious physical similarity that it must have occurred to many different cultures. What is, however, probably unique to the Japanese-Korean and Altaic evidence for this word is that we do have, in this one instance, a pretty clear idea of the direction in which the etymological metaphor developed—from body lice to the marine animals, rather than the other way around.

In the consideration of these and related questions of etymology, we are fortunate in that a good deal is known about the linguistic details of the earlier forms of the original Malayo-Polynesian language, thanks in particular to the work of a number of German scholars of the past generation. What we know in this connection generally confirms our conclusion that similarities in forms and their meanings between Japanese and any of the Malayo-Polynesian languages are to be attributed to early borrowings but not to genetic relationship. This is because the recon-

struction of Malayo-Polynesian, by application of the comparative method to hundreds of surviving languages, shows us that
the earliest forms that may be recovered for Malayo-Polynesian
are quite different in linguistic structure from what we also
know about the earliest forms of Japanese, as well as those of
the other Altaic languages.

These differences include radical differences in phonological inventory and patterning, as well as very different systems
of morphology and syntax. If two or more languages are indeed
genetically related, the further back into their histories we go,
the more we expect that their earlier forms will resemble each
other; this follows logically from the definition of what is meant
by "genetic relationship." But when we study and compare
Japanese and Malayo-Polynesian, just the opposite proves to be
true. The further back we go in our pursuit of Japanese linguistic
origins, the closer we approach a stage that reveals similarities
with the other Altaic languages on every level of linguistic structure. The further back we pursue Malayo-Polynesian, the more
our findings diverge from Japanese, and from the Altaic system.
The sounds are different, the ways in which the sounds are put
together to make words are different, the ways in which words
are formed, and in which they are employed in turn to make
up sentences, are different; everything is different. If a real
probability of genetic relationship existed between Japanese
and the Malayo-Polynesian family of languages, just the opposite
should be true—the further back in time we go, the more things
should begin to look the same. The only conclusion that is tenable, in the light of the evidence, is that similarities in linguistic
forms and their meanings between Japanese and Malayo-Polynesian are the result of borrowings.

Scholars in both Japan and the West have from time to
time considered the possibility that Japanese may be a "mixed
language." This term and the quite special concept behind it were
first applied to Japanese by the Soviet linguist E. D. Polivanov
(1890-1938), in several papers that he published between 1914
and 1930. (Polivanov died before he was able to fulfill the full
promise of his scholarly work, apparently a victim of one of
Stalin's many purges of Soviet intellectuals.) By the concept
of a mixed language, Polivanov meant that Japanese was neither

an Altaic language nor a Malayo-Polynesian language, but that elements of both had entered into its composition at a very early period—so early that in the course of subsequent historical developments they had become intertwined in such a way that it is no longer possible to distinguish clearly, on the basis of surviving linguistic evidence, between them.

If Japanese were such a language, then indeed it would merit the designation of mixed or hybrid. But many serious obstacles stand in the way of an unqualified acceptance of Polivanov's views, or of any hypothesis that would make Japanese a "mixed language," at least in this special definition of the term. Polivanov's own views were set forth in extremely brief form, and were illustrated with only a few examples. And not all of these examples will stand up under careful scrutiny; too often his thesis falls down because his data are not accurate. His control of Altaic materials was sounder than his command of Malayo-Polynesian, but here too there are problems in his data, which again are hardly extensive. At best, Polivanov's ideas in this connection were expressed only in the form of intuitive exercises of the scholarly imagination. The early termination of his career made it impossible for him to substantiate his early speculation with more extensive documentation.

Another serious obstacle in the way of accepting Polivanov's view of Japanese as a mixed or hybrid language is the continued and substantial reluctance, among historical linguists in particular, to admit that mixed languages, at least in the particular sense Polivanov intended, really do exist anywhere in the world, or have ever existed. There does not appear to be enough evidence to support such a view. Indeed, what evidence we do have points in just the opposite direction. When languages come into contact, various things can happen, but language mixture, or the generation of mixed or hybrid languages, is apparently not one of them. Languages can borrow from one another, or they can replace one another, but they do not appear to mix with one another in the way that Polivanov argued for Altaic and Malayo-Polynesian in the case of Japanese.

Again, it is safer to begin with examples in which the historical facts can be documented, and then argue what events most likely took place in other circumstances where such evidence is not forthcoming, than to arrange our argumentation in the opposite order. We know what happened, for example, when Spanish came to Mexico. The result of the European conquest and colonization of Mexico was a mixed race, and a mixed population, but not a mixed language. The language that survived was and is Spanish, and it is not a mixed, or a hybrid language, though of course it is different today from European Spanish. The same parallel exists for many other places in the world. We find plenty of mixed races—indeed, all races are mixed, and there are no "pure races" except in the mischievous imaginations of ethnic zealots—but we do not find instances of mixed languages that we can document from historical evidence.

Given this situation, any attempt to take Japanese, for which we lack very early historical documentation, and make of it an unprecedented example of a mixed or hybrid language, at least in the special sense in which Polivanov and others following him have sought to employ that term, appears at the very least to be theoretically unsound and methodologically unwise. It is basing an argument on what is unknown and undemonstrated, instead of on what can be ascertained to be fact; it is, in essence, arguing from the exception and trying to make it into the rule.

Attempts to make of Japanese a mixed or hybrid language also run counter to the consensus of Western scholarship in another, equally important fashion. We have already stressed that the most significant direction or thrust of most modern studies of Japanese linguistic origins, particularly in the West, has been to show that in its historical development Japanese is a language like any other human language, a linguistic system whose origins we can expect to account for in terms of the same historical processes of linguistic development that are known to be common to many other languages of Asia and of the world. Polivanov's "mixed language" hypothesis would work in precisely the opposite direction. If successfully upheld, it would mean that Japanese would then become the sole documented example of a true mixed language; once again, Japanese would be unique in the world, and divorced from the common run of human linguistic history. Perhaps these implications of isolation and unique development, implicit in Polivanov's thesis, help to account for some of the interest in reviving his views that one notes in contemporary Japanese scholarship.

Words, however, can easily be made to mean what we wish them to mean, and the terminology of linguistics or any other science is no exception. If we are careful to separate our thinking and our methodology from Polivanov's quite special interpretation of the term, we may still find that there are times when it will be unobjectionable to employ the designation "mixed language" as a useful categorization for Japanese.

Just as there are surely no pure races, so also—in this general, non-Polivanov interpretation—are there no unmixed languages. We know that Japanese, like every other language for which we have any firsthand evidence, has borrowed from many different languages in the course of its long history and development. Some of these languages were themselves, like Japanese, genetically related to the original Altaic language; many others were not. All of them contributed to the Japanese language at one time or another in various ways, and some of them are still making almost daily contributions. Japanese is, in this sense, surely a mixed language, just as English, or Chinese, or Russian is a mixed language.

In order to emphasize this aspect of the history of Japanese, it is probably still useful to keep the term "mixed" in our active linguistic vocabulary, particularly since its use in this sense will stress what we have wished to stress all along about the history of this language, namely that Japanese has undergone changes and developments quite like those that other languages in the world have undergone. If Japanese were unmixed, or pure, in this general sense of those terms, it would again be a unique example among the world's languages; but again, it clearly is not.

At the same time, it must be stressed that this kind of "mixing"—which is not the mixing to which Polivanov and his theories had reference—is a phenomenon that is common to all languages; moreover, it is one that does not necessarily, in or of itself, obscure the genetic relationship of the language concerned. The Latin that the Roman armies and colonists brought to ancient Gaul did not there mix with Gaulish to become a "hybrid" language. Latin in Gaul changed in ways unlike the changes that Latin underwent in other parts of the Roman Empire, but these changes do not obscure the fact that French was, and is, a Romance language—a later, changed form of Latin. If the kind of mixing that all languages undergo—by which we mean principally the borrowing back and forth of linguistic materials throughout history—did obscure the genetic relationship of language, then we would be in the dark about the genetic relationship of every language in the world, because in this general sense—not in Polivanov's—every language in the world is a mixed language, just as every race is a mixed race.

The fact that English is equally "mixed," in the sense of having many different layers of loanwords—often borrowed from languages that are themselves genetically related to English—does not either disguise or negate the fact that English is a Germanic language, or that it is a later, changed form of Indo-European. Russian has many loanwords that came into the language as a result of generations of contacts between Russian speakers and speakers of various Altaic languages; but these loans neither change nor obscure the fact that Russian is a Slavic language, and also another form of Indo-European. Japanese is, similarly, an Altaic language, and the evidence for this genetic relationship is complicated, but not disguised or obscured, by the many elements that have been "mixed" or borrowed into the language in the long course of its history, either from other Altaic languages such as Korean or from non-Altaic languages such as Chinese and Malayo-Polynesian.

4. Japanese Scholarship

No consideration of the origins of the Japanese language can be complete without paying some attention to the various problems that Japanese scholarship has encountered, particularly in the past three decades of academic freedom, in its study of this question. Anyone who reads the literature, both popular and scientific, that is published in this field in Japan almost daily, or who attempts to keep abreast of the work of Japanese scholars who are concerned with this subject, soon comes to realize two important facts.

One is that the sheer bulk of the literature and the scale of the Japanese scholarly effort directed toward the consideration of this question are enormous. So much is written and published in Japan about the origins of the Japanese language that anyone—particularly the scholar who does not live in Japan, and for whom Japanese books and articles are not always easily available—may be forgiven for having missed some important publication here or there, or even for forming conclusions on the basis of less than complete control of the evidence. The sheer quantity of published materials works against complete familiarity with all the relevant literature by any single scholar.

The other important fact is that a surprising amount of Japanese scholarship concerned with this question is still operating under the unnecessary inhibitions imposed by the completely obsolete chronological restrictions of the pre-1945 fascist-nationalist orthodoxy, generally without realizing that it is this totally discredited system of dating early Japanese civilization that is still hampering every variety of serious inquiry in this field. Indeed, a careful survey of representative work done in Japan on the question of the origins of the Japanese language inclines many of us in the West toward the view that no other single factor has been as restrictive of the efforts of all Japanese historical-linguistic scholarship.

Even though no one in Japan today would seriously argue that it is necessary to compress the entire historical development of Japanese civilization and culture within the short time span between 660 B.C. and the present, so strong was the indoctrination on this point by the pre-1945 educational authorities, and so severe were the penalties for any deviation from this artificial and blatantly unhistorical norm, that even today, three decades after these restrictions on free academic inquiry were completely lifted, the inhibitions clearly persist. Too many Japanese scholars still approach the question of the origins of the language as if they were actually convinced that whatever happened must have happened within the first six centuries before our era. As a result they labor needlessly—and fruitlessly, in my view—to evolve systems that will account for the necessary developments within this extremely narrow time span. We have already seen many of the reasons why this cannot be done. Chief among them is that there simply is not enough room in such a system to account for the archaeological evidence, nor to make it possible to relate well-attested developments in Japan to equally well-documented developments on the Asiatic continent.

By the seventh century B.C., the formative stages in the

development of Japanese civilization, culture, and language were over and done with. Whatever had happened earlier to bring about these distinctive developments in human civilization, and to set Japan on the direction in which it was to move, had already taken place. If one were to point to any single reason as the principal one for why Japanese scholarship has not been able to achieve a *teisetsu* on this question of the origins of the Japanese language, it would have to be the unfortunate persistence of the totally discredited pre-1945 chronological system for early Japanese history in the thinking of Japanese scholars. No one today officially takes the system seriously; but no one has really forgotten about it either. It remains a powerful if latent force behind Japanese scholarship, where it continues to work a tremendous amount of mischief. (We have already identified another reason that helps explain the persistence of the discredited pre-1945 view of early Japanese chronology in the traditional scholarly bias against nonagricultural and preliterate civilizations and peoples.)

The persistence of this chronological orthodoxy also does more than any other single factor to explain the tremendous vogue that theories of supposed invasions of Japan by "horse-riding peoples" *(kiba minzoku)* continue to enjoy, both among the general Japanese reading public and also among some serious scholars of early Japan. With the evolution of these "horse-riding peoples" theories, the Japanese popular imagination was finally presented with an attractive alternative that seemed to solve many of the problems that plagued a more sober consideration of the facts. By going along with the "horse-riding peoples" speculations, it was possible to have one's prehistoric cake and eat it too: these speculations provided a convenient and pleasing, if quite unsupported, means for escaping from the unpleasant necessity of recognizing the importance of just those motley peoples and early stages in the development of human civilization against which Japanese scholarship had traditionally been the most severely biased.

No one knew just who these "horse riders" could have been—nor does anyone know today. But the strong implication is that they were some sort of foreign elite—not just anybody, but people of importance, people to be reckoned with. While little else of specific detail is generally attributed to them, it is always made out that they were people of quality, hence worthy to have been involved in Japanese prehistory—above all, worthier of such a role than any motley, nonagricultural, preliterate unknowns from the continent or, even worse, from the Korean peninsula. The popular imagination, fed by a never-ending stream of quasi-scholarly speculation, soon concluded that if one had to believe that one's native land had been invaded and occupied in prehistoric times—much as it was once more being invaded and occupied by a foreign elite at the time these speculations were becoming most rife—then the least one could do was to assume that the invaders had been "our kind of people"—elite, horse-riding aristocrats, not such bad types after all. Little of this, one soon understands, can possibly be of serious interest to the prehistorian, archaeologist, or linguist; but the student of social pathology will find rich materials for his research in these speculations.

At any rate, what is actually important for our present consideration of the origins of the Japanese language with respect to these "horse-riding peoples" and their supposed invasions of early Japan is not so much whether such events took place as it is when could they have happened and how could they have played a formative role in the development, and origin, of the Japanese language.

The hypothesis that the critically formative event in the development of early Japanese culture, state, and civilization was at least one major invasion by "horse-riding peoples" who came over from the Asiatic mainland is itself fraught with problems; fortunately most of them lie outside the scope of this book. The principal advantage of such a hypothesis is that it does admit the importance of outside influences on early Japan, and does relate developments in Japan to the situation in the rest of early Asia, particularly Korea. Both of these are certainly attempts in the right direction.

Its principal drawbacks have to do with the way in which the hypothesis has been developed, and particularly the fact that it has arisen almost entirely as a response to negative evidence. Nature is not the only thing that abhors a vacuum; so does scholarship. Too much of the "horse-riding peoples" hypothesis has been evolved for no other reason than to explain things for which no other explanation is apparently forthcoming. When there is no evidence to be had, it is a simple matter to argue that this or that must have happened, and to invoke the impact of visitors from outside the system, whether they turn out to be horse riders from the continent or little men in flying saucers from outer space. Above all, the hypothesis is weak in its handling of the archaeological materials, particularly because it invokes absolutely no concrete linguistic evidence in support of its views.

But even apart from these internal weaknesses of the "horse riders" hypothesis, its main limitation, as far as the origins of the Japanese language are concerned, lies in the fact that it would place the formative period for all aspects of Japanese civilization, including the language, well into early historical times. The invasions in which the "horse riders" hypothesis deals are supposed to have taken place at the end of the fourth century of our era. Such invasions may very well have taken place at that time—even major, disruptive ones of the type envisioned by the adherents of this hypothesis. But if they did, they came to a country in which the species *Homo sapiens* had already been domiciled for millennia. The "horse riders," if they ever existed, were late, very late intruders upon a cultural and linguistic scene that had already advanced millennia away from its truly formative stage.

It seems likely enough that something quite important happened in Japanese life near the end of the fourth century A.D. That something might very well have been an invasion from the continent. But if it did take place, it need have left no more impressive traces behind it in the language and culture of the country than did the occupation of Japan by Allied armed forces following the defeat of 1945. By A.D. 500, Japanese civilization and the Japanese language were already going concerns, whatever their ultimate origins may have been.

The strong latent tendency of Japanese scholarship to try to contain all the necessary stages in the development of the language within the historical period, or at most to move only slightly back in time from that period, shows itself in a wide variety of writing and speculation. Recently, for example, a Japanese scholar has argued that Japanese and the Tibeto-Burman

[172]

languages are genetically related. On the face of it, this seems most unlikely; and the methodology and development of his hypothesis do not inspire confidence in his conclusions. But at least the scholar in question deserves full marks for being, unlike the majority of Japanese scholars, willing at least to consider the possibility that Japanese may have a genetic relationship with some other language or languages and, even more important, that such a genetic relationship may one day be demonstrated with the necessary power of conviction.

Nevertheless, this same scholar unwittingly demonstrates the still active inhibition of the pre-1945 orthodox chronology by attempting to make a case for his Japanese-Tibeto-Burman linguistic unity as having existed during the Yayoi period. According to his thesis, the speakers of this original language brought it to Japan from the continent in Yayoi times, in other words, well within the old, orthodox limits of chronology set by the 660 B.C. of the pre-1945 system.

Of course, we now understand enough about the archaeological evidence from Japan, as well as a sufficient amount concerning the linguistic evidence from the rest of Eurasia, to realize at once that such a recent time limit for these major developments is totally unrealistic. This scholar's thesis of a genetic relationship between Japanese and the Tibeto-Burman languages has other serious problems that stand in the way of its acceptance; but even if those questions were somehow resolved, his eagerness to fit such a system of historical development within the narrow chronological confines of post-Yayoi Japan continues to demonstrate the persistent inhibition of scholarly inquiry exercised by outmoded concepts and limitations that should properly have been left where they fell by the roadside in 1945.

But even apart from the persistence of outmoded attitudes and approaches, there must be other reasons behind the reluctance of Japanese linguistic scholarship to come to grips with the question of the origins of the Japanese language; and although the reasons behind this phenomenon are of a degree of complexity that makes it impossible to treat them here with rigor or thoroughness, it will still perhaps be informative to attempt at least to list what appear to Western scholars to be the principal factors that contribute to this situation.

[173]

At the outset, we might recall that the failure of modern Japanese linguistic scholarship to arrive at what it would call a *teisetsu* on this question of the origins of the Japanese language might, in theory at least, be attributed to any one of three different causes.

First, it might be the Japanese language itself that is responsible. The language might be somehow different from other human languages, or in some other way distinctive or unique, so that its history would resist investigation by the methodology that has demonstrated itself to be of value in establishing the history of many other human languages. The language might have some particular spiritual essence that distinguishes it from other languages that have no such mystical element as part of their make-up, and it might be the presence of this mysterious ingredient in the language that inhibits attempts to learn more than we now know about its history, hence also about its origins.

This approach to the question, with all that it implies, has seriously been advanced by Japanese scholars from time to time, and it is discouraging to observe that it is once more being written and spoken about in all seriousness. Some scholars in Japan today have even revived a word from Old Japanese to express this mystical or spiritual quality that they suppose to be present in the Japanese language, and which they argue makes it impossible to treat the language as if it were simply another of the languages of mankind. This term is *kotodama* "the spirit of the Japanese language," though it must be noted in passing that to employ the word in this particular sense is also to do violence to its history within Japanese language and culture. The entire modern revival of the *kotodama* myth and its mystique is hence not only a willful obfuscation of linguistic science but also a conscious tampering with Japanese antiquity.

At any rate, all such theories must clearly be rejected, if we are to have scientific inquiry concerning Japanese on any level at all, and particularly if we are to study its history and pursue its origins. The current neo-revival of the cult of *kotodama* and all that it represents, including its many perversions of earlier Japanese thought and culture, must be firmly rejected. We cannot continue to call ourselves linguists and still believe that the origins of Japanese are obscure simply because of the existence of *koto-*

dama, though many colleagues in modern Japan apparently continue to do just that.

Second, we might consider the possibility that any obscurity that may presently obtain concerning the origins of the Japanese language is the result of a lack of materials, either for early forms of Japanese or for early forms of other nearby languages, such as Korean, that might reasonably be expected to be related to it. We have already seen why this is surely not the reason behind the inability, or unwillingness, of Japanese scholarship to agree on a *teisetsu* concerning the origin of the language. For the early forms of Japanese we have plenty of materials. Even more important, when genuinely earlier written records are lacking, as in the case of Korean or the Tungusic languages, we know that the application of the comparative method of historical linguistics to living languages—which we do certainly have in abundance—can more than make up for this lack. Thus, lack of materials, which is second in popularity only to *kotodama* as a scapegoat in much modern Japanese writing on this subject, must also be absolved of guilt.

This brings us to the third of these possible causes; the first two are clearly without merit, and nothing can be laid to their blame. If it is not the language itself that is responsible, and if it is also not the materials that we have available that are responsible, only one further possibility exists: it must be the way in which the scholarship has been conducted. In other words, it must be the way in which the subject has been studied, and not the subject itself, that continues to block progress; all other possible reasons have been eliminated.

Having reached this conclusion, it is possible to identify a large number of problems in the methodology and approach of much recent scholarship on this question, many of which seem fair candidates for membership in this last category. In the brief listing that follows are ten items that appear to be the most important, arranged roughly according to the role they have played in determining the course of these studies in Japan, particularly in the period since 1945.

First, it seems necessary to assign priority to the persistent and continuing unfamiliarity of Japanese academic circles with the comparative method of historical linguistics, and with the possibilities that this methodology offers for the pursuit of linguistic history. To the extent that this method has been taught and studied in Japanese universities at all, it has almost always been rigidly compartmentalized, and restricted to the study of Western languages. This has led to the erroneous impression throughout Japanese academia that the method is something that can be employed with profit only in the study of Western languages, and that it is without utility for the study of Japanese. Nothing could, of course, be further from the truth.

The second category is closely related to the first, out of which it grows by a natural cause-and-effect relationship. As a result of the neglect of the study of the comparative method, comparison between Japanese and other languages, on those rare occasions when it has been attempted in a serious fashion, has almost always been limited to the confrontation of words that "look alike." Hence it has remained on the relatively trivial and nonsignificant level of lexical comparisons, without generally reaching the level of true comparative grammar, the heart of the comparative method. Again, this lack of true comparison on the level of grammar, in the full sense of the term, is the result, more than anything else, of the lack of the study of the comparative method in Japan. Not understanding what the comparative method really is, or what it can accomplish, scholars have unfortunately let themselves become sidetracked into mere lexical comparisons rather than becoming involved in true questions of comparative grammar. This has contributed heavily to the continuing obscurity of the origins of the Japanese language.

Third, the traditional approach to the structure of the Japanese language, and particularly to Japanese grammar, that is commonly taught and studied throughout the Japanese school system, is so heavily oriented toward the traditional writing system that it obscures rather than clarifies the structure of the language. Hence it also tends to obscure any historical connections with other languages that might otherwise have come to common notice long ago. The comparative method, and comparative grammar, can only operate with valid linguistic data. The approach of traditional Japanese school grammar, particularly what that school grammar has to say about the inflected forms of the language, makes the facts of the language secondary to the canons of the writing system. Generation after generation of scholars drilled by rote since childhood in the numbing intricacies of this system of school grammar have experienced tremendous difficulty in freeing their thinking from its unnatural confines.

Fourth place in this list must be assigned to the neglect of the study of foreign languages other than English in post-1945 Japan. In particular, the striking neglect of original studies of the languages of Asia that might reasonably be expected to be genetically related to Japanese, such as Korean and the Altaic languages of mainland Asia, is much to be regretted. In order to apply the comparative method, and in order to have comparative grammar in the true sense of the term, a high degree of familiarity with all the languages being compared is essential. Too often, even in the past few decades, Japanese scholarship has been content to cite linguistic data concerning other languages at second- or even thirdhand. Many cases could be cited of scholarly works attempting to consider this question of the origins of Japanese, but employing data for other languages that are not only manifestly inaccurate but have continued to be cited incorrectly in Japan for decade after decade, in books where such errors in linguistic forms and their meanings go uncorrected in printing after printing. Lack of firsthand familiarity with other languages leads to this careless handling of linguistic data; and out of such careless handling, and the perpetuation of erroneous citations of linguistic forms in book after book, nothing that will contribute to solving the question of the origins of Japanese can reasonably be expected.

The fifth problem is closely related to the fourth. Not only have too many scholars been content to cite data from other languages at second- or even thirdhand, but they have been so unfamiliar with the firsthand linguistic data for other languages that they have continued to cite and recite a handful of old, long-standing lexical comparisons between Japanese and a few other languages, without attempting to locate new comparisons on their own. This problem is particularly critical in the comparison of Japanese and Korean, where a number of well-worn word comparisons—only a few of which rise above the level of superficial "look-alikes"—have held the field for almost a century,

[177]

being quoted over and over by author after author. Meanwhile, in the comparison of Japanese with Korean, as well as in the comparison of Japanese with all the other Altaic languages, rich new resources of potential comparative materials lie untouched and uninvestigated.

Especially rich and particularly untouched, in almost every instance, are the materials potentially available from the comparison of all these languages that would actually involve considerations of comparative grammar, and hence contribute in a substantial fashion to the clarification of the origins of Japanese. But these materials are not cited because they are not known; and they are not known because they are not looked for.

Closely allied with this factor is the sixth, a tendency to assume that what has been learned to date about the comparison of Japanese with other languages is all that will ever be learned, and that the handful of "look-alike" lexical comparisons that have been so frequently cited—or mis-cited—in the Japanese literature for the past few generations actually represents the totality of the evidence available.

Surprisingly often one reads in a Japanese book or magazine article something to the effect that only such-and-such a number of "comparisons" are available between Japanese and Korean, or that there are "very few" similarities between Japanese and some other language, or similarly conclusive and apparently final summations of the problem. Behind such claims is the assumption that everything that can be learned about this subject has been learned, and that the materials available have been exhaustively studied. When such absurd claims are made by otherwise responsible scholars, the general reading public may be forgiven for believing that they represent a true and accurate reflection of the actual state of affairs; but of course, we realize that they do not.

Japanese scholarship on the origin of the language has not even begun to work through the available linguistic evidence. More has been done in this connection in the West than in Japan, but even in the West a tremendous amount remains to be done. We generally cannot say that only so many comparisons can be established between Japanese and this language or that, or that the comparison of Japanese with this language or that does not reveal anything of value or interest, for the simple reason that in almost every case the work in question has not been undertaken with anything resembling the degree of rigor that would be necessary to support such sweeping statements. The race is not yet over; the results are not yet in.

To anyone not familiar with much of the Japanese literature in this field, some or all of these comments may appear to be somewhat sensational charges. Anyone who spends much time reading this literature will, however, think of article after article and book after book which these categories describe. It would be invidious, though not all difficult, to cite many examples for each of the six categories above; fortunately, this is hardly necessary. But anyone unfamiliar with the literature who is curious about such things may be directed to a single example that simultaneously illustrates and documents each of these problems within the space of a few pages. The book is Ōno Susumu's *Nihongo no kigen,* a standard work in the field, first published in 1957, and since then kept continuously in print; by 1976 it had reached its twenty-third printing, with several more most likely following since then. The curious reader is invited to inspect page 170 of this book. There he will find a Mongolian word cited which is not Mongolian at all, but actually Manchu; together with this, two of the words cited there from Chuvash Turkish are misspelled, as are two of the forms cited from Old Turkish. Page 125 contains at least one nonexistent Korean word, a lexical "ghost," compared there with a Japanese word. Meanwhile, pages 168-69 firmly state that very few Turkic-Japanese comparisons are possible, clearly implying that the author has made an attempt to find more but has failed.

The point is not only that these errors in citing foreign-language materials, and these misrepresentations of scholarly positions, occur in a standard work of general circulation but that they have remained unchanged through nearly thirty successive printings. It would be difficult to find a more striking demonstration of all these particular problems, in the concrete form in which they continue to plague Japanese scholarship in this field, than that provided by this book.

Professor Ōno's book also provides an excellent introduction to our seventh problem, the reluctance of Japanese scholars

[179]

to study and utilize scientific literature published in foreign countries. This has had an especially deleterious effect in this field. As we have seen, the study of the origins of the Japanese language happens to be one of the areas of linguistic investigation in which some of the most important work has been done outside of Japan; this has been true ever since Boller published his work in Vienna over 120 years ago.

By continuing to ignore publications originating in countries other than Japan, our Japanese colleagues unnecessarily limit the contributions that they themselves might make to this field. For example, we have just noted that as late as 1976 Professor Ōno was still repeating, without change, his 1957 claim that the total number of comparisons that can be made between Turkic and Japanese is extremely small. But two years earlier, in 1974, a Soviet scholar, E. Azerbajev, published in the *Izvestija* of the Kazakh Academy of Sciences an important study based on his own comparison of Japanese with materials from several of the Turkic languages. Working only in one limited area of the comparative phonology that may be established between the two languages, Azerbajev was able to bring together an impressive number of quite convincing parallels, and to establish regular sound laws. What appears in Professor Ōno's book concerning the comparison of Japanese and Turkic may or may not have been correct when it was first written in 1957, but it surely was not accurate in 1976; to continue to repeat this misinformation in reprinting after reprinting can only be explained by neglect of the relevant literature in the field. Of course, no variety of science, including the science of historical linguistics, can make genuine progress or advancement under such circumstances.

One further example of the problems created by the neglect of non-Japanese scientific literature by Japanese academic circles may be cited, since it is representative of many other instances and also of great importance in its own right. In 1975, Professor Karl H. Menges, one of the world's most renowned Turkologists, published in Wiesbaden an important study of the relationship of Japanese to the other Altaic languages. To date, this study, which ranges over the entire question of the origins of Japanese, and upon which this book has drawn extensively, has been totally ignored by Japanese scholars. Not only have its contents and findings not been made available to the general reading public interested in such matters, but even in specialized works on the problem, one finds not the slightest indication that Japanese scholars have even been curious, much less interested, in learning what this eminent European scholar has to say about the subject. Until this lamentable state of affairs is remedied, it is difficult to see how Japanese studies in this field can be expected to make any significant advance.

The last three problem areas that deserve at least a brief mention are all of a rather general, even theoretical nature, but this does not mean that they are any less important than the more concrete questions just listed. Some of them have already been noted, in passing, in this book. First—and number eight in the present list—there is the question of a certain amount of misunderstanding concerning what the comparative method can do; this of course goes along with the general lack of firsthand knowledge of and experience with this method. Because the method itself is still insufficiently familiar to Japanese scholarship, its goals and possibilities are not well understood. It is most commonly misunderstood to be a way to "prove that languages are related." Since this is not true, such a misunderstanding of its goals in turn results in many related misunderstandings concerning its methods and findings.

Second, and following in turn directly from the above, there is a lack of understanding concerning the nature of the findings of the comparative method, particularly of the fact that they are not, nor are they ever intended to be, proofs, but only the accumulation of more and more convincing evidence in support of the original hypothesis or assumption of relationship around which the work itself progresses. False expectations lead only to disappointment. When one erroneously believes that the comparative method, or any of the techniques of historical linguistics, can provide proof, then one is disappointed when such proof is not forthcoming. Misunderstandings and disappointments of this sort can only be prevented by sounder theoretical understanding of the method, its essential assumptions, and its working principles.

Finally, there is the pervading spirit of defeatism that for one reason or another continues to mark much of the Japanese writing and publishing in this field. So much of what is done appears to be predicated on an assumption of nihilism, to the effect that nothing important is known about the subject today (which is surely not true) and also that nothing significant can possibly be found out about it in the future (which seems to be quite as unlikely as the former assumption is manifestly incorrect). Behind this· attitude of defeatism lie many reasons and causes; just what they consist of is less important than the inhibition they continue to exercise over the progress of scientific knowledge in this field.

The question of the origins of the Japanese language is one that cannot be significantly advanced solely by scholars working in any one place or within any one academic tradition. Japanese scholars cannot, it is now clear, solve it on their own, or even notably advance it, if they continue to work in isolation from the efforts of scholars in other countries. It is equally clear that scholars in the West cannot contribute to this question without the continued help and support of their Japanese colleagues. Today we know a great deal about the origins of the Japanese language—more, perhaps, than is generally recognized. But what we know and understand about this important subject is not sufficient, nor is it surely more than a fraction of what we may one day achieve, if all of us who are interested in this problem, in both Japan and the West, work together toward its clarification.

Further
Reading
and
Documentation

For a general orientation on the question of the genetic relationship of Japanese to other languages, chapter 2, "Genetic Relationship," in my book *The Japanese Language* (Chicago: University of Chicago Press, 1967), pp. 59-89, will provide a useful introduction, even though subsequent studies have shown that certain of the positions taken there, particularly with respect to the Proto-Korean-Japanese linguistic unity postulated by Samuel E. Martin (*Language* 42 [1966] :185-251), have required subsequent modification. A more detailed treatment is to be found in my book *Japanese and the Other Altaic Languages* (Chicago: University of Chicago Press, 1971), though here, too, the approach to the comparison of Korean and Japanese requires substantial modification. Most highly to be recommended of any treatment of the general question now available is Karl H.

[183]

Menges, *Altajische Studien, II. Japanisch und Altajisch,* Abhandlungen für die Kunde des Morgenlandes, XLI, 3 (Wiesbaden: Franz
Steiner, 1975); and a useful introduction to his views is also
provided by the same scholar's important review of *Japanese and
the Other Altaic Languages* in *Central Asiatic Journal* 18 (1974):
193-201. Reviews of Menges's *Japanisch und Altajisch* published
thus far include one by Nicholas Poppe in *Journal of Japanese
Studies* 2 (1976):470-74, Theodora Bynon in *Bulletin of the
School of Oriental and African Studies* 41 (1978):196, and by the
author in *Journal of the American Oriental Society* 99 (1979):
120-21. Charles Haguenauer, *Origines de la civilisation japonaise,
Introduction à l'étude de la préhistoire du japon, première partie*
(Paris: Imprimerie Nationale, 1956; no more parts published),
is difficult to use, but contains, inter alia, many important
observations on the historical connections and genetic relationship
of Japanese with other languages. Haguenauer's posthumous
*Nouvelles recherches comparées sur le japonais et les langues
altaïques,* Bibliothèque de l'Institut des hautes études japonaises,
Collège de France (Paris: L'asiathèque, n.d., Avertissement of
1975), is largely polemical in content, and does the memory of
this important pioneer scholar little credit. A short, nontechnical
introduction to the question, stressing the important contributions
of non-Japanese scholars to its study during the past century and
more, is now available in my paper, "The Origin of the Japanese
Language," *Japan Foundation Newsletter* 6, no. 6 (February-
March 1979):6-12. The best introduction to the entire problem
of the origins of the Japanese language available to the English-
language reader is the group of articles published under the general
heading "Symposium: Japanese Origins," *Journal of Japanese
Studies* 2 (1976):295-436. The four papers in this symposium
provide reliable introductions to the question of origins as they
involve the language with disciplines such as prehistory, archaeology, and comparative (historical) linguistics; they also provide
bibliographical coverage for a large number of other important
works in the field. Among works on this subject written in English, the translation of Ōno Susumu, *Nihongo no kigen,* Iwanami
shinsho, vol. 289 (Tokyo: Iwanami shoten, 1957), as Susumu
Ohno, *The Origin of the Japanese Language* (Tokyo: Kokusai
bunka shinkokai, 1970), is most easily available. Unfortunately,

this translation does not give an accurate version of Ōno's original, which itself is full of problems (discussed in the review of the translation in *Monumenta Nipponica* 26 [1971]:455-69); thus the work cannot be recommended to the general reader without the most serious reservations. The Japanese-language publications are immense in number and uneven in quality; no comprehensive treatment of the problem that can be recommended without reservation exists in Japanese at the present time. For an introduction to many of the recent Japanese publications in this general area of scholarship, see my article "Recent Works on the Japanese Language," *Journal of Japanese Studies* 4 (1978): 427-45, which includes references to a number of fairly useful works of recent date that are likely still to be in print. For the specialist, the projected series *Altaic Elements in Old Japanese* is now beginning to provide comprehensive treatments of individual etymologies relating to the Altaic origin of Japanese. Thus far two volumes have been published: John Street and Roy Andrew Miller, part 1 (Madison: the authors, 1975), and John Street, part 2 (Madison: the author, 1978). Subsequent volumes of this series will greatly advance the general understanding of this entire question, as well as serving the specialist in historical linguistics.

The reader who would like to acquire some of the necessary background concerning the nature and history of the various Altaic languages will be excellently served by two general introductions to the subject, Nicholas Poppe, *Introduction to Altaic Linguistics*, Ural-Altaische Bibliothek, vol. 14 (Wiesbaden: Otto Harrassowitz, 1965), and Karl H. Menges, *The Turkic Languages and Peoples: An Introduction to Turkic Studies*, Ural-Altaische Bibliothek, vol. 15 (Wiesbaden: Otto Harrassowitz, 1968). These two books will also introduce the essential bibliography on the subject in addition to the original insights they provide for their subject-matter. Also highly recommended are two recent papers by Nicholas Poppe, "Altaic Linguistics—An Overview," *Sciences of Language* (Tokyo) 6 (1975):130-86, and "Remarks on Comparative Study of the Vocabulary of the Altaic Languages," *Ural-Altaische Jahrbücher* 46 (1974):120-34; the first of these two articles is particularly valuable for the summation it provides (pp. 180 ff.) of Poppe's views concerning the genetic relationship between Japanese and the other Altaic languages. For more specialized purposes, the present state of the reconstruction of Proto-Altaic phonology is available in Poppe's *Vergleichende Grammatik der altaischen Sprachen, Teil 1, Vergleichende Lautlehre,* Porta Linguarum Orientalium, Neue Serie, IV (Wiesbaden: Otto Harrassowitz, 1960), the reconstructions of which are most usefully indexed in John Street, *On the Lexicon of Proto-Altaic: A Partial Index to Reconstructions* (Madison: the author, 1974), which has been put under contribution several times in the present book for citing Proto-Altaic forms and meanings. Poppe's *Vergleichende Grammatik* covers only the reconstruction of Altaic phonology; he is presently dealing with morphology in a series of individual papers which it is hoped will soon be reworked into a comprehensive reconstruction of Altaic morphology. In the meantime, an older work but still useful for all aspects of Proto-Altaic, including phonology and morphology alike, is G. J. Ramstedt, *Einführung in die altaische Sprachwissenschaft, I, Lautlehre, II, Formenlehre, III, Register,* ed. Pentti Aalto, Mémoires de la Société Finno-ougrienne, vol. 104, parts 1, 2, 3 (Helsinki: Suomalais-Ugrilainen Seura, 1957, 1952, 1966), which remains indispensable to the reader interested in further work in this field. G. J. Ramstedt, *Studies in Korean Etymology,* vol. 1, Mémoires de la Société Finno-ougrienne, vol. 95, part 1 (Helsinki: Suomalais-Ugrilainen Seura, 1949), is also of great value, particularly when supplemented by Pentti Aalto, "Additional Korean Etymologies," *Suomalais-Ugrilainen Seura, Helsingfors, Aikakauskirja* 57 (1954):1-23. Unfortunately, much of the *Einführung* had to be published posthumously; nor did Ramstedt have the opportunity to bring his *Studies,* published the year before his death, to the degree of completion that he would have wished. Despite these problems, however, Ramstedt's *Einführung* and *Studies* both remain landmark works for any scholar of the Altaic languages and their history, including the Altaic relationship of Japanese. For the general principles of historical linguistics, particularly as they relate to the study of Japanese linguistic origins, my paper "The Relevance of Historical Linguistics for Japanese Studies," *Journal of Japanese Studies* 2 (1976):335-88, is available; beyond that, the relevant sections of Leonard Bloomfield, *Language* (New York: Henry Holt, 1933), particularly chapter 18, "The Comparative Method," pp. 297 ff., will provide the interested reader with all the background necessary for understanding the principles and issues involved, and is highly recommended.

Chapter 1

On the definition, scope, and distribution of Japanese, see *The Japanese Language,* especially chapter 1, pp. 1-58. On the oldest written records for the Japanese language, see the account by Murayama Shichirō and Roy Andrew Miller of the important archaeological discovery of an inscribed sword from the late fifth century, announced in September 1978 (though the sword itself was excavated ten years previously, in August 1968!), in "The Inariyama Tumulus Sword Inscription," *Journal of Japanese Studies* 5 (1979):405-38. We presently lack a good account of Old Japanese phonetics and phonemics that may be recommended; Roland A. Lange, *The Phonology of Eighth-Century Japanese* (Tokyo: Sophia University, 1973), is readily available, but the findings of his study are contrary to what we otherwise know about Old Japanese (see the review in *Journal of Oriental Studies* (Hong Kong) 13 [1975]:194-200); thus the book must be used with great caution, if at all. In the meantime, information on the subject will be found in the more reliable though brief accounts in *Japanese and the Other Altaic Languages,* pp. 62 ff., and my monograph *'The Footprints of the Buddha': An Eighth-Century Old Japanese Poetic Sequence,* American Oriental Series, vol. 58 (New Haven: American Oriental Society, 1975), pp. 56 ff. On the implications and applications of such Japanese technical linguistic terms as *kigen, keitō,* and so on, see my paper "The Origins of Japanese," *Monumenta Nipponica* 29 (1974):93-102. The recent revival of interest in the issue of the "origin of language" properly so-called is described in Frits Staal, "Oriental Ideas on the Origin of Language," *Journal of the American Oriental Society* 99 (1979):1-14. Examples of Japanese scholars suggesting highly unlikely genetic relationships for the Japanese language are so numerous in the Japanese-language literature that one cannot even begin to cite representative examples; fortunately, few of these have yet to find their way into English or other Western-language translations, so they are little known outside Japan. Most active in this field over the past few years have been Gō Minoru and Nishida Tatsuo. Gō has published a large number of popular books and newspaper articles in which he professes to find "just the same words as Japanese" in obscure languages of the New Guinea region. Representative of his work is his paper "Nihongo wa doko kara kita ka—kita to minami kara mita Nihongo," in *Nihon Bunka no Genryū* (Tokyo: Shin-Jinbutsu Ōrai-sha, 1974), pp. 11-42; he has followed this with a large number of popular newspaper articles that will surely one day find their way into book form. Gō's work is distinguished by its unfamiliarity with the principles of historical linguistics, and by his totally unprincipled citation of linguistic forms from languages that are apparently as obscure to him as they are to his readers, since efforts to verify his citations from the sources that he claims to be employing are almost always futile. Nishida attempts to relate Japanese to the Tibeto-Burman language family; his work is distinguished by its extremely careless citation of Japanese forms and their meanings, as well as by its total disregard of the historical principle in linguistics. See my paper, "Is Tibetan Genetically Related to Japanese?" pp. 295-312, in *Proceedings of the Csoma de Kőrös Memorial Symposium Held at Mátrafüred, Hungary,* 24-30 September 1976, ed. L. Ligeti, Bibliotheca Orientalis Hungarica, vol. 23 (Budapest: Akadémiai Kiadó, 1978), for citations of Nishida's publications and a refutation of his views. The *locus classicus* for Bloomfield's perceptive remark concerning the difficulty in sticking to the study of language—that is, the subject matter of linguistics—is found in his *Language* (pp. 3-4).

Chapter 2

Fujioka's paper was originally published under the title "Nihongo no ichi," *Kokugaku'in Zasshi* 14, no. 8 (1908):1-9; no. 10 (1908):14-23; no. 11 (1908):12-20; like much academic publication in Japan at the time, it appeared in the form of a transcript of a public lecture. The scientific inutility of negative criteria such as constitute the major part of Fujioka's "articles" is discussed in my paper "The Origin of the Japanese Language," *Monumenta Nipponica* 26 (1971):455-69, and the arguments seconded by Murayama Shichirō, *Nihongo no kigen* (Tokyo: Kōbundō, 1973), p. 103. Anton Boller, "Nachweis, daß das Japanische zum ural-altaischen Stamme gehört," *Sitzungsberichte der philos.-histor. Classe der kais. Akademie der Wissenschaften, Wien* 23 (1857):393–481, is a paper that, in Japan at least, is cited rather more frequently than it is studied; examples of Japanese-Altaic etymologies original with Boller that are still perfectly sound, and that have been neglected by most of the scholars who have not taken the trouble to consult his monograph, are easy to identify—for example, for the negative-privative, Boller, p. 467, rediscovered in *Japanese and the Other Altaic Languages,* p. 13, and further vindicated by Menges, *Japanisch und Altajisch,* p. 99; so also Boller, p. 477, Menges, p. 121.

For the Mongolian and Turkic subgroups of Altaic, the student is excellently served by two reliable introductory treatments, both in English, that are at the same time original works of research that continue to serve the specialist in these areas: for Turkic, Karl H. Menges, *The Turkic Languages and Peoples: An Introduction to Turkic Studies,* and for Mongolian, Nicholas Poppe, *Introduction to Mongolian Comparative Studies,* Mémoires de la Société Finno-ougrienne, vol. 110 (Helsinki: Suomalais-Ugrilainen Seura, 1955). For Old Turkish, the only grammar written in English is Talât Tekin, *A Grammar of Orkhon Turkic,* Indiana University Publications, Uralic and Altaic Series, vol. 69 (Bloomington: Indiana University, 1968), but the work is unfortunately unreliable in many of its details, and should not be employed by the student who cannot at the same time consult the originals and secondary works in other European languages that Tekin cites, often incorrectly; for multiple examples of the unreliability of this source, particularly as they adversely affect a number of significant Turkic-Japanese comparisons, see Menges, *Japanisch und Altajisch,* pp. 64–65, 110–11, and passim: "Manche Lesungen und Übersetzungen sind bei T. Tekin überhaput falsch. . . ." Instead, even the elementary student must go directly to Annemarie von Gabain, *Alttürkische Grammatik, mit Bibliographie, Lesestücken und Wörterverzeichnis, auch Neutürkisch,* Porta Linguarum Orientalium, vol. 23 (Leipzig: Otto Harrassowitz, 1950), for the grammar, and to V. M. Nadeljaev et al., *Drevnetjurkskij slovar'* (Leningrad: Izdatel'stvo "Nauka," 1969), for the lexicon, of earlier forms of Turkic. For Old Mongolian, Nicholas Poppe, "Ancient Mongolian," in *Tractata Altaica, Festschrift Denis Sinor* (Wiesbaden: Otto Harrassowitz, 1976), pp. 463-78, is of great value. For the Tungusic subgroup, there are two important works in English, both by Karl H. Menges: "The Function and Origin of the Tungus Tense in *-ra* and Some Related Questions of Tungus Grammar," *Language* 19 (1943): 237-51, and "Problems of Tungus Linguistics," *Anthropos* 73 (1978):367-400. The first of these articles has particularly important data for the historical study of the relationship of Japanese to the Tungusic subgroup of Altaic, since the verb forms that Menges studied in that article have well-preserved and quite easily identified cognates in the Japanese verb. But neither of these papers is introductory in nature, and both presuppose considerable prior acquaintance with the Tungusic languages and the problems of their history. For such an introduction one must turn instead to Menges's book-length "article" entitled "Die tungusischen Sprachen," in *Handbuch der Orientalistik,* 1.5.3 (Leiden and Cologne: E. J. Brill, 1968), pp. 21-246. For the lexicon of the Tungusic languages, we are now well served by the long-awaited and extensive comparative-etymological dictionary under preparation by Soviet colleagues for many years, V. I. Cincius [Tsintsius], ed., *Sravnitel′nyj slovar′ tunguso-man′čžurskix jazykov: Materialy k ėtimologičeskomu slovarju,* 2 vols. (Leningrad: Izdatel′stvo "Nauka," 1975, 1977), which in the years ahead will tremendously facilitate all historical linguistic work involving the Tungusic languages, as well as the study of the Altaic languages in general. For the reconstruction of Proto-Tungus, a useful introduction is Johannes Benzing, "Die tungusischen Sprachen, Versuch einer vergleichenden Grammatik," *Abhandlungen der geistes- und sozialwissenschaftlichen Klasse, Akademie der Wissenschaften und der Literatur, Mainz* 11 (1955): 949-1099; of greater scientific value, but almost impossible to find today, is V. I. Cincius, *Sravnitel′naja fonetika tunguso-man′čžurskix jazykov* (Leningrad: Akademija Nauk, 1949). A representative Soviet reference work dealing with the Tungusic peoples of the U.S.S.R., M. G. Levin and L. P. Potapov, eds., *Narody Sibiri* (Moscow: Akademija Nauk, 1956), is easily accessible through the English translation by Scripta Technica, ed.

Stephen P. Dunn, *The Peoples of Siberia* (Chicago: University of Chicago Press, 1964); it contains a detailed map locating the Tungusic speakers who live in Soviet territory, and is of great value for archaeology and ethnology, but unfortunately hardly mentions linguistic data or questions. There is no really satisfactory treatment of Manchu available in any language, but an excellent dictionary has now appeared, Jerry Norman, *A Concise Manchu-English Lexicon* (Seattle: University of Washington Press, 1978). On the Jurchen language, the student must still begin with an old work, Wilhelm Grube, *Die Sprache und Schrift der Jučen* (Leipzig: Otto Harrassowitz, 1896, but also available in many subsequent reprintings in China and Japan ca. 1940), supplementing this with Karl H. Menges, "Die Sprache der Žürčen," in *Handbuch der Orientalistik*, 1.5.3, pp. 245-56. Unfortunately, the only study of this important language to appear in English, Gisaburo N. Kiyose, *A Study of the Jurchen Language and Script: Reconstruction and Decipherment* (Kyoto: Hōritsubunka-sha, 1977), is unreliable in almost every respect, and cannot be recommended.

The study of Korean as an Altaic language is somewhat more advanced than similar studies relating to Japanese; nevertheless these works, too, present special problems, and the literature can be used only with caution. Bruno Lewin, "Japanese and Korean: The Problems and History of a Linguistic Comparison," *Journal of Japanese Studies* 2 (1976):389-412, provides an excellent and reliable introduction to most of the questions in this field. Samuel E. Martin, "Lexical Evidence Relating Korean to Japanese," *Language* 42 (1966):185-251, was, at the time of its publication, an important advance in the field, but subsequent studies have shown that it cannot be followed in many of its details, particularly in its overliteral reconstruction of a Proto-Korean-Japanese linguistic unity. G. J. Ramstedt, *Studies in Korean Etymology*, remains basic and essential despite the many problems already alluded to above. Soviet colleagues are particularly apt to cite this source in an uncritical fashion—thus, for example, some of the articles in the *Sravnitel´nyj slovar´ tunguso-man´čžurskix jazykov,* cited above, must be treated with more than usual caution. Most of the lexical comparisons of Korean with other languages, including the major Altaic languages, are the original work of a Japanese scholar named Shiratori Kurakichi (1865-1942), and published by him, inter alia, in a series of articles in the journal *Tōyō Gakuhō*, vol. 4, nos. 2, 3, 5; vol. 5, nos. 1, 2, 3; vol. 6, nos. 2, 3, in the period 1914-16. These papers are now easily available, with some corrections of typographical errors that appeared in the original publication and useful indexes, in the *Shiratori Kurakichi zenshū*, vol. 3: *Chōsenshi kenkyū* (Tokyo: Iwanami shoten, 1970), pp. 1-280. It seems clear that Ramstedt had copies of Shiratori's papers, and that many of Shiratori's comparisons found their way into his notes, and from there into the *Studies in Korean Etymology*. Had Ramstedt lived to see his *Studies* through the press in the way he would have liked to do, there can be little question that he would have acknowledged the important role that Shiratori's work played in his studies. Lee Ki-moon, "A Comparative Study of Manchu and Korean," *Ural-altaische Jahrbücher* 30 (1958): 104-20, similarly puts Shiratori's work under heavy contribution; one searches with difficulty in Lee's paper for Korean-Manchu comparisons that were not first discovered by Shiratori.

The principal unresolved problem in the comparison of Korean with other languages, including Japanese, remains one of time-levels. Almost all comparisons undertaken to date have involved only modern Korean, or at the most the so-called Middle Korean, which is, however, only from the mid-fifteenth century, and so does not in most respects take us significantly further back into the internal linguistic history of the language than do the modern forms. Martin's "Lexical Evidence . . ." based its reconstructions on the comparison of modern Japanese forms with modern Korean, or in some cases with Middle Korean. Relating these comparisons to Old Japanese instead was done in my paper, "Old Japanese Phonology and the Korean-Japanese Relationship," *Language* 43 (1967):278-302. The Old Korean written records, while available in considerable quantity, present more formidable philological problems than are encountered in any other branch of Altaic, and it has taken longer to approach the question of the genetic relationship of Korean directly from the evidence that survives for Old Korean. A beginning is now at last being made; see my two papers, "Some Old Paekche Fragments," *Journal of Korean Studies* 1 (1979):3-69, and "Old

Korean and Altaic," *Ural-Altaische Jahrbücher* 51 (1979):1-54, where for the first time Old Korean linguistic evidence is employed on the historical-comparative level.

The student interested in the Uralic languages and their comparison will be well served by Björn Collinder, *An Introduction to the Uralic Languages* (Berkeley and Los Angeles: University of California Press, 1965).

Chapter 3

This account of the earliest Altaic migrations is heavily in debt to the work of Karl H. Menges; see in particular the relevant passages in his *Turkic Languages and Peoples,* especially pp. 16 ff. More on the problems of the Tungusic migrations in particular will be found in the same scholar's monograph *Tungusen und Ljao,* Abhandlungen für die Kunde des Morgenlandes, vol. 38, part 1 (Wiesbaden: Franz Steiner, 1968). Karl Jettmar, "Zum Problem der tungusischen 'Urheimat,'" *Wiener Beiträge zur Kulturgeschichte und Linguistik* 8 (1952):484-511, has relatively little to contribute, but is worth noting since it is still virtually the only specialized "Urheimat" study in the field. Menges's great contribution to the solution of this question lies in his suggestion of a succession of early homelands, elaborated upon in the text. The attempt of earlier scholars to select a single site produces more problems than it solves; thus, Ramstedt, *Einführung. . .,* 1:15, placed the Altaic "Urheimat" in the "Hingangebirge," that is, the Hsing-an (Xīng-ān 興 安) mountain range that reaches from Inner Mongolia into northern Manchuria (cf. Menges, *Turkic Languages and Peoples,* pp. 55-56; Murayama Shichirō, *Nihongo no tanjō* [Tokyo: Chikuma shobō, 1979], pp. 10-11).

The discussion of the historical implications of the various words for "one" and other number words refutes the views of Gerhard Doerfer, *Türkische und mongolische Elemente im Neupersischen, unter besonderer Berücksichtigung älterer neupersischer Geschichtsquellen, vor allem der Mongolen- und Timuridenzeit,* Akademie der Wissenschaften und der Literatur, Veröffentlichungen der Orientalischen Kommission, 4 vols. (Wiesbaden: Franz Steiner, 1963-75), 1:80 ff. Doerfer would find in the data cited an argument against, rather than for, the genetic relationship of the Altaic languages. The numbers have some-times, even before Doerfer, mistakenly been used as material for arguments against the genetic relationship of the Altaic lan-guages; one important result of the introduction of Japanese materials onto the scene of Altaic historical-linguistic studies has been the demonstration of how the numerals in the various languages, including Japanese and Korean, provide important evidence for the earliest historical connections of all these lan-guages; on this, cf. *Japanese and the Other Altaic Languages,* § 5.3, pp. 219 ff.; Menges, *Central Asiatic Journal* 18 (1974): 197-98; and Menges, *Japanisch und Altajïsch,* pp. 92-96.

Similarly, the treatment of the words for "a stone, a rock" in the various languages refutes the views of A. Róna-Tas, "Obščeje nasledije ili zaimstvovanija? (k probleme rodstva altajskix jazykov)," *Voprosy Jazykoznanija,* 1974, no. 2, pp. 31-45, particularly p. 33, and also corrects Mongolian forms and their meanings that he there gives incorrectly. Róna-Tas argues that since "Mo. *körü*" (an incorrect form) and Mo. *čilaγun* "both mean the same thing"—and they do not—it must necessarily follow that the second of these Mongolian forms is an old borrowing into Mongolian from Turkic, where the word supposed to account for Mo. *čilaγun* is none other than Tk. *tāš*. That such concatenations of erroneous data and faulty logic have made a favorable impression in certain quarters (e.g., Larry V. Clark, *Journal of the American Oriental Society* 98 [1978]: 143, who there refers to the "high level" of such argumentation; or by the same author, "Mongol Elements in Old Turkic?" *Journal de la Société Finno-ougrienne* 75 [1977]:129, who there invokes the Róna-Tas argumentation as if it were an automatic rule that mechanically determines what is and what is not a loanword) only demonstrates vividly how much basic work remains to be done in the field of Altaic historical linguistics. All the Tungusic citations for "stone" are collected conveniently in Cincius, *Sravnitel´nyj slovar´,* 1:263b, s. v. *žolo I;* they include Ev. *ǰolo* "large stone, boulder," Lam. *ǰōl* "stone," and Goldi *ǰolo* "id." The details of the historical relationship of the Japanese word *ishi* to the Altaic root in question are somewhat more involved than the presentation in the text implies; for an account of the

[194]

rest of the relevant evidence, and in particular for an explanation of the relationship of the Proto-Tungusic *-ō- vowel in the first syllable of these words to the Japanese forms, see my remarks in "Old Korean and Altaic," *Ural-Altaische Jahrbücher* 51 (1979): 40, note 160.

The scientific literature on the reconstruction and significance of the two Proto-Altaic *l_2 and *r_2 phonemes is enormous, with important contributions in almost every language except Japanese; a good introduction for the student is Eric P. Hamp, "The Altaic Non-obstruents," in *Researches in Altaic Languages*, ed. L. Ligeti, Bibliotheca Orientalis Hungarica, vol. 20 (Budapest: Akadémiai Kiadó, 1975), pp. 67-70.

The importance of the original Altaic system of secondary verb-stem derivation for the history of Japanese was first recognized, and explored in a preliminary fashion, by Haguenauer, *Origines de la civilisation japonaise . . .*, pp. 503 ff., in a section entitled, "Examen comparé de certains suffixes dérivatifs du japonais." But Japanese scholars for their part have neglected this important source of information for the prehistory of the language; even synchronic accounts of the system of derivation involved are all but lacking, with the possible exception of Yoshida Kanehiko, *Nihongo gogengaku no hōhō* (Tokyo: Taishūkan, 1976), from which some information on the system may be gleaned, especially his § 2, pp. 85 ff. But the standard Japanese works on derivation and morphology, such as Sakakura Atsuyoshi, *Gokōzō no kenkyū* (Tokyo: Kadokawa shoten, 1966), do not even mention the subject. The original Altaic system was first studied and reconstructed—apart from the light that the Japanese and Korean evidence can now shed on it—by G. J. Ramstedt, "Zur Verbstammbildungslehre der mongolisch-türkischen Sprachen," *Journal de la Société Finno-ougrienne* 28, no. 3 (1912):1-86. Recent important contributions by Nicholas Poppe have further clarified the reconstruction, and in particular amplified the part that Tungusic materials play in it; see, for example, "Über einige Verbalstammbildungssuffixe in den altaischen Sprachen," *Orientalia Suecana* (Uppsala) 21 (1972):119-41. To date, little has been published on the Japanese reflexes of this system, apart from my article "The Origin of the Japanese Language," *The Japan Foundation Newsletter*

6, no. 6 (February-March 1979):6-12. On the Japanese evidence
for original Altaic *-l-* and *-r-* suffixes to secondary verbs, see
my paper, "Nani ga Nihongo no keitō wo fumei ni shita no ka?"
Gekkan Gengo 6, no. 9 (1977):76-81, 109, and "Some Old
Paekche Fragments," *Journal of Korean Studies* 1 (1979):58.

The pseudo-scientific techniques of "glottochronology"
and "lexicostatistics" continue to enjoy great popularity in
Japan, despite the curious fact that what is probably the most
convincing single refutation of both these ideas is the work of a
Japanese scholar, Izui Hisanosuke, "Sūri to iwayuru gengo
nendairon no yūkōsei ni tsuite," in his volume *Gengo no kōzō*
(Tokyo: Kiinokuniya shoten, 1967), pp. 153-74. Equally conclusive are the remarks in L. Ligeti, "La théorie altaïque et la lexico-
statistique," in *Researches in Altaic Languages,* ed. Ligeti, pp.
99-115.

Further details for all the comparisons of Japanese words
with other Altaic cognates presented in this section, including
other Altaic forms and complete references to the specialized
literature in which all non-Japanese forms here cited may be
verified as to form and meaning, are found in my paper "The
Relevance of Historical Linguistics for Japanese Studies," *Journal
of Japanese Studies* 2 (1976):376-78, where additional etymologies of the same type will also be found.

On the etymological sources of the Japanese plural in
-ra, see Menges, "Die tungusischen Sprachen," pp. 57-58, and
Turkic Languages and Peoples, p. 111. The original Altaic language
was rich in plural markers, one of which was the *-l-* that is preserved in Japanese *-ra,* and which also gave Proto-Tungusic *-l*
plurals. The same suffix also survives in Turkic, but there it is
generally in the form of a compound suffix *-l-ar,* where the
final *-ar* continues an inherited Altaic collective suffix.

On the Tungusic aorists in original *-ra-* and *-rĭ-*, the
first important contribution, and still one of the most important articles in the entire field, is Karl H. Menges, "The Function
and Origin of the Tungus Tense in *-ra,*" *Language* 19 (1943):
237-51, now to be supplemented by many passages in his "Die
tungusischen Sprachen." Additional important data on these
forms are found in brief presentation in Murayama Shichirō,
"Tungusica-Japonica," *Ural-Altaische Jahrbücher* 48 (1976):

186-87, and in fuller detail in his book *Nihongo keitō no tankyū* (Tokyo: Taishūkan shoten, 1978), pp. 259-92, where the importance of these forms for the history of the Japanese verb is further explored. These Tungusic forms also provide important clues for associating the verb classes of the traditional Japanese school grammar with their Altaic origins, as explained in my paper "Altaic Origins of the Japanese Verb Classes," now in the press for publication in May 1980, in *Bono Homini Donum: Essays on Historical Linguistics in Memory of J. Alexander Kerns,* eds., Yoël Arbeitman and Allan R. Bomhard (Amsterdam: John Benjamins). One important contribution in Japanese on this subject ought not to be overlooked, Yamamoto Kengo, "Tsungūsu-Mōko shogo ni okeru meishi gokan keisei gobi *-ri* ni tsuite," *Gengo Kenkyū* 14 (1949):49-62, an unhappy reminder of what this exceptionally capable scholar might have accomplished in the field of Altaic studies had he lived longer.

More on the "nomadize" words can be found in Poppe, *Vergleichende Grammatik,* pp. 38, 139 (cf. also the reconstruction in Street, *On the Lexicon . . .,* p. 20), and, with all relevant Tungusic forms, in Cincius, *Sravnitel´nyj slovar´ . . .,* 1:609b-610b, s. v. *nulgī.*

A useful and reliable introduction to the problems of prehistory and archaeology for the student of the questions here under consideration is provided in Richard Pearson, "The Contribution of Archaeology to Japanese Studies," *Journal of Japanese Studies* 2 (1976):305-33. Newspaper accounts of the excavation of the Lake Nojiri Venus figure are found in the *Asahi Evening News,* March 29, 1975; *Japan Times,* March 30, 1975; *Mainichi Shinbun,* March 31, 1975; and the *Kyoto Shinbun* (evening edition), April 17, 1975.

In general, the account in the text at this point is heavily in debt to Kamaki Yoshimasa, "Kyūsekki jidairon," in *Iwanami Kōza, Nihon Rekishi, 1, Genshi oyobi Kodai, 1* (Tokyo: Iwanami shoten, 1975), pp. 35-74, especially his pp. 48 ff. and pp. 67 ff. On the "comb-pattern pottery" and its importance, much use has been made of Tanabe Shōzō, *Nazo no joō, Himiko, Yamataikoku to sono jidai,* 2d ed. (Tokyo: Tokuma shoten, 1974), especially pp. 142 ff. The Japanese scholars rarely attempt to correlate linguistic data with findings from other disciplines; this makes the contribution by Tokugawa Munemasa, "Tōzai no kotobaarasoi," in *Nihongo no Rekishi, Nihongo Kōza,* ed. Sakakura Atsuyoshi (Tokyo: Taishūkan shoten, 1977), pp. 243-86, particularly welcome, despite its inconclusive nature. Most useful of all in its deft combination of linguistic evidence with the findings of prehistory and archaeology, and highly recommended to the student, is Richard Pearson, "Japan, Korea, and China: The Problem of Defining Continuities," *Asian Perspectives* 19, no. 1 (1978):176-89.

On the importance of the words for "catching fish," cf. Menges, *Japanisch und Altajisch,* p. 53: " . . . sozusagen als das ῡš/īš der Ur-Japaner κατ ' 'εξοχ ήν." The Turkic forms are found in Martti Räsänen, *Versuch eines etymologischen Wörterbuchs der Türksprachen,* Lexica Societatis Fenno-ugricae, vol. 17, part 1 (Helsinki: Suomalais-Ugrilainen Seura, 1969), p. 174b. The Korean etymology is due to Ramstedt (cited in Räsänen); the entry in *Studies in Korean Etymology,* p. 69, s.v. *il* ("see *nil"*), is an error, corrected by Pentti Aalto in *Studies in Korean Etymology,* vol. 2, Mémoires de la Société Finno-ougrienne, vol. 95, part 2 (Helsinki: Suomalais-Ugrilainen Seura, 1953), p. 57, and again in his "Additional Korean Etymologies," p. 9, with references in both instances to further literature. *Japanese and the Other Altaic Languages,* p. 121, was less than precise about the forms and meanings of the word in Old Japanese; the language had a doublet, with both *izar-* "to catch fish at sea," and *azar-* "to catch, gather seafood" being attested. The first of these two forms was specialized for the activities of human beings, while the second was also employed in reference to animals searching for food for themselves or their young. The two forms are related by the so-called *i*-breaking phenomenon, as correctly explained by N. A. Syromjatnikov, "O perelome glasnyx *i* i *ï* v japonskom jazyke," *Voprosy Japonskoj Filologii* 2 (1973): 107 (and several of his other papers, cited inter alia, in my "Wissenschaftliche Nachrichten," *Zeitschrift der Deutschen Morgenländischen Gesellschaft* 126 [1976] :*69*, note 13), though Syromjatnikov did not recognize the correct Altaic etymology of this word. Internal linguistic evidence in Japanese shows that of this doublet, it is the *izar-* form that is linguistically "older," both because of the "unbroken *i*" in the first syllable

and because of the -z-, which the other, later form shifted analogically to -s- (or one could say, preserved unchanged as -s-). But
it is important to note that here "older" is a technical linguistic
term, referring to the relative chronological levels of the various
portions of this form in historical-comparative terms; both words
"coexisted" in the Old Japanese language at the same historical
period.

Old Silla *isi* "moss, lichen" is attested in a gloss to the
Samguk Sagi, a text of 1145, chapter 44, p. 445, in the edition
of the Chōsen Shigakkai (Seoul: Chikazawa shoten, 1941).
Manchu *nisi.kte* is surely a cognate Tungusic form, but it must
be a loan into Manchu from some other Tungusic language (even
though no other Tungusic forms are registered, e.g., Cincius,
Sravnitel´nyj slovar´. . ., 1:600b), since the inherited form in
Manchu for the Proto-Tungusic suffix **-kta* would be Ma. -ha/
-ho/ -he (Benzing, "Die tungusischen Sprachen," §80, p. 1020).
Otto Karow, *"sŭ yŭ, sŭ yuē* in der altajapanischen Literatur:
Hochsprache und Mundarten der Naraperiode," *Monumenta
Nipponica* 6 (1943): 164-65, studies the earliest Japanese attes-
tation for the word *nori* in a most useful fashion; this is now
available in the reprinted volume of this scholar's work, *Otto
Karow Opera Minora, Zum 65. Geburtstag des Verfassers aus-
gewählt und eingeleitet von Hans Adalbert Dettmer und Gerhild
Endreß* (Wiesbaden: Otto Harrassowitz, 1978), pp. 174-75.

On the Sobata site, see *Nihon no reimei* (Kyoto: Kokuritsu
Hakubutsukan, 1974), p. 24, and also the chronological chart
for Mid-Jōmon, p. 139. For the most recent Korean finds of
comb-pattern pottery sites, see Mikami Tsugio, "Chōsen hantō
no kōkogaku, Sengo no chōsa wo chūshin to shite," pp. 453-67
in *Nihon kōkogaku no genjō to kadai,* ed. Nihon Rekishi Gakkai,
(Tokyo: Yoshikawa Kōbunkan, 1974), especially the list of
sites at his pp. 454-55, with references there to the relevant
Korean publications. Note also that several Japanese reference
handbooks and other sources prefer to read the name of the
Kyushu site as "Sohata," though "Sobata" has become standard
in the Western-language literature. The shell mound in question
is located near the modern town of Uto, which is near Kumamoto
City in modern Kumamoto Prefecture. With particular reference
to the comb-pattern pottery *(kushigaki renjōmon, kushimemon*

doki, or *kushigakimon doki),* and especially identifying the Korean counterpart wares for the comb-pattern objects from Sobata-type sites in Kyushu, see Pearson, "Contribution of Archaeology," p. 317 and pp. 328-29, his Fig. 1, "Comparative sequence of ceramic forms in Kyūshū and the Korean Peninsula: Jōmon and Comb Pattern"; Pearson, "Japan, Korea, and China," p. 181 (the Korean influence on Sobata pottery); and Pearson, "Paleoenvironment and Human Settlement in Japan and Korea," *Science* 197 (23 September 1977):1239-46, especially p. 1240, where he describes "close similarities between the Early Jomon incised pottery of the Sobata type of Kyushu and the incised pottery of Korea of the same age (roughly 4000 to 3000 B.C.) which is termed Comb Pattern or Geometric," in conjunction with "the development of increased fishing activities [that] may have stimulated movement between Kyushu and Korea," after the Jōmon marine transgression reduced the amount of low-lying land and altered coastlines, leading to more intensive subsistence patterns to maintain food levels on less territory, and to the dislocation and migration of populations as a result. "In summary, it is proposed that incised pottery of the comb-pattern or Sobata type, polished black pottery, and plain pottery are all cases of diffused stylistic categories of material culture, which meet descriptive and distributional criteria of similarity and can be said to represent genetic cultural connections between the Japanese islands and the Korean peninsula" (Pearson, "Japan, Korea, and China," p. 185). In the same passage, Pearson continues as follows: "If I might be granted one last idle speculation [why idle? RAM], I would suggest that the Liaoning-Manchurian area may be the area of 'linguistic symbiosis' postulated by Miller (1967:45-47) [an error for 1971:45-47, and a reference to a passage in *Japanese and the Other Altaic Languages,* RAM], between Northern and Peninsular Altaic languages." It is gratifying to find this overall correlation between independently evolved linguistic data on the one hand and archaeological findings on the other; taken together, the force of conviction carried by the total is considerably more than the simple sum of the parts. Archaeological evidence also provides data substantiating the thesis of successive waves of multiple migrations or invasions advanced in the text: "It could be stated that the transfer of incised pottery took place in the 4th millennium, that of black polished ceramics in the 2nd and early 1st millennia, and that of plain coarse pottery in the latter half of the last millennium" (Pearson, p. 185)—precisely the kind of scenario that is postulated in the text for the transmission of Altaic linguistic forms. I have also to acknowledge here the considerable assistance received in connection with my understanding of the Sobata site and the importance of its type of ware in the course of a conversation with Professor J. Edward Kidder in Tokyo on October 20, 1977, following the delivery of this lecture.

On the Turkic developments of Proto-Altaic *-d-, see Menges, *Turkic Languages and Peoples,* pp. 87-91; on Chuvash -r- for *-d- (the so-called Chuvash "rhotacism"), p. 97, where Japanese *yar-* "give" provides yet another example of a Japanese version of this same special Chuvash development (cf. "Old Korean and Altaic," *Ural-Altaische Jahrbücher* 51 [1979]:51, note 183); more on the same sets of changes in Ramstedt, *Einführung . . .,* 1:21-22 and 1.87.

On Proto-Altaic *padâk and the various attested forms that underlie this reconstruction, see Street, *On the Lexicon . . .,* p. 22; Poppe, *Vergleichende Grammatik . . .,* pp. 52, 124; Ramstedt, *Einführung . . .,* 1:52, 1:130; Ramstedt, *Studies in Korean Etymology,* pp. 180-81; Cincius, *Sravnitel'nyj slovar'. . .,* 2:318a-b, where the Tungusic forms now brought together, e.g., Ev. *āt* "root, base (of a mountain, of a word, etc.)," clarify the query concerning the nature of the Tungusic evidence for this root earlier expressed by Aalto in a footnote to Ramstedt's *Einführung . . .,* 1:52 (the meanings of the Tungusic cognates fit in with the sense of the word as reconstructed for the Altaic linguistic unity). Typical Turkic forms showing representative developments of *-d- include Uig. *adak,* MTk. *aδak,* and modern Tk. *ayak* "foot, leg" (these and others in Räsänen, *Versuch . . .,* p. 5a). The final velar of these and other Turkic forms is a suffix for deriving deverbal nouns (Menges, *Turkic Languages and Peoples,* p. 162), hence its lack of correspondence in Chuvash, and in some of the other languages, including Japanese, should occasion no particular surprise; it would also be possible, perhaps preferable, to write the Proto-Altaic reconstruction without this final *-k, simply as *padâ, and in a sense the final *-k of

[201]

padák overweights the form in the direction of a portion of the Turkic evidence. From this it also follows that the roots that we reconstruct such as **ayu-*, **ari-*, **aru-* might just as well be termed verbal roots; but at the stage to which these reconstructions relate, a distinction between nominal and verbal roots is without significance, particularly in the Tungusic subgroup of Altaic. More on this is found in Menges, "Problems of Tungus Linguistics," pp. 371, 373-74, and especially pp. 389-90; Menges, "Die tungusischen Sprachen," p. 79 and passim. This is the feature for which Murayama Shichirō uses the symbol ±; for example, in his *Nihongo keitō no tankyū,* pp. 261, 268, and passim, the plus sign for noun stems or roots, the minus for verbs, but the combination (plus-minus) for that early stage of Altaic, particularly of Tungusic, where the distinction appears to be without significance, in contrast with its later striking nature in Turkic and Mongolian, particularly in the former.

Amateurs of linguistic comparison who confuse the "meaning" of forms with their translation-glosses are well illustrated by Gerhard Doerfer, for example, in his *Türkische und mongolische Elemente im Neupersischen,* where innumerable ex cathedra etymological judgments are based on nothing more substantial than his lack of understanding of this simple principle; in vol. 3, p. 646, of this work one finds a typical example, involving the semantics of **padák* and related terms in Altaic. Poppe, *Central Asiatic Journal* 12 (1968):157, effectively refutes Doerfer's views, showing in the process that they are not only based on a misunderstanding of the process of historical linguistic comparison but also unfairly misrepresent the views of earlier, and better informed, scholars.

Old Japanese *kuzi* "chestnut" is registered in a *Fudoki* fragment cited and studied in Karow, "Hochsprache und Mundarten . . .," pp. 153, 168 (or in the reprint volume, pp. 163, 178); it is sad commentary on the present state of Japanese lexicography that this account by a German scholar of the previous generation appears to be the only place this important form has been registered, or discussed in the literature. On the importance of the chestnut *(Castanea)* for the early Japanese food economy, see Pearson, "Paleoenvironment and Human Settlement," especially pp. 1240-41, where he shows that although *Castanea* became more important as the Yayoi cultivators took charge of the Japanese ecology, the species itself was already a part of the pre-Yayoi-settlement forest vegetation. Further important data on the role of *Castanea* in early Japan is in Richard and Kazue Pearson, "Some Problems in the Study of Jomon Subsistence," *Antiquity* 52 (1978):21-27, with references to the literature establishing *Castanea* as one of the major Jōmon subsistence plants. On the question of early Japanese names for nut-bearing trees, the note by Karl H. Menges, *Ural-Altaische Jahrbücher* 49 (1977):165, is of considerable value.

On the Old Paekche language, see "Some Old Paekche Fragments" and "Old Korean and Altaic," cited above.

The question of the relationship of Korean *mal* and Japanese *masu* was first discussed in the *Journal of Japanese Studies* 2 (1976):349-51, but this is now to be restudied in view of the further discussion in the *Ural-Altaische Jahrbücher* 51 (1979):48.

The words for "bird" and "chicken" are comprehensively studied in another often overlooked paper by Otto Karow, "Der Ursprung des Torii," now available in the *Opera Minora* reprint volume, pp. 82-83. The Proto-Turkic reconstruction is from Doerfer, *Türkische und mongolische Elemente im Neupersischen*, 2:482-83, Abs. 887. On the etymology of Japanese *yak-* and *tak-*, the explanation of the text is now to be preferred to that earlier proposed in *Japanese and the Other Altaic Languages*, pp. 90 ff.

For an introduction to the question of Malayo-Polynesian elements in Japanese, the student will be well served by Murayama Shichirō, "The Malayo-Polynesian Component in the Japanese Language," *Journal of Japanese Studies* 2 (1976):413-36. This prolific scholar has in recent years published a veritable series of books devoted to the study and identification of the Malayo-Polynesian elements in Japanese, not to mention many shorter articles and contributions that cannot be listed here; his major books on this subject include the following: (1) with Ōbayashi Taryō, *Nihongo no kigen* (Tokyo: Kōbundō, 1973); (2) *Nihongo no gogen* (Tokyo: Kōbundō, 1974); (3) *Nihongo no kenkyū hōhō* (Tokyo: Kōbundō, 1974); (4) *Kokugogaku no genkai* (Tokyo: Kōbundō, 1975); (5) *Nihongo keitō no tankyū* (Tokyo: Taishūkan shoten, 1978); (6) *Nihongo no tanjō* (Tokyo: Chikuma shobō, 1979); (7) with Kokubu Naoichi, *Genshi Nihongo to minzoku bunka* (Tokyo: San'ichi shobō, 1979). All these are important to the student of this problem; fortunately—and unlike most Japanese scholarly publications—they include indexes of forms cited and studied, which greatly facilitate their use. The reconstruction of Proto-Malayo-Polynesian was principally accomplished by Otto Dempwolff, in his *Vergleichende Lautlehre des austronesischen Wortschatzes,* published between 1934 and 1939 as vols. 15, 17, and 19 of the *Zeitschrift für Eingeborenen-Sprachen,* Berlin. The student will find a recent treatment in English, Otto Christian Dahl, *Proto-Austronesian,* Scandinavian Institute of Asian Studies, Monograph Series no. 15, 2d rev. ed. (Lund: Studentlitteratur, 1977), to be a very useful introduction to the subject, as well as providing reliable information about progress in the field since Dempwolff's original reconstruction. For Murayama's most recent affirmation of the essentially Altaic nature of Japanese, over and above the Malayo-Polynesian elements that he has specialized in studying, see his *Nihongo keitō no tankyū,* pp. 291-92.

The etymology of Proto-Altaic *sil_2 is discussed in *Japanese and the Other Altaic Languages,* p. 119.

The etymology for Japanese *kani* "crab" in the text is original with John Street (personal communication, March 19, 1975), and will eventually be further treated by him in a forthcoming number of *Altaic Elements in Old Japanese.* Turkic data for this etymology are from Räsänen, *Versuch . . .,* p. 251b.

A selection of E. D. Polivanov's important papers, including much of his pioneering work on the history and genetic relationship of Japanese, was published following his posthumous political rehabilitation in the USSR under the title *Statʾi po obščej jazykoznaniju* (Moscow: Akademija Nauk, 1968). A more useful volume for the student of Japanese is the translation by Murayama Shichirō of all of Polivanov's significant contributions on Japanese, entitled *Nihongo kenkyū* (Tokyo: Kōbundō, 1976). An English version, somewhat indifferent in quality of translation, of the Moscow volume was published by Mouton (The Hague, 1968), under the title *Articles on General Linguistics,* Janua Linguarum, Series Major, vol. 72.

Contemporary Japanese interest in Japanese as a "mixed

language" is difficult to evaluate. In Western linguistic science such concerns would have to be expressed today in terms of what are generally called "pidgins" and "creoles." The term *Mischsprache* was originally associated with pidgin and creole studies by Hugo Schuchardt (1842-1927), but no longer has any significant currency in linguistic science, except in Japan. Elsewhere the consensus is that it is races that end up mixed, not languages. A number of essays in *Pidginization and Creolization of Languages,* ed. Dell Hymes (London: Cambridge University Press, 1971), may be recommended to the student interested in this question. Especially relevant to the question of Japanese as a "mixed language" in the historical sense (all languages are "mixed" at any given stage, including the present) is David Decamp, "Introduction: The Study of Pidgin and Creole Languages," in Hymes, pp. 13-39, particularly for its demonstration of the ways in which pidgin and creole studies cast considerable doubt on the concepts of "basic vocabulary" and the technique of glottochronology, and also for pointing out that "there is no way of knowing whether a language of unknown history has ever passed through the pidgin-creole cycle" (p. 25). This remains the unsolved crux of attempts in Japan to explain the history of Japanese entirely in terms of a "mixed language": attempts to argue that Japanese has "a pidgin in its past" (Franklin C. Southworth, "Detecting Prior Creolization," in Hymes, p. 270) are necessarily circular in that they employ the assumption of prior pidginization-creolization in order to explain the unknown history—unknown to those who would see in Japanese a "mixed language"—of Japanese, whereas it is only in cases where earlier linguistic history is securely attested that assumptions concerning pidginization and creolization can be made. Revaluation of contemporary Japanese scholarly interest in Japanese as a "mixed language" in terms of current pidgin and creole studies remains a pressing task for linguistic science.

Chapter 4

Egami's views are easily scrutinized in an English version, "The Formation of the People and the Origin of the State in Japan," *Memoirs of the Tōyō Bunko* 23 (1964):35-70, which accurately reproduces the argumentation of his widely read book on the subject, Egami Namio, *Kiba minzoku kokka, Nihon kodaishi e no apurōchi,* Chūkō shinsho, vol. 147 (Tokyo: Chūō Kōronsha, 1967; 24th printing of 1973). Summations of Egami's arguments are found in the English text, pp. 51 ff., and in the Japanese original, pp. 171-73. Representative examples of Egami's neglect of linguistic data, as well as his mangling of what linguistic evidence he does attempt to introduce, will be found in the English text, pp. 40, 56, among many others, and in the Japanese original, pp. 210, 221, 222, and passim. In the former, for example, we are told that "some words signifying 'rice plant', such as *nep, ni,* and *nun,* in the languages spoken by the Indo-Chinese peoples who are supposed to have inhabited South China before the moving in of the Chinese, bear some phonetic similarity to the Japanese *ine"* (p. 40); furthermore, "in all these cases words which are difficult to understand as Japanese are readily and rationally understandable as Korean" (p. 56). Gari Ledyard, "Galloping Along with the Horseriders: Looking for the Founders of Japan," *Journal of Japanese Studies* 1 (1975):217-54, makes valiant efforts toward salvaging what there is to be saved of the Egami hypothesis; but since Ledyard himself is the first to admit (p. 220, note 9) that he does not know what is meant by "linguistic evidence," he is unable to do anything with or to this Achilles' heel of Egami's argumentation.

On the possibility of a Tibeto-Burman genetic relationship of the Japanese language, and Nishida Tatsuo's studies in that connection, see the citation above.

The *kotodama* phenomenon is treated—but apart from its involvement with questions of the genetic relationship of the language—in my article "The 'Spirit' of the Japanese Language," *Journal of Japanese Studies* 3 (1977):251-98.

Large numbers of original etymologies between Turkic and Japanese are suggested in E. Azerbajev, "Nekotoryje voprosy japonsko-tjurkskix jazykovyx svjazej," *Izvestija AN Kaz. SSSR, Serija Filologičeskaja* 4 (1974):42-48.

A single Japanese scholar has apparently seen Menges, *Japanisch und Altajisch* (cited in *Journal of Japanese Studies* 4 [1978] :432), but he does not comment on its contents.

Index

GENERAL

Abbreviations, 87n
Active. *See* Verbs
Agriculture, 118
Altai Mountains, 55
Altaic languages, 37, 63, 88; original homeland of, 37, 48-58, 69, 76, 132; linguistic diversity in, 49-52; second homeland of, 54-56, 58, 63, 70-71, 75, 79, 92-95, 98-99, 101-2, 112, 116-17, 133; numbers in, 58-68; transitive, intransitive in, 85; recovery of common vocabulary of, 85; plurals, 88; major dispersal of, 133; comparative historical phonology of, 135

—lexical evidence: for original language, 99-100; for "nomadize," 100-101; for "work; fishing," 113-14; for "moss, lichen," 115-16
—linguistic unity: favoring of internal variants in, 93-94; and time limits of comparative method, 108; secondary stages of attested in later languages, 136
—original language: general, 65, 94, 97; derivation of secondary verbs, 80-85; special relationship to Tungusic, 98-103; doublets in, 99-100; recovery of meaning in, 100-101; earliest

[207]

80, 82-83; factitives, 83; voicing in Japanese with *-l-*, 83-84; analogical formations, 84; transitive-intransitive contrast, 85; term, 89; assimilations, 91; conditional, 91; imperfect, 91; negatives, 91; phonetic changes in, 92. *See also* Nouns, deverbal

Vocabulary: recovery of common Altaic, 85; additions to, 97; evidence for multiple invasions, 134

Voice. *See* Verbs

Voicing: *-s-* > *-z-* with *-l-*, 83, 113-14, 161

Volga River, 53

Writing system, of Japanese, 176

Written records: earliest Japanese, 4-5; limitations of, 12; invention of, 24; in China, 25, 158; earliest Altaic, 39-42; Japanese, 41,

72, 75-76, 81, 175; Korean, 41, 151-52; comparative method and, 43-44; distinct from reconstructions, 69; Japanese and Korean, 72; and terminology for periods of linguistic history, 87n; in establishing borrowings, 96; and carbon-14 dating, 120; and transition from Yayoi, 126; in application of comparative method to Romance, 149; problem of absence of early examples, 153; and Japanese numbers, 158-59

Yamato River, 129

Yayoi period, 118, 125-26, 173; term, 125; transition, 126-28; Bronze Age and, 127; Middle Yayoi, 128-30, 133; comb-pattern pottery intrusion, 128-29, 133. *See also* Ceramics

Yodo River, 129

JAPANESE AND KOREAN

This portion of the index registers only those Japanese and Korean lexical elements (words, roots, and bound suffixes) that are discussed etymologically in the text; additional Japanese and Korean words, including technical terms, that are discussed in other connections are entered in the general index above. In the text Japanese forms are romanized in several ways in order to reflect different historical stages of the language, according to the point under discussion in a given passage. In this index all Japanese forms that have survived down into the modern language (New Japanese) have been uniformly romanized in the Hepburn system, but a few Old Japanese forms that have not so survived are entered here in the usual romanization of Old Japanese, and are marked (OJ). The Korean forms in this index are modern (New Korean) except for those marked Middle (MK) or Old (OK).

Japanese

Index

sak- "split into two," 84
sak- "bloom," 91
saka "an incline," 83
sakar- "defy," 83
sakar- "be split apart," 84
sakat- "to butcher," 84
sakura "cherry blossoms," 92
shik- "moisten," 87
shik(k)o "urine," 87
shimo "frost," 88
shir- "know," 82
shiragah- "do something in a way to
  be noticed," 82-83
shirake- "sober up," 82
shiri "buttocks," 87
shita "below," 82, 85
shitagah- "follow upon," 85
shitak- "tread underfoot," 82
sisi (OJ) "meat," 158
sugur- "pluck off," 82

tab- "eat," 87
tadu (OJ) "crane," 139
tagir- "boil, churn," 84
tagit- "rushes, boils up," 84
tak- "burn," 157, 203
taka "high," 83
takar- "be(come) high," 83

taki "cascade," 84
tar- "be sufficient," 85
tas- "fill up," 85
toki "crested ibis," 155-56
tori "bird," 155-56
tsugar- "attach," 83
tsuk- "be exhausted," 84
tsuka "haft," 83
tsukar- "be exhausted," 84
tsukarakas- "make to be exhausted," 84
tsuna "rope," 83
tsunag- "pursue quarry," 83
tsuru "crane," 139

una "nape," 83
unag- "wear at throat, neck," 83
ura "bottom, inside; sole," 137-38

wak- "be separate," 83
wakar- "become separate," 84
wakat- "break apart," 84
wana "noose," 82
wanak- "throttle," 82
wi- (OJ) "be," 87

yak- "bake," 157, 203
yar- "give," 201

Korean

achim "morning," 152-53

īl "job, work," 113
is (MK) "moss," 115
isi (OK-Silla) "moss," 199

kŏi "crab," 161-62

mal "a measure," 154-55
mŏki- "keep animals,"100
mul "water," 82

mulk- "be watery," 82

noh- "set free," 100

patak "bottom; sole," 137

sam "hemp," 152

talk "chicken," 155-56
tha- "burn," 157
tol "stone," 72-73, 75

[217]

PUBLICATIONS ON ASIA OF THE SCHOOL OF
INTERNATIONAL STUDIES

1. Boyd, Compton, trans. and ed. *Mao's China: Party Reform Documents, 1942-44.* 1952. Reissued 1966. Washington Paperback-4, 1966. 330 pp., map.

2. Siang-tseh Chiang. *The Nien Rebellion.* 1954. 177 pp., bibliog., index, maps.

3. Chung-li Chang. *The Chinese Gentry: Studies on Their Role in Nineteenth-Century Chinese Society.* Introduction by Franz Michael. 1955. Reissued 1967. Washington Paperback on Russia and Asia-4. 277 pp., bibliog., index, tables.

4. *Guide to the Memorials of Seven Leading Officials of Nineteenth-Century China.* Summaries and indexes of memorials to Hu Lin-i, Tseng Kuo-fan, Tso Tsung-tang, Kuo Sung-tao, Tseng Kuo-ch'üan, Li Hung-chang, Chang Chih-tung. 1955. 457 pp., mimeographed. Out of print.

5. Marc Raeff. *Siberia and the Reforms of 1822.* 1956. 228 pp., maps, bibliog., index. Out of print.

6. Li Chi. *The Beginnings of Chinese Civilization: Three Lectures Illustrated with Finds of Anyang.* 1957. Reissued 1968. Washington Paperback on Russia and Asia-6. 141 pp., illus., bibliog., index.

7. Pedro Carrasco. *Land and Polity in Tibet.* 1959. 318 pp., maps, bibliog., index.

8. Kung-chuan Hsiao. *Rural China: Imperial Control in the Nineteenth Century.* 1960. Reissued 1967. Washington Paperback on Russia and Asia-3. 797 pp., tables, bibliog., index.

9. Tso-liang Hsiao. *Power Relations within the Chinese Communist Movement, 1930-34.* Vol. 1: *A Study of Documents.* 1961. 416 pp., bibliog., index, glossary. Vol. 2: *The Chinese Documents.* 1967. 856 pp.

10. Chung-li Chang. *The Income of the Chinese Gentry.* Introduction by Franz Michael. 1962. 387 pp., tables, bibliog., index.

11. John M. Maki. *Court and Constitution in Japan: Selected Supreme Court Decisions, 1948-60.* 1964. 491 pp., bibliog., index.

12. Nicholas Poppe, Leon Hurvitz, and Hidehiro Okada. *Catalogue of the Manchu-Mongol Section of the Toyo Bunko.* 1964. 391 pp., index.

13. Stanley Spector. *Li Hung-chang and the Huai Army: A Study in Nineteenth-Century Chinese Regionalism.* Introduction by Franz Michael. 1964. 399 pp., maps, tables, bibliog., glossary, index.

14. Franz Michael and Chung-li Chang. *The Taiping Rebellion: History and Documents.* Vol. 1: *History.* 1966. 256 pp., maps, index. Vols. 2 and 3: *Documents and Comments.* 1971. 756 and 1,107 pp.

15. Vincent Y. C. Shih. *The Taiping Ideology: Its Sources, Interpretations, and Influences.* 1967. 576 pp., bibliog., index.

16. Nicholas Poppe. *The Twelve Deeds of Buddha: A Mongolian Version of the Lalitavistara.* 1967. 241 pp., illus. Paper.

17. Tsi-an Hsia. *The Gate of Darkness: Studies on the Leftist Literary Movement in China.* Preface by Franz Michael. Introduction by C. T. Hsia. 1968. 298 pp., index.

18. Tso-liang Hsiao. *The Land Revolution in China, 1930-34: A Study of Documents.* 1969. 374 pp., tables, glossary, bibliog., index.

19. Michael Gasster. *Chinese Intellectuals and the Revolution of 1911: The Birth of Modern Chinese Radicalism.* 1969. 320 pp., glossary, bibliog., index.

20. Richard C. Thornton. *The Comintern and the Chinese Communists, 1928-31.* 1969. 266 pp., bibliog., index.

21. Julia C. Lin. *Modern Chinese Poetry: An Introduction.* 1972. 278 pp., bibliog., index.

22. Philip C. Huang, *Liang Ch'i-ch'ao and Modern Chinese Liberalism.* 1972. 200 pp., illus., glossary, bibliog., index.

23. Edwin Gerow and Margery Lang, eds. *Studies in the Language and Culture of South Asia.* 1974. 174 pp.

24. Barrie M. Morrison. *Lalmai, A Cultural Center of Early Bengal.* 1974. 190 pp., maps, drawings, tables.

25. Kung-chuan Hsiao. *A Modern China and a New World: K'ang Yu-Wei, Reformer and Utopian, 1858-1927.* 1975. 669 pp., transliteration table, bibliog., index.

26. Marleigh Grayer Ryan. *The Development of Realism in the Fiction of Tsubochi Shōyō.* 1975. 133 pp., index.

27. Dae-Sook Suh and Chae-Jin Lee, eds. *Political Leadership in Korea.* 1976. 272 pp., tables, figures, index.

28. Hellmut Wilhelm. *Heaven, Earth, and Man in the Book of Changes: Seven Eranos Lectures.* 1976. 230 pp., index.

29. Jing-shen Tao. *The Jurchen in Twelfth-Century China: A Study of Sinicization.* 1976. 217 pp., map, illus., appendix, glossary, bibliog., index.

30. Byung-joon Ahn. *Chinese Politics and the Cultural Revolution: Dynamics of Policy Processes.* 1976. 392 pp., appendixes, bibliog., index.

31. Margaret Nowak and Stephen Durrant. *The Tale of the Niśan Shamaness: A Manchu Folk Epic.* 1977. 182 pp., bibliog., index.

32. Jerry Norman. *A Manchu-English Lexicon.* 1978. 318 pp., appendix, bibliog.
33. James Brow. *Vedda Villages of Anuradhapura: The Historical Anthropology of a Community in Sri Lanka.* 1978. 268 pp., tables, figures, bibliog., index.
34. Roy Andrew Miller. *Origins of the Japanese Language.* 1980. 217 pp., maps, bibliog., index.